THE PLURAL AC

To my son Nathan

I slept constantly during these two days of the journey to Sicily, where I had not returned since the death of my mother. Someone seemed to have called me. I did not properly understand who, but I was happy to leave my house in Rome.

As soon as I entered the house, I felt that I was not alone. Something was going on in the shadows, in the corners of the rooms; shadows that looked at me so insistently that in the end, naturally, I turned round:

'But of course, Mama, it's you who called me.'

'It is me, Luigi.'

'And that's your music. I recognize it. I remember when you sung it to us.'

'I called you to tell you everything that I wasn't able to explain to you, because you were so far away, before I leave this life.'

'"Be strong", that's what you want to say today, Mama.'

'You're laughing at me . . . Don't cry, Luigi.'

'I'm crying because you can't think of me any more. When you were sitting there, in that corner, I often said to myself: "If she is thinking of me so far away, it means that I'm alive for her." That was my support in life, my comfort. Now that you're dead and don't think of me any more, I am no longer alive for you. I never shall be again.'

'I get tired quickly, my son, trying to follow all your talk. All this has become too hard for me. And yet I feel that I can still tell you something: learn to see things with the eyes of those who don't see any more, and although you'll feel pain, no doubt, this pain will make those things more sacred and beautiful for you. Perhaps it's only to tell you this that I've made you come here to me.'

'I know now what your eyes are looking at, Mama. The sail of that fishing-boat, isn't it? You told us a hundred times about that famous journey, and a hundred times I wanted to write about it.'

(extract from *Kaos*, a film by Paolo and Vittorio Taviana,
after *A Year's News* by Luigi Pirandello)

THE PLURAL ACTOR

BERNARD LAHIRE

Translated by David Fernbach

polity

First published in French as *L'homme pluriel* © Armand Colin, 2001

This English edition © Polity Press, 2011

Liberté • Égalité • Fraternité
RÉPUBLIQUE FRANÇAISE

This book is supported by the French Ministry of Foreign Affairs, as part of the Burgess programme run by the Cultural Department of the French Embassy in London (www.frenchbooknews.com)

Ouvrage publié avec le concours du Ministère français de la Culture – Centre national du livre

Published with the assistance of the French Ministry of Culture – National Centre for the Book

Polity Press
65 Bridge Street
Cambridge CB2 1UR, UK

Polity Press
350 Main Street
Malden, MA 02148, USA

All rights reserved. Except for the quotation of short passages for the purpose of criticism and review, no part of this publication may be reproduced, stored in a retrieval system, or transmitted, in any form or by any means, electronic, mechanical, photocopying, recording or otherwise, without the prior permission of the publisher.

ISBN-13: 978-0-7456-4684-8
ISBN-13: 978-0-7456-4685-5 (pb)

A catalogue record for this book is available from the British Library.

Typeset in 10.5 on 12 pt Sabon
by Servis Filmsetting Ltd, Stockport, Cheshire
Printed and bound in Great Britain by MPG Books Group, Bodmin, Cornwall

The publisher has used its best endeavours to ensure that the URLs for external websites referred to in this book are correct and active at the time of going to press. However, the publisher has no responsibility for the websites and can make no guarantee that a site will remain live or that the content is or will remain appropriate.

Every effort has been made to trace all copyright holders, but if any have been inadvertently overlooked the publisher will be pleased to include any necessary credits in any subsequent reprint or edition.

For further information on Polity, visit our website: www.politybooks.com

CONTENTS

Preface to the English edition   viii
Acknowledgements   xx

Prologue   1

Act I Outline of a Theory of the Plural Actor

Scene 1 The Plural Actor   11
On Singleness   11
The single self: a commonplace illusion, but socially well
   founded   15
The socio-historical conditions of singleness and plurality   18
The plurality of social contexts and repertoires of habits   26
The Proustian model of the plural actor   32
Splitting of the self and mental conflict: crossings of social space   36

Scene 2 The Wellsprings of Action   42
Presence of the past, present of action   42
The many occasions for maladjustment and crisis   45
The plurality of the actor and the openings of the present   47
Conditional dispositions   50
The negative power of the context: inhibition and latency   56
'Code switching' and 'code mixing' within the same context   60
Actors uncertainly swinging   62

Scene 3 Analogy and Transfer   66
Practical analogy and the triggers of action and memory   66
Involuntary action and memory   69

The role of habits	72
From analytic transfer to the interview relationship	74
A relative transferability	77
From general to partial schemes	82
From generalized transfer to limited and conditional transfer	86
Scene 4 Literary Experience: Reading, Daydreams and Parapraxes	89

Act II Reflexivities and Logics of Action

Scene 1 School, Action and Language	101
The scholastic break with practical sense	101
Saussure, or the pure theory of scholastic practices on language	108
The social conditions of departure from practical sense	110
Scene 2 The Everyday Practices of Writing in Action	115
Embodied memory, objectified memory	117
Everyday breaks with practical sense	120
'Doing it like that'	123
Memory for the unusual	124
The longer term and preparing the future	126
Managing complex practices	128
The official, the formal and tense situations	129
The presence of the absent	132
Temporary disturbances of practical sense	134
The use of plans: lists of all kinds	136
The relative pertinence of practical sense	139
Scene 3 The Plural Logics of Action	143
The ambiguity of a singular practice	143
The sporting model of practical sense and its limitations	147
Intentionality and the levels of context	154
Plurality of times and logics of action	156

Act III Forms of Embodiment

Scene 1 The Place of Language	163
The world of silence	163
The punctuation of action and its theorization	169
Language and the forms of social life	172
The mysterious inside	173

Scene 2 What Exactly is Embodied? 175
Processes of embodiment–internalization 175
The polymorphic embodiment of written culture in the world
    of the family 183
Negative identifications and the force of implicit injunctions 189

Act IV Workshops and Debates

Scene 1 Psychological Sociology 195
An exit from sociology? 197
The objectivity of the 'subjective' 201
The singular folds of the social 203
Multi-determinism and the sense of freedom 206
New methodological requirements 207

Scene 2 Pertinent Fields 211
On excessive generalization 211
The varying scale of context in the social sciences 213
Experimental variation and loss of illusions 214
The historicizing of universal theories and fields of pertinence 217

Notes 223
References 253
Index 264

PREFACE

When I came to write this preface to the translation of a book published more than ten years ago, I still remembered very clearly how it had originally been conceived as a theoretical parenthesis and clarification in the wake of several years of empirical research. This research focused variously on social inequalities in relation to the written culture of the school, popular practices of writing (modes of appropriation of texts, and domestic and occupational practices of writing), cases of unlikely educational success in a working-class milieu, intergenerational cultural transmission, and students' relationship to study, knowledge and culture as a function of the type of higher education pursued. But this parenthesis, with the objective of settling a certain number of theoretical questions that forced themselves on me in the course of these successive projects, turned out to be a springboard that rapidly led well beyond what I had initially imagined.

In this book I take issue with a series of sociological currents and authors (including myself), but chiefly with major theoretical questions or problems either formulated or reformulated by Pierre Bourdieu. When I began to write it, Bourdieu was an author both much acclaimed by the scholarly community and particularly mistreated by it at the scientific level. It seemed to me, however, that the shabby way in which his work was treated arose as much from servile disciples who were happy (and unfortunately are still happy) to apply untiringly a model whose universal pertinence was beyond doubt in their eyes, as from opponents or even enemies who were in too great a hurry to cast him into outer darkness or relegate him to the past of a so-called classical sociology.

In order to keep scientific thinking alive, it is necessary regularly to accept submitting to discussion, rather than enclosing oneself in the endless repetition of pre-established concepts and arguments. The question here, which had already been raised before Bourdieu's death, is that of the mode of appropriation of the legacy that he left us. There are two main ways of taking up this legacy. The first consists, at best, of applying his theories indefinitely to new terrains and, at worst, of resting content with using his vocabulary and grammar, giving (oneself) the impression of thinking when all that has been done is to set in motion the machine for producing texts 'in the Bourdieu style'. A number of sociological works then resembled a kind of involuntary pastiche, and still do today. The second way of taking up the legacy presupposes making the effort, and taking the intellectual risk, of continuing to imagine and create beyond what Bourdieu himself thought and formulated, rediscovering in this way the attitude that he was himself able to adopt when he invented, either with or against other authors, a new way of doing sociology and conceiving the social world. It is an attribute of any major body of work that it gives rise to this kind of opposition between repetition/commemoration and reinvention, between veneration and creative criticism. And those researchers most faithful to Pierre Bourdieu's work are not, in my mind, where people are generally in the habit of seeing them.

What I discuss here first and foremost is the theory of habitus, and in the most detailed manner possible (certain very precise conceptual points), mobilizing for this purpose results of empirical work that make it possible to qualify or challenge certain formulations or propositions.[1] The theory of habitus is a theory of socialization (and of its products as crystallized in the form of an embodied 'system of dispositions'), a theory of action (the question of the relative weight attributed to the embodied past and to the present of a context of action, or the question of the transferability of schemas or dispositions that constitute the habitus) and a theory of practice (emphasizing the non-reflexive or pre-reflexive character of actors envisaged as individuals caught up in the urgency of practice, who are most commonly adjusted to the situations that they are led to live). This whole series of points is the object of discussion and clarification here, and, in a certain number of cases, of questioning.

On reflexivity, for example, it clearly appears that, in his opposition to intentionalist theories of action (strategic analyses, theories of rational action, philosophies of action in terms of projects, etc.), Bourdieu neglected all those everyday situations in which actors are led to adopt an external point of view on their practices, to plan some of their activities, to elaborate projects and even to 'calculate' certain decisions. Taking seriously the sporting metaphors that he used, following Maurice Merleau-Ponty, to speak of the sense of a game (the positioning of a football player, the feints of a boxer, the practical anticipation of a tennis player, etc.), we may think of all the situations of training, outside the actual time of performance, when the coach comments on gestures or actions, either directly or subsequently (thanks to video recording), in order to bring to awareness a certain number of mistakes or imperfections to be corrected. Social actors are not constantly comparable with sports players caught up in the urgency of the match and improvising *on the field* as a function of their embodied dispositions. They also go over what they have done and imagine, project or plan what they are going to do. They make use, as the case may be, of writing, reading, discussion with others, or the objectification of their actions that video resources make possible.

Moreover, the adjustment of 'embodied structures' to 'objective structures' that is presupposed and very widely used to support the idea of a pre-reflexive actor (in the sense that the actor lives in the self-evidence of things to do and not do) does not long resist analysis of the multiple and diversified realities of maladjustment and crisis (minor or major) that put in question the 'ontological complicity' between the embodied (dispositions) and the objectified (situations, the institution, the field, etc.). 'Out of place' and 'maladjusted' individuals are more numerous than the theory of habitus assumes: migration, social and occupational mobility, the many situations in which individuals are transplanted in one way or another (hospital, boarding school, prison, concentration camp, etc.), cultural shocks – whether of civilizations, as in the case of great colonial enterprises, or internal to a given society, for example when compulsory education leads children to be faced with forms of cultural apprenticeship, knowledge and social relations that are quite foreign to their original milieu – are all occasions where a lack of fit forces actors to modify or radically change their habits.

But it is on the question of dispositions and the weight that is attributed to them in relation to that of the context of action, their strength or durability, their transferability and their homogeneity, that the problems raised by the theory of habitus are concentrated. If we wanted to caricature the two major pitfalls that any researcher should seek to avoid on the question of the theory of action and the actor, we could say that there are on the one hand models that ascribe a crushing weight to the actor's past, and more particularly to the very earliest experiences lived in the course of infancy (most often assumed to be homogeneous), and on the other hand models that describe and analyse moments of an action or an interaction, or a given state of a system of action, without ever concerning themselves with this past.

In the first case, it is only past experiences that are reconstructed in order to understand present actions, which are seen in some sense as no more than successive actualizations of an active past. In the second, actors are constrained exclusively by the logic of the present situation (context of interaction, system of action, organization, market or field).[2] In the first type of model of action, study of the singular characteristics of the different contexts of action is neglected, and in the second there is an elision, whether deliberate or not, of everything in the present action that depends on the embodied past of the actors (dispositions, mental and behavioural inclinations or habits).[3]

The scientific programme I offer in *The Plural Actor* is that of a sociology that is indissociably both dispositional and contextual. It consists in taking into account the embodied past, the earlier socializing experience of the actors studied (experiences that are crystallized in the form of more or less strong and constant dispositions – dispositions to believe, feel, think and act in a certain fashion), while not neglecting or cancelling the role of the present (the different present contexts of action). The issue here is to make evident the weight of embodied social dispositions while not claiming that we are at every moment – or engaged at every moment, in every one of our acts – in a kind of synthesis of everything that we have previously experienced, and that each new context (whether in the field of practices or the context of interaction) is simply a terrain of expression or actualization of this embodied past that can be synthesized in the form of a matrix or formula.

I still believe today that it is quite illusory to think that the sociologist can be in a position to reconstruct a synthesis of this kind (a unifying principle or generating formula of all our practices, as Bourdieu again put it) that can account for either the practices of groups or those of singular individuals. Behaviours and practices can only be understood as the intersection of embodied dispositions – which we can never assume in advance to be firm, lasting, transferable, homogeneous and mutually coherent – and contextual constraints that do not so much solicit this or that part of a legacy of dispositions, more or less so as the case may be, as rather and more globally a system of dispositions. Habitus, as it is defined by Pierre Bourdieu, definitively appears as a particular case of the possible. It corresponds to a type of individual inheritance of very coherent dispositions. An inheritance of this kind can only arise in extremely homogeneous conditions of primary and secondary socialization. But the socio-historical conditions for this are only rather rarely met with in highly differentiated societies.[4] The title of this book, *The Plural Actor*, should not lead to confusion: I would never maintain – and have never said – that the individual actor is necessarily and universally plural. The right question to raise here is: What are the social and historical conditions of production of an individual actor who is dispositionally plural?[5]

It is because the dispositions that make up each individual legacy of dispositions are not necessarily coherent or homogeneous among themselves, moreover, that each new situation experienced by the actor plays an important role as a filter, selector or trigger and is the occasion for an application or suspension, a flourishing or an inhibition, of this or that part of the embodied dispositions. Rather than an actor applying invariably and across every context the same system of dispositions (or habitus), what we more commonly see is a more complex mechanism of suspension/application or inhibition/activation of dispositions: a mechanism that evidently presupposes that each singular individual can be the bearer of a plurality of dispositions and straddle a plurality of social contexts. What determines the activation of a particular disposition (or series of dispositions) in this context is then the product of the interaction between the internal and the external balance of forces: the balance of forces between dispositions that are more or less firmly established in the course of past socialization (internal) and that between the elements of the context (objective characteristics of the situation, which can be associated with different individuals) that weigh more or less heavily on the actor (external).

The Plural Actor was thus an opportunity for me to emphasize the lack of sociological work studying the same individuals across a plurality of stages, the haste of researchers to deduce, on the basis of analyses of particular practices (family, educational, occupational, cultural, political, etc.), general dispositions, attitudes or relationships to the world assumed to be transferable from one context to another (domain or sub-domain of practices, type of interaction, etc.) and the need for new methodological requirements in order to grasp the social variation of individual behaviour according to the context of action. The research that I subsequently sought to conduct thus substituted for 'empirical laziness' and the 'demon of abusive generalization', which I pinpointed here, a high degree of empirical experience and a concern for the contextualization and the comparison of behaviours.

I began to speak of a 'psychological sociology',[6] then of sociology on the individual scale',[7] in order to denote the kind of work that it is indispensable to conduct if the aim is to make the 'social in the embodied state', or the 'individualized social', something more than a mere rhetorical evocation, designed simply as a reminder that the social exists as much within actors as outside them. An individual – a constructed object rather than a complex empirical reality that is unattainable as such – can be defined as a social reality characterized by a possible[8] dispositional complexity, a complexity that is manifested or observed only in the diversity of domains of practice or stages of action within which the practices of this individual are inscribed. The possibility of such a sociology on the individual scale thus begins when one has available, for the same individual, at least two behaviours to compare in different contexts. In a technical vocabulary, but one that has the advantage of precision, we can say that, after being interested in variations in behaviour between societies or epochs, then, in intergroup or interclass variations within a society, sociology is now in a position to constitute as sociological object the inter-individual variations of behaviour (asking, for example, how children belonging to the same family can have significantly different educational and professional destinies) and, better still, intra-individual variations in behaviour.[9]

The idea of grasping certain individual complexities (i.e. the fact that an individual is the bearer of heterogeneous dispositions, and not completely 'the same' in different contexts of social life) has nothing in common with the illusory search for the complex totality of a singular person. But the researcher is not obliged, under the pretext that it is impossible to understand exhaustively what is most singular about each individual, to opt conversely for a caricature of individual styles, profiles or habitus. The legitimate reduction of the complexity of individual dispositional legacies that certain scholarly work effects by privileging intergroup comparison (including when this exemplifies groups by resorting to the study of individual cases reduced to ideal-type figures) should not prevent the researcher from working on this complexity.

This is without even taking into account, or assessing the consequences of, the fact that sociology has become steadily more interested both in socialized individuals as such (in case studies or work that presents, among other types of 'data', individual portraits, methodologically supported by life story or in-depth interview) and in groups, categories, structures, institutions or situations (whatever their scope and type). By speaking indifferently of the 'habitus' of groups or classes along with the 'habitus' of singular individuals

(Martin Heidegger or Gustave Flaubert), Bourdieu did not take into account that the change of scale in observation and analysis[10] modifies the degree of precision of the conceptual tool that he used. The somewhat caricaturized ('ideal-typical') illustration of 'class habitus' (a notion that, moreover, loses its specificity and turns out to be very close to the more everyday one of 'culture') is comprehensible and scientifically legitimate. But when you want to understand how embodied dispositions actually operate, the way in which they are formed, the way in which they are transferred or not, are actualized, suspended or transformed as a function of the specific context of action, you come across a series of limits and problems that necessarily lead to reformulating the initial definitions.

The metaphor of 'the social in a folded or unfolded state', which I have used frequently on previous occasions, can prove useful in this argument. When sociologists study Protestantism, for example, describing its pertinent properties or features or analysing the operation of its institutions and attitude, its ethos or the values attaching to it, they speak of a phenomenon that, despite being quite tightly defined historically and geographically, involves thousands or even millions of individuals in history, whether ordinary Protestant ascetics or famous theologians, all committed to a greater or lesser extent, and more or less strongly defined by their denominational membership. The result is that to speak of 'Protestantism' means making a tremendous abstraction in relation to these thousands or millions of ways of living Protestanism (and making it live). The necessarily ideal-typical description of Protestant culture is a dis-individualized, de-singularized, de-particularized description, but one that is inevitably based on the traces of multiple activities and actions, representations that are individual, particular, singular. And the same argument can be made in relation to the educational system, the state, an economic mode of production, etc. – in other words, all those macro-social objects to which the social sciences have accustomed us, implying a multitude of individual actors and yet not capable of being summed up in any individual action or life. By way of historical, statistical or ethnographic reconstruction, anthropologists, historians and sociologists thus regularly carry out abstract totalizations that transcend each individual case and cannot be enclosed in any particular case.

Statistical procedures that produce equivalence for the needs of coding, such as the typifying operations of a more qualitative sociology, dis-individualize social facts and deliver an unfolded version of the social (one that conflates individual singularities). The classic procedure gives access to this or that social fact by de-singularizing it – i.e. detaching it from singular individuals and disembarrassing it of aspects that are then viewed as secondary. As a result the individual appears far too concrete and complex to be capable of study. Sociologists have been right historically to campaign in favour of this abstraction, a necessary one in order to grasp certain social and historical regularities and invariances. And yet, if we accept that the social world does not present itself externally to individuals, or live internally within them, in an unfolded and abstract fashion, that rather it exists in a folded or creased state – i.e. in the form of nuanced and concrete combinations of contextual and dispositional properties – we can then try, in apprehending social facts, to take account of this situation as far as is possible.

Each individual is in some form the 'depository' of dispositions to think, feel and act that are the product of his or her multiple socializing experiences, more or less lasting and intense, in various collectives (from the smallest to the largest). In this folded version of reality that I am seeking to develop, individuals are not reducible to their Protestantism, their class membership, their level of culture or their gender. They are defined by the entire series of their experiences, past and present. Whether synthesized or struggling within them, in combination or contradiction, whether harmoniously articulated, coexisting more or less peacefully or confronting one another, there are elements and dimensions of their culture (in the broad sense of the term) that are generally studied separately by researchers in the social sciences. If an individual has attended school, sociologists or historians of education will speak of the educational practices he or she has experienced, the skills that teachers have attempted to inculcate in them, the methods applied to this end, etc. With a Protestant, researchers will doubtless analyse the Protestant ethic as it was in this time and milieu; with an artisan, sociologists, ethnologists and historians of labour will also establish much in the way of knowledge of the moral and professional world, the values and modes of life of artisanal existence, and so on. But the social world is made up in such a way that it does not follow these scientific and institutional dissections: it is in fact the same individual who is at the same time a man, educated, artisan, Protestant, etc. After the social has been unfolded, it may sometimes be useful to refold it again. This folded version of the social world cannot be substituted for the unfolded one, but it should eventually make it possible to render this more complex.

The dispositional and contextualist programme of a sociology on the individual scale, such as the present book seeks to sketch out, has given rise to misunderstandings that it may be useful to note and try to dispel, by way of concluding this preface.

First of all, in the logic of academic classifications, my procedure has often been situated on the side of 'qualitative' and 'micro-sociological' approaches, even ranked among studies of 'atypical cases'. I can understand such a reading, bound up with the recognition that my work on cases of unlikely educational success gained, based as this was on the very thorough examination of a limited series of family configurations.[11] The same feeling may have been subsequently reinforced by the experimental work I conducted on eight socially differentiated individuals on six occasions and, at length, on some very different themes – school, family, work, friends, leisure and cultural activities, sport, food, health, dress – in order to straddle domains of activity and dimensions of existence that were sufficiently diverse, with the object of entering into intra-individual variations in detail and questioning some apparently self-evident assertions concerning mechanisms of transferability of dispositions.[12]

This initial research enabled me to develop a project of wider scale[13] on intra-individual variations in cultural practices and preferences. But analysis of individual cultural profiles shows that these variations arise from the differentiated structuration of our societies. In fact, the series of intra-individual variations in the cultural behaviour studied can be ascribed to heterogeneous and sometimes contradictory socializing influences: the effect of a trajectory of upward or downward social or occupational mobility, the effect of a diversified network of cultural relations, the effect of a relative heterogamy in cultural terms, the effect of the internalization of educational preferences that vary from those of the milieu of origin, the effect of combined constraints experienced by young people in the school situation (between peer group, school and family), the effect of contradictory socializing influences on the part of competing cultural influences (family, school, television, press, etc.), the effect of heterogeneous cultural influences even within the family of origin, etc. Contrary to what one might have initially believed – like the nineteenth-century psychologists before the premises of differential psychology initiated by Francis Galton – intra- and inter-individual variations in phenomena are not 'error' or 'noise' that the sociologist should systematically eliminate with a view to establishing general laws or general social facts (transcendent in relation to individuals). They are, rather, bound up with the macro-social structures of the societies within which individuals develop.

The same programme of studying intra-individual variations and multiple socializations has also allowed me – by combining quantitative data and individual portraits – to comprehend better the situation of writers living in a market regime, often grasped exclusively in their literary milieu, whereas, as distinct from manual workers, doctors, researchers or employers, who spend their whole working time in a single professional universe and draw the essential part of the income from this work, the great majority of them are not reducible to their membership of the literary world and so live a situation of double life: compelled to combine literary activity and a 'second trade', and alternating constantly between writing time and the time of extra-literary remunerative activity. This kind of 'double life' situation, pluri-secular and structural, has consequences for the rhythm and nature of literary creation.[14]

We can thus see from these two examples how directing attention to the individual level of the social and to the question of intra-individual variation in practices does not enclose the researcher in a clinical study or the qualitative sociology of individual singularities, but makes it possible to raise afresh the classic questions of sociology.

A further misunderstanding, partly bound up with the first one, is far more problematic in so far as it has a political resonance. Certain authors have ranked me with people who believe that social classes no longer exist, who are no longer interested in them, or who, by their choice of analysis, make all kinds of macro-social objects disappear (institutions or milieus as well as groups or classes). Yet one need only see the importance of social classes in my successive works, including the case studies that always situate the individual studied in social space, to refute this kind of classification. Study of the social in the folded state would make no sense if it could not base itself on study of the social in the unfolded state. Leaving macroscopic analysis of the gaps between social groups and classes to direct one's interest to intra-individual variations in socially situated individuals does not mean questioning the existence of these gaps. No one would criticize a researcher who studies molecules, microbes or atoms of denying the existence of planets. Yet this is the kind of commentary that can be read or heard in sociology. The objects of sociology are so hot politically that, when they start to work on questions of inter-individual or intra-individual variations, researchers can be suspected of disseminating the objects of their research and having a kind of implicit 'political agenda'.[15]

More surprising still is the way in which *The Plural Actor* and the studies that were particular realizations of its programme have been ascribed to a 'less deterministic' view of an actor supposedly more free and conscious. What I emphasize is, on the contrary, the fact that actors are *multi-socialized* and *multi-determined*, and that it is for this very reason that they are not in a position to 'feel' or have a practical intuition of the weight of these determinisms. When the actors are plural and the forces at work on them differ according to the context in which they find themselves, they can only have the sense of a freedom of behaviour. It could be said that we are too multi-socialized and multi-determined to be able to be readily aware of our determinisms. If people insist on calling the product of this multi-determinism a 'sense of freedom', what is wrong with that? But this feeling has nothing in common with the sovereign and conscious freedom that certain philosophies of action present to us.

We can basically see that the misunderstandings in the reception of this book around the questions micro/macro, qualitative/quantitative, individuals/social classes and determinism/freedom are all more or less directly bound up with a questioning or disquiet as to the reasons that impel sociologists to study the social on the individual scale. By choosing this kind of perspective for the knowledge of reality, are they not in the process of espousing the movement of individualization that is under way in our social formations, of actively supporting individualist ideologies, even neo-liberal ones?

Outside the specific dynamic of the sociological field, what makes this kind of sociology, this kind of interest, run clearly in the direction of an advance in the scientific autonomy of the discipline[16] is that it responds, in my view, to the historical necessity of conceiving the social in a strongly individualizing society. At a time when the individual tends to be ever more commonly conceived or dreamed of as an isolated, autonomous, responsible being endowed with reason, opposed to 'society' and defending his or her 'authenticity' or 'singularity' against it,[17] sociology has the duty more than ever before of bringing to light the social fabrication of individuals and proving that the social is not reducible to the collective or the general, but dwells in the most singular folds of each individual. It should seek to propose a vision of man in society that is finer and more scientifically correct than the caricatures made of it when the individual is represented on the basis of cases that serve to exemplify or illustrate social groups, historical eras or institutions.

The social world is within us as much as outside of us. As the origin of our unhappiness as well as our happiness, individual and collective, it is differentiated and complexified to the point of producing the sentiment that the intimate, the singular, the personal, is by nature distinct from society (as two clearly different objects) and even opposed to it. It is a paradox or ruse of the social world that it has produced, in a particularly advanced state of differentiation, the very widespread sensation of a subjective life that is non-social or extra-social. This individualistic story is accepted on all sides. The individual, the internal forum or subjectivity as site of our ultimate freedom is one of our great contemporary myths. People may prefer to share these myths or to rid themselves of them. It seems to me that abandoning any illusion of an undetermined 'subjectivity', 'interiority' or 'singularity', any illusion of free will or 'personal' existence outside of the social world, in order to show the forces and counter-forces, both internal (dispositional) and external (contextual), to which we are continuously subjected from our birth and which make us feel what we feel, think what we think and do what we do, is a valuable advance in knowledge.

Lyons, October 2009 – Rio de Janeiro, November 2009

ACKNOWLEDGEMENTS

The help of the Institut Universitaire de France was of prime importance in allowing me the time and resources needed to develop the research and reflections on which this book is based.

I want to thank in particular Aaron Victor Cicourel, professor at the University of San Diego, and Troy Duster, director of the Institute for the Study of Social Change and professor of sociology at the University of Berkeley, for having made possible my productive stay at Berkeley in February–March 1977. This enabled me to work actively on preparing and writing this book.

The propositions, arguments and illustrations that you will read here are to a certain extent the developments of those contained in my article 'Éléments pour une théorie des formes socio-historiques d'acteur et d'action', published in the *Revue européenne des sciences sociales* (vol. 34, no. 106, 1996). I am sincerely grateful to this journal and its editor, Giovanni Busino, for having enabled me to publish this crucial step in my work.

Scientific argument is often enriched by the opportunity for verbal presentation and the spontaneous reactions this arouses – still better, by informal and impassioned dialogue. I would therefore like to mention all those who gave me such opportunities to speak about my work, whether still in progress or already complete, and among them in particular Jean-Claude Passeron, François de Singly, Jean-Michel Chapoulie and Jean-Pierre Briand, Anne-Marie Chartier and Jean Hébrard, Benoît Falaize, Samuel Joshua, Marie Bonafé, Claire Meljac, Maria Thereza Fraga Rocco and Beatriz Cardoso.

PROLOGUE

It is impossible to avail oneself of the scientific spirit if one is not in a position, at every moment of thinking life, to reconstruct the whole of one's knowledge.
    (Gaston Bachelard, *The Formation of the Scientific Mind*)

The development of the theory of kinetic energy owed more to Leibniz's desire to prevail over Descartes than to the Cartesians' respectful fidelity to their master's physics; and the acerbic footnotes of Granet and Maspéro were more significant for Sinology than the panegyrics of their respective endorsers.
    (Jean-Claude Passeron, *Le Raisonnement sociologique*)

Against all appearance, this is not strictly speaking a theoretical text. Or, rather, it is not going to champion a finished point of view, anticipating the results of empirical research – which is what is usually understood by theory. It will instead propose a framework of reflection, draw new lines of research, and try never to universalize the scientific findings on which it is based, whether they are narrow or wide. In a particular sense of the term, therefore, it is not theoretical; it neither can be nor wants to be, and even defends the idea that any interpretative framework must be modified as a function of the objects studied.

A theory (a conceptual system, a paradigm, an interpretative or explanatory model), in fact, very often presents itself as a somewhat mysterious and original vision of the social world. The more original, strange and one-sided it is, the harder it is to grasp its foundations and the greater the seductive power or fascination it exercises. A theory is then an approach that claims to cover the totality of the social world and deal with any problem by drawing on the same resources, an approach that ignores its own origins and denies its own limits. In this perspective a theory is always total, never partial. At least this is the way in which 'grand theories' like to see themselves. One can succumb to the charms of unconsciousness and mystery. Or one may prefer lucidity, clarity and scientific pragmatism.

Rational actor theories (or rational choice theories), theories of habitus, of the actor-as-strategist, of the actor in interaction, theories of experience and lived worlds, etc., objectively conflict with one another today, without any real clash or confrontation, in a scientific space where the crossing of arguments and the results of comparative empirical research might permit certain advances. And one could say about sociology the same as Jean-Pierre Cometti has of philosophy: 'The paradox is that philosophy has become one of those fields of intellectual activity in which discussion tends to become nonexistent, advantageously replaced as it is by diligent commentaries inspired by the pre-existing convictions around which insular consensuses are formed' (Cometti, 1996, p. 21).

It is customary for theories of action and the actor to come into conflict around a series of interpretative tensions: between theories that privilege the actor's singleness and homogeneity (his or her identity, his or her relationship to the world, his or her 'self', his or her system of dispositions . . .) and those that describe for us an endless fragmentation of 'selves', roles, experiences, etc.; a tension, again, between theories that place the determining weight on the actor's past and those that virtually ignore this; and, finally, a tension between theories of conscious action, of the actor as strategist, rational calculator, vector of intentionalities or voluntary decisions (theories that sometimes believe they can deduce from these calculating, conscious, rational capacities a fundamental freedom on the actor's part) and theories of unconscious, subconscious or non-conscious action that present actions as pre-reflexive adjustments to practical situations.

Throughout the present work I shall use the word 'actor', though this is not particularly current in French sociology given its implicit link with ideas of 'freedom' and 'rationality' that certain theories of action end up imposing, but it has the advantage of going together with the term 'action'. In current theories of the social, the vocabulary ranges through the terms actor, agent, subject, individual, member, author, social being, person, personality, etc. Territorial markers that trigger conditioned theoretical reflexes, the words used to denote 'people in the forms of social life', thus generally serve also as classificatory signals. By using them, their authors themselves choose to (let themselves) be classified, to rehearse their clan identity, to denote both the camp they belong to and their potential enemies, enclosing themselves in advance, before having even asserted any proposition at all on the social world, in the confined social spaces of schools, currents or theoretical traditions. Sticking to the word 'actor' does not mean for me adopting a theatrical metaphor (actor, stage, role, cues, backstage, scenario, script . . .), or proposing an umpteenth version of the theory of the free (because!) rational actor, or romantic theories of 'man as actor of his destiny', but rather making use of a relatively coherent network of terms: 'actor', 'action', 'act', 'activity', 'activate', 'reactivate', and so on. But how are we to avoid the automatic associations of ideas attaching to the word 'actor', except by explicitly asking the reader to read this term here without its customary adversarial connotations (e.g. anti-agent), which we in no way intend to reactivate?

Any theoretical reflection is necessarily developed in a critical relationship to others; that is commonplace enough. And yet 'dispute' is stigmatized in an academic world that more often generates a façade of consensus along with assassination behind the scenes, the hyper-euphemizing of public judgements and the extreme violence of 'strokes' or 'private' assertions, rather than an interest in or passion for reasoned discussion and the frank criticism of theses (rather than of the individuals that support them, which is not at all the same). Criticism is respectable and should be rehabilitated.

In the present work, I shall not discuss with the same intensity and systematicness the whole series of theories of action that exist in the field of the social sciences, even if they are all present in my arguments to one degree or another. I thus claim a freedom of choice in my dialogues. My own sociological procedure has been inspired principally by the theory of practice and habitus developed by Pierre Bourdieu. A dialogue with this theory, from my point of view, does not mean discussing just one theory among others. Contrary to what a certain form of interpretative democracy might suggest, not everything is equivalent in the world of interpretation of the social sciences (Lahire, 1996b). I see Bourdieu as proposing one of the most stimulating and complex theoretical orientations in the social sciences – one of those that most successfully integrates theoretical and methodological subtleties (succeeding in particular in making productive use of a number of philosophical problems) into the great current of critical sociologies (critiques of the forms of exercise of power, of inegalitarian structures and of relationships of domination). In France, Bourdieu's sociology is either hated (even ignored) or worshipped. If we overlook the former totally negative attitude, we may note that adoration is not appropriate to scientific life. It is sometimes even necessary to impose a certain social (relational) distance, to dare to raise certain questions, to authorize oneself to contradict, refute, complete or inflect the thought of an author. The present work thus invites the reader to think both with and against Bourdieu, most often in fact differently from him. Since we are invited, as Foucault said of the thought of Nietzsche, not to fear 'to use it, to deform it, to make it groan and protest' (Bourdieu and Wacquant, 1992, p. xiv), we shall not fear to exercise a critical activity. The only thing that really matters, in the end, is the result of the discussion.

If, moreover, we really want to take into account the fact that the author of this book is himself split and divided, that the criticisms he addresses to other authors are largely addressed to himself, and that through these criticisms he is seeking to convince himself as much as his readers; if, therefore, we really accept that this text is as much an internal dialogue between different 'parts' of the author as a dialogue between him and the authors cited, then perhaps he will more readily be granted the right to criticize.[1] More generally, one can argue and criticize better after internalizing the reasoning deployed by others, in its full complexity and without caricature. The systematic internalization of the most varied scientific 'points of view' on the social world is the best means towards developing one's own 'point of view' in due course.

The outline of a theory of the plural actor, and the reflections proposed here on the different forms of reflexivity in action, on the plurality of logics of action, on the forms of embodiment of the social and the place of language in the study of action and of the processes of internalization, have been developed in a constant concern not to have only one type of action in mind and theorize this by an excessive generalization, but, on the contrary, systematically to vary possible cases, sometimes even up to borderline cases that are almost absurd (reasoning *ad absurdum* being a good way of grasping the logic of normal cases that generally escapes attention), by basing myself on varied empirical research, both my own and that of many other scholars in the social sciences. This attention to the diversity of reality makes it possible, on the one hand, to avoid unconsciously theorizing – i.e. unduly generalizing – a particular case of the real, as is done by the majority of theories mentioned and, on the other hand, to divine behind each of these theories the relatively limited examples, cases or series of cases that these unknowingly describe or dissect. For a large proportion of these, their conceptual tensions reproduce and fix in the theoretical order real social differences: between types of action, dimensions of action or types of actors.

The sum of these developments leads on to the programme of a psychological sociology, which offers conditions for the sociological study of the most singular folds of the social. 'All sociology is psychology, but a psychology *sui generis*', as Durkheim maintained. In fact, sociological theories of action, or at least the more complex of these, have long since integrated models of cognitive, mental and bodily functioning drawn from the psychological sciences (from experimental psychology through to psychoanalysis) without, however having ever really controlled such borrowings, and especially without having subjected them to the test of empirical investigation in so far as this was not at the centre of the models of sociological explanation. If, as a consequence, I mention various psychological works throughout the present book (cognitive psychology, cultural psychology, psychoanalysis, etc.), this is not in order to import fraudulently illicit (conceptual) products, but rather to put in question again what was silently borrowed from these fields of research several decades ago, especially from the studies of Piaget. The point is to open a number of little boxes that were sealed in the 1970s and have not been opened since.

It seems as if a part of sociology has been living with psychological findings that are partly outdated today, and partly subject to doubt today (how could it be otherwise?), as if these were embedded in its theories of action and cognition. It is necessary therefore to return to all the evidence that was left unquestioned, but was in fact no more than summaries of scientific findings drawn from a section of the psychological works of a particular era: notions of schemes, of their transferability or transposability, of analogical transfer, of general and systematic application of schemes, etc.

It is also surprising that, while philosophical debates around explanation in terms of disposition are still lively, particularly in the English-speaking countries, there is such a watertight barrier between the worlds of philosophy and sociology that these debates are prevented from having any effect in clarifying sociological practice. It is not that sociologists need philosophers to dictate their theories, but rather that philosophy – or at least a proportion of philosophical reflections – can sometimes contribute usefully to illuminating the concepts used by sociologists in their inquiries into the social world. There is such a fear in France of the idea that sociology might fall back into social philosophy (something that is clearly undesirable) that a large number of sociologists live with a permanent theoretical bad conscience. Any conceptual discussion is suspected of 'intellectualism', 'useless verbiage' or 'bad philosophy'. Of course, the same sociologists who make such an outcry about theoreticism (the supreme academic insult in certain clans of the sociological tribe) have no compunction about theorizing themselves; as we all know, it is always someone else's theory that is hollow and mere words . . .

A suspicion of uselessness, of luxurious waste of time, marked by an absence of concrete investigation or troublesome work 'in the field', weighs on those who reflect on their discipline, their knowledge and their methods. Some people disqualify in advance any theoretical, methodological or epistemological reflection as being futile, sterile, pretentious or verbose. It is of course always those with a very particular interest in maintaining the scientific order as it stands, with a theory, methodology and epistemology that is taken for granted and 'goes without saying', who have no interest in seeing the rise of new arguments (which are bound to be pretentious, ill-minded or stupid), especially when these open up conceptual boxes that were thought to have been sealed for ever. Such disqualification, however, is that much more difficult, or at least forced to reveal its motivation, when those undertaking this reflection have not abandoned the path of investigation, and are all the more happy to return to it once their collective reflections have improved the quality of their empirical work and broadened their sociological imagination as applied to the construction of objects of study. Theoretical, methodological and epistemological reflection, when it is a lesson drawn from research work and an invitation to return anew to the task, is in no way an unavoidable and rather terroristic preliminary to investigation that might even prevent such investigation for fear of making a mistake. It is, rather, its systematic disqualification that is a disguised form of intellectual terrorism.

In order to elaborate the outlines of a theory of the plural actor, I have found support in sociology, anthropology, historiography, philosophy and psychology (drawing particularly on the work of North American scholars), as well as in the critical reflections of Marcel Proust in *Against Sainte-Beuve* and in the *de facto* sociological analyses that his fictional writing often displays. Even before Durkheim, I can claim the French sociological heritage of Maurice Halbwachs, whose analyses of memory are sensitive to the multiple belonging of individual actors, their successive or simultaneous socializations in different groups, and the plurality of 'points of view' that they can mobilize. The references or supports that I draw on are thus not homogeneous, or even inscribed in a single field of knowledge, and yet I fully inscribe my own approach in the space of sociological knowledge. There will be no trace of interdisciplinarity or pluridisciplinarity in these apparent mixtures, which are always placed at the service of the coherent construction of sociological reflection.

Even so, it might be thought odd that the contents page of a work purporting to speak of 'action' should include reflections on literary experiment (and daydreams), on educational practices and the everyday practices of writing, or again developments around the processes of embodiment. My wager is that reading the book as a whole will remove the initial disquiet or surprise and lead the reader to conclude that these diverse elements – apparently 'off the subject' – will finally prove useful and even necessary in order to elaborate my theory of the plural actor and the plurality of logics of action.

But the reader may legitimately wonder about the usefulness of a sociological theory of action and the actor outside the scientific realm. In point of fact, I see the various descriptions and analyses of action as always having socio-political correlates, implicitly if not explicitly. According to whether the wellsprings of action are understood in this fashion or that, the ways of transforming the existing order of things or of maintaining it intact, modifying or preserving behaviour patterns, may be very different. Theories of action are therefore, at bottom, always political theories: by answering the question 'What is acting?', they prepare the ground for reforms in ways of acting. If we are in a position to grasp the processes that lead actors in a society to act as they do, it then becomes possible to act on their actions and change them.[2] This is a fascinating perspective, but also a dangerous one (the least democratic uses of sociological knowledge being always possible), yet one that deserves to be opened up, if only to provide the means for counteracting the effects of all *technê* of manipulation (political, cultural, symbolic, educational), indissociable as they are from contemporary modes of the exercise of power. To touch on the programmes or matrices of socialization of actors is, as the author of the *Nicomachean Ethics* already put it, leading them to act differently, in a way that one can hope will be more virtuous and democratic:

> By doing the things that we do in the presence of danger, and by being habituated to feel fear or confidence, we become brave or cowardly. The same is true of appetites and feelings of anger; some men become temperate and good-tempered, others self-indulgent and irascible, by behaving in one way or another in the appropriate circumstances. Thus, in one word, states of character arise out of activities. This is why the activities we exhibit must be of a certain kind; it is because the states of character correspond to the differences between these. (Aristotle, 1998, p. 29)

Act I

Outline of a Theory of the Plural Actor

> It follows that a theory of action should not be so abstract or speculative as to distance us from understanding the concreteness of 'real life' and of 'life in general'. Reading some theories of action, it is easy to get lost in their abstractions and their dense commentaries directed towards points made by other theorists; so that after reading these writings it takes a leap of imagination to become immersed again in events, happenings, understandings, and the problems, passions and struggles of actual people, and their institutions and other collectivities.
> (Anselm L. Strauss, *Continual Permutations of Action*)

Scene 1

THE PLURAL ACTOR

> Those who make a practice of comparing human actions are never so perplexed as when they try to see them as a whole and in the same light; for they commonly contradict each other so strangely that it seems impossible that they have come from the same shop.
> (Montaigne, *The Complete Essays*, 'Of the inconsistency of our actions')

On Singleness

Like the terrestrial globe, the ensemble made up of various theories of the actor has two great poles: that of the singleness of the actor and that of an internal fragmentation. On the one side, the quest is for their vision of the world, their relationship to the world or 'the generating formula of their practices'; on the other, the multiplicity of embodied knowledge and skills, of lived experience, is accepted, likewise of 'egos' or 'roles' that are internalized by the actor (repertoire of roles, stock of knowledge, reserve of available knowledge, etc.). In both cases, however, the choice of singleness or fragmentation is made *a priori*; it constitutes an undiscussed postulate and in some cases is based more on ethical assumptions than on empirical observations.

The chief interest of the first position was well expressed by Pierre Bourdieu, when he explained that 'the virtue, at once heuristic and explanatory' of his theory of habitus 'is never seen better than in the case of practices that are often studied separately' (Bourdieu and Wacquant, 1992, p. 131).[1] But this leads at the same time to insisting, too exclusively no doubt, on the 'systematic' and 'unifying' aspect of habitus:

Taste, the propensity and capacity to appropriate (materially or symbolically) a given class of classified, classifying objects or practices, is the generative formula of life-style, a unitary set of distinctive preferences which express the same expressive intention in the specific logic of each of the symbolic sub-spaces, furniture, clothing, language or body hexis. Each dimension of life-style 'symbolizes with' the others, in Leibniz's phrase, and symbolizes them. An old cabinetmaker's world view, the way he manages his budget, his time or his body, his use of language and choice of clothing are fully present in his ethic of scrupulous, impeccable craftsmanship and in the aesthetic of work for work's sake which leads him to measure the beauty of his products by the care and patience that have gone into them. (Bourdieu, 1984, pp. 173–4)

This kind of example, which sometimes condenses or combines the set of properties that are statistically most attached to a social group, is useful for illustrating macro-sociological models. However, it may become a deceptive caricature once it does not just have this illustrative status, but is taken as a particular case of the real. For the social reality embodied in each singular actor is already less smooth and less simple than this. Besides, if the results of large-scale investigations indicate those properties, attitudes, practices, opinions, etc., that are most common to one or other social group of category, they do not say that each individual composing the group or category, or even the majority of them, combine all or even the majority of these properties.

If we expected the opposite (as many trainee sociologists do, and many professional sociologists as well), then an encounter with the subjects of investigation (i.e. individuals in their irreducible singularity) would be quite disturbing. How many students in the social sciences complain at not having selected in their studied population 'real workers', 'real managers' or 'real craftsmen', believing the problem to be methodological, whereas the actual mistake is one of the conception of the social world. What should be done about actors who do not combine the totality of properties that characterize the group as a whole? Unskilled workers who read more than is expected of them, and who upset the envisaged social problematic of class tastes and distastes? Those who, in some respects, in some areas, seem very close to salaried employees or intermediate professions?

It is not a matter of questioning the existence of actors corresponding to the model of the craftsman Bourdieu cites (and whom the sociologist may well encounter in his research), but one of stressing the fact that not all actors are cast in the same mould. Bourdieu's example mobilizes a phenomenological scheme that is presented in Husserl's philosophy – i.e. the idea of the fundamental unity of subjectivity: 'Who would want to separate knowing subjectivity from affective subjectivity, from the subjectivity that aspires, desires, wants and acts, from the subjectivity that in some sense evaluates and works towards a goal? Subjectivity cannot be decomposed ... into separate elements to be juxtaposed like parts external to one another in the same subjectivity' (Husserl, 1990, pp. 66–7). The philosophical inheritance, which does not pose any problem in itself, requires all the same to be validated empirically rather than considered pertinent *a priori*. What proves that subjectivity does not function by simply piling up or storing knowledge and experience rather than by synthesis and unification? If the postulate (which should rather be a hypothesis) of coherence and homogeneity of the different types of embodied experience (in the form of schemes) is undoubtedly more intellectually appealing than that of dispersal, separation or generalized fragmentation (we must ask what are the social foundations of the exercise of such a seductive power), elements of confirmation still need to be found in empirical work. As we shall see, however, experimental psychology,[2] as well a part of contemporary cultural psychology, does indeed produce tangible scientific results that seriously put in question the premises of singleness. In the face of such research findings, the hypothesis becomes more embarrassing than anything else, no matter how seductive it may be.

In relation to theories of 'cognitive style' (Berry, 1976; Witkin, 1967), for example, based on the idea that the same cognitive style underlies cognitive conduct on the most varied subjects, psychologists have shown through empirical studies stylistic incoherences between one field (e.g. perception) and another (e.g. social interaction), as well as incoherences in terms of style of response to different tasks that supposedly belong to the same cognitive field (e.g. recognition of forms) (Cole, 1996, p. 94).

But the same kind of challenge can be heard as well in both anthropology and history. Several anthropologists start from the principle that the society, community, tribe, etc., that they study are necessarily homogeneous ensembles in which each situation is homologous to all others. This supposed homology of situations (domains of practices) makes it possible to believe that one can reconstruct, in the study of a single situation, a reduced model or a metaphor of the society as a whole (e.g., for Clifford Geertz, cock-fighting in Bali or the puppet theatre as metaphor or metonym of Balinese society). At bottom, however, is there not the same interpretative scheme in the theory of habitus, *mutatis mutandis*, if not at the level of the whole society, then at least at that of a 'life style' attached to a 'class of conditions of existence'? Each dimension of this life style 'symbolizes with' the others and 'symbolizes' them, just as each field of practice in a society is in a metaphorical relationship with all others. What may appear terribly homogenizing in one case (society) seems unchallenged in the other (habitus, life style).

In the same way, in history, the critique of the notion of 'mentality' by Geoffrey E. R. Lloyd again attacks the unitary and homogenizing conceptions that often go together with it. It is difficult in fact to validate historically the idea of the existence of a 'single mentality' in a group or in an individual, whatever the social activity under consideration:

> One point at which the talk of mentalities does not just fail to provide an accurate description, but positively misleads, relates to the *diversities* that exist between inter-personal exchanges of different types within the same culture at the same period ... Those who participated in the political assemblies and law-courts, and who attended the debates of the sophists, did not, we may be sure, *always* behave in that marked adversarial fashion: they did not *always* bring to bear the keen critical acumen in the evaluation of evidence and arguments that they *often* did in *those* contexts. If rationality in the sense of a demand for an account to be given – *logon didonai* – was often the watchword of the new-style enquiries, as of much political debate, that certainly did not mean an end to irrationality, and the very same groups who deployed the watchword were capable of ignoring it or of suspending the criteria it implied, and not just in politics but in science as well. (Lloyd, 1990, p. 142)

Lloyd also stresses the fact that the same populations that appropriated certain aspects of rational thought could perfectly well continue to adhere – in practice – to magical and religious beliefs. One part of themselves could engage in rational thinking while another part remained in the frameworks of magical thinking, since 'these "thoughts" are tied to "socially circumscribed" social contexts' (ibid., p. 143). Rather than evoking general mentalities, Lloyd cautiously prefers to appeal to the historical analysis of social contexts in which these 'mentalities' are enunciated, manifested and deployed (the 'circumstances of their formulation', the 'types of social interaction', etc.).[3] The theses of singleness and homogeneity (of both culture and actor) are thus by no means self-evident.

The single self: a commonplace illusion, but socially well founded

> A proper name is something extremely important in a novel, a capital thing. You can no more change the name of a character than his skin. It is like trying to whiten a black man.
> (Gustave Flaubert, *Correspondance*, to Louis Bonenfant)

At the opposite pole to the thesis of singleness, Erving Goffman – among others – set out to criticize unitary conceptions of the actor, which, according to him, in a certain sense echoed the everyday conceptions of the self:

> We come to expect that all his acts will exhibit the same style, be stamped in a unique way. If every strip of activity is enmeshed and anchored in its environing world so that it necessarily bears the marks of what produced it, then surely it is reasonable to say that each utterance or physical doing that the individual contributes to a current situation will be rooted in his biographical, personal identity. Behind the current role, the person himself will peek out. Indeed, this is a common way of framing our perception of another. So three cheers for the self. Now let us try to reduce the clatter. (Goffman, 1974, pp. 293–4).

Seeking 'the' generating formula of an actor's practices, reconstituting 'the' style ('cognitive' or 'of life') that persists and is expressed in the most varied fields of activity – isn't this sharing the commonplace illusion of singleness and invariability? We well know how 'lunatics', 'weathercocks', 'opportunists' or 'chameleons',[4] those who change their opinion and their behaviour depending on their interlocutor or the situation, are not well thought of: at the opposite pole are those whose behaviour is 'frank' and who proudly display their pride at not being moved ('influenced') by the most varied situations they encounter. Everything happens as if there were a specific symbolic and moral profit (as the very terms of inconstancy, versatility and unfaithfulness to oneself suggest) in believing oneself 'identical' or 'faithful' to oneself at every time and place, whatever the events experienced or tests undergone ('I've not changed'; 'I'm always the same'.)[5] How many hagiographies of artists or intellectuals stress, as one of their most positive features, the fact that the individual in question basically had just one single idea or line of thought, which they developed throughout their career (the novelist who always writes the same book, the painter who always paints the same canvas . . .)? By recalling that 'commonplace experience of life as a unity and a totality' is a social (and literary) construction, Bourdieu seeks none the less to escape the idea of a self reduced to 'the rhapsody of individual sensations', by appeal to habitus as an 'active principle, irreducible to passive perceptions, the unification of practices and representations' (1986a, p. 70). The concept of habitus (sociology) thus comes to the rescue of a socially well-founded illusion (common sense), without conceding anything to empiricism.[6]

Goffman, therefore, vigorously challenges these commonplace myths of an invariable personal identity:

> What they discover from their gleanings will apparently point to what this fellow is like beyond the current situation. But every situation he is in will provide his others with such an image. That is what situations can do for us. That is a reason why we find them (as we find novels) engrossing. But that is no reason to think that all these gleanings about himself that an individual makes available, all those pointings from his current situation to the way he is in his other occasions, have anything very much in common. (Goffman, 1974, p. 299)

This, however, does not prevent us from immediately perceiving the opposite risk of falling into a kind of radical empiricism that would not grasp anything more than a dusty haze of identities, roles, behaviours, actions and reactions with no kind of connection among them.[7]

However, this scientific illusion (which sociologists have to take into account in their interpretation of the social world, but which they should not stumble over) does not lack a social foundation. There are many permanent institutions, just as there are several more ephemeral occasions, that celebrate the unity of the self – to start with, the 'proper name' that consecrates the whole singularity of the 'person'. These personal and emotional coordinates with which their bearers identify themselves symbolically (as opposed to the more precise and singular numerical identifications that are less conducive to the projection of identity: social security number, credit card number, gas customer number . . .), or into which they project themselves – and which immediately seem to evoke the totality of a person in the eyes of those who know them – are astonishing unificatory abstractions in relation to the diversity of social reality. Child, adolescent or adult, father, lover, football player, stamp collector, political comrade or factory worker, the same biological body is denoted by the same name and surname.[8] Quite naturally, the abstraction ends up taking bodily form, supported by the evidence of the body's biological unity. Socially, however, the same body passes through different states and is the irrevocable bearer of heterogeneous and even contradictory schemes of action or habits.

The realism of the name is constantly reinforced by administrative demands (public or private), which are so many injunctions to exhibit one's identity and recall its singularity, as well as by the various identity papers (identity card, passport, residence permit, driving licence, social security card, blood-group card) that often refer to nothing other than themselves (e.g. on the identity card: name, surname, height, particular features), as well as certain spatio-temporal and national coordinates (e.g. date and place of birth, nationality, home address).[9] It is also the name that provides the basis of the stylized manuscript representation (one therefore indissociable from the singular person and his body) constituted by the signature, a singular mark *par excellence*. Name and surname, signature, these semantically weak signs claim to enclose us fully, and are summary but powerful unifiers or our personal identity.

Actors are also given other occasions and other means for reducing the diversity of individual practices and events to the unity of a coherent and unified self, at least in some of their dimensions (educational, professional, familial, sexual . . .). One can think of the curriculum vitae (accompanying the rationalization and technicization of entry into the labour market) as a technique of presentation of self, or of the various 'narratives of self' produced in the confidences made to those near and dear (friends or members of the same family), or, more rarely, to persons unknown (life stories solicited by social-science researchers or 'heard' by psychologists, psychoanalysts, specialists in social work, etc.), which give actors the possibility of elaborating partial syntheses, putting order and coherence where this did not necessarily exist.[10] And, finally, there are the more official kinds such as funeral orations, obituaries, panegyrics, official biographies, etc., which provide models of a totalizing and unificatory presentation. In all cases, we can say that the work needed to maintain the illusion is that much more laborious for actors who are precociously and lastingly enrolled in social groups and worlds that are multiple, heterogeneous and contradictory.

If the first tradition lays too great a weight on unity and singleness, the second grants too much importance to fragmentation. We finally have to reject both, the unificatory 'formula', 'system' or 'principle', on the one hand, and the generalized fragmentation or dispersed fractioning, on the other. From this point of view, Pierre Naville showed a very fine sense more than fifty years ago in describing the multiplicity of our systems of embodied habits, bound up with different fields of existence and social worlds that we traverse:

You will find in this particular individual more or less coordinated systems of habits, and above all the professional ones that are the basis of social existence. But you will also find all kinds of other behaviours: conjugal, parental, religious, political, in relation to food, play, etc. In sum, the personality is the sum of activities revealed by direct observation of behaviour during a period long enough to provide certain data; in other words, it is simply the end product of our systems of habits. (1942, pp. 220–1)

The particular pertinence of Naville's formulation will become clear through later discussions. For the moment, let us simply emphasize the articulation that this quotation maintains between systems of habits and fields of practices. What we can criticize the two theoretical tendencies cited above for is not their theorizing in one particular way or another, but rather their theorizing in a general and universal fashion, as if actors at all times and in all places had to correspond to the model of the actor that they have constructed. But the question of the singleness or plurality of the actor is as much a historical (or empirical) question as a theoretical one. The question must therefore be asked in the following terms: what are the socio-historical conditions that make possible a plural actor or an actor characterized by a profound singleness?

The socio-historical conditions of singleness and plurality

> These supple variations and contradiction that are seen in us . . .
> (Montaigne, *The Complete Essays*)

> I well believe, Gentlemen, that the age of a civilization must be measured by the number of contradictions it accumulates, by the number of incompatible customs and beliefs that jostle and temper one another: by the plurality of the philosophies and aesthetics that coexist and cohabit in the same head.
> (Paul Valéry, *Variety*)

One thing is clear: for us to be dealing with an actor who displays a homogeneous and coherent system of dispositions or schemes, quite specific social conditions are required, ones that are not always met with, and indeed are met with only exceptionally. Émile Durkheim, who used the notion of habitus in the sense of a very coherent and lasting relation to the world, evoked this concept in connection with two particular historical situations: 'traditional societies' and 'the boarding-school regime'. In the first case, Durkheim wrote: 'The lesser development of individuality, the smaller scale of the group, and the homogeneity of external circumstances all contribute to reducing the differences and variations to a minimum. The group regularly produces an intellectual and moral uniformity of which we find only rare examples in the more advanced societies. Everything is common to everyone' (Durkheim, 1976, p. 5). And it is certainly no accident that Pierre Bourdieu gave the notion of habitus new currency precisely so as to grasp adequately the functioning of a traditional and weakly differentiated society – i.e. the Kabyl. Given the great homogeneity, great coherence and great stability of the material and cultural conditions of existence, and the principles of socialization that followed from these, the actors fashioned by such societies are endowed with a stock of embodied schemes of action that are particularly homogeneous and coherent.

In the second case, Durkheim used the term 'habitus' in connection with Christian education as a milieu that totally envelops the child with a unique and constant influence. Habitus, for Durkheim, corresponds perfectly to the boarding-school situation, where the child is cloistered for board and lodging as well as lessons; this is a truly total institution in Goffman's (1961) sense. As a small-scale model of the undifferentiated community, however, the total institution owes its originality and exceptionality to the fact that it lives embedded in a society that is highly differentiated. Like traditional societies,[11] it is characterized by a restricted number of actors in all domains of existence, domains which are otherwise experienced more commonly in different places and with different actors (in our work, play, family, sporting, religious activities, etc., we are customarily led to frequent actors and sites that are more or less institutionally differentiated). On the other hand, the total institution has to struggle against possible contact between its actors and the outside world (with its exogenous values), and in any case it includes two major categories of actor: those who organize the institution and those who undergo its programme of socialization. The total institution is thus a world that presents itself as 'total' and unique within the context of a differentiated society.

And it is this institution that constitutes 'the natural means of realizing in an integrated way the Christian idea of education' (Durkheim, 1977, p. 119):

> To be able to act thus powerfully on the deepest recesses of the soul it is patently essential that the different influences to which the child is subjected are not dispersed in different directions but are, rather,

vigorously concentrated towards one and the same goal. This can be achieved only by making children live in one and the same moral environment, which is constantly present to them, which enshrouds them completely, and from whose influence they are unable, as it were, to escape. (Ibid., p. 29)

Education is then 'organized', Durkheim goes on to say, 'in such a way as to be able to produce the profound and lasting effect demanded from it' (ibid., pp. 30–1). It follows that individuals can have general and coherent dispositions that are transferable from one sphere of activity or one practice to another if – and only if – their social experiences have always been governed by the same principles. Far from this being regularly the case, it may well be a historical exception.[12]

Erwin Panovsky also indicates very clearly, in his celebrated *Gothic Architecture and Scholasticism*, what an 'exception' is the historical context he is studying, one that makes it possible to explain the deep homology of structure between Gothic art and scholastic philosophy on the basis of the scheme of 'mental habit' or 'habit-forming force'. Panovsky's remark deserves to be taken seriously, instead of considering this admission of the exceptionality of the period and geographical zone studied as simply a rhetorical effect that the author produces with the aim of attracting the reader to his object of research. In order for this 'habit-forming force' to be observable, socio-historical conditions must be right for it, as Panovsky tells us by insisting on the particular homogeneity of the historical conditions in which the architects of the time lived – a homogeneity that was the result of an educational monopoly: 'Often it is difficult or impossible to single out one habit-forming force from many others and to imagine the channels of transmission. However the period from about 1130–40 to about 1270 and the "100-mile zone around Paris" constitute an exception. In this tight little sphere Scholasticism possessed what amounted to a monopoly in education' (1957, pp. 21–2).

Pierre Bourdieu wrote a postface to the book, and was broadly inspired by Panovsky's implicit sociology in developing and reinforcing his theory of habitus. But he did not stress in his commentary the exceptionality of the context studied here. Taking this into account would no doubt have forced him to relativize the singleness, durability and transposability of the constitutive schemes or dispositions of habitus.

Paradoxically, however, the same author's first works, on Algeria in the 1960s, were what led him towards the construction of a theory of the actor and of action that was more sensitive to the plurality of schemes of embodied experience and habit-forming forces.[13] In *Le Déracinement*, in fact, Pierre Bourdieu and Abdelmalek Sayad analysed the situation of 'doubling, which generally offered the colonized a solution through which he escaped the contradictions of a double existence' (Bourdieu and Sayad, 1964, p. 69). They wavered, moreover, according to phases of this work, and in a particularly interesting fashion, between this model of 'doubling' (mental and social), which assumes that the actors of the social world apply different and often contradictory manners of speaking and acting within different social worlds (the family on the one hand, the colonial world on the other), and that of 'cultural lingua franca', which rather implies a mixture and confusion of genres and registers and, in the end, a contradiction at the very heart of each practice.[14]

The counter-model of these cases of forced doubling or cultural pidgin compelled by the colonial situation is of course that of the traditional cultural universe, supposedly homogeneous and coherent: 'What actually is the *niya*, an almost untranslatable notion, if not a certain way of being and acting, a permanent, general and transposable disposition towards the world and other people?' (Bourdieu and Sayad, 1964, p. 88). 'Because his being is above all a certain manner of being, a habitus, a permanent and general disposition towards the world and others, the peasant can remain a peasant even when there is no longer the possibility of behaving as a peasant' (ibid., p. 102). It is thus the model of traditional Algerian peasant society, one with a weak division of labour, on which the theory of habitus is ultimately built, by this token carrying the cases of doubling or cultural pidgin on the back of exceptional and somewhat monstrous historical situations. The paradox lies in the fact of having at the end of the day retained the model of habitus adapted to an approach to weakly differentiated societies (pre-industrial, pre-capitalist) in order to study societies that are highly differentiated, and which by definition necessarily produce actors that are more differentiated both between one another and internally.

And yet there are such great differences between *demographically weak traditional societies*, on the one hand, in which people have strong personal knowledge of one another and each can exert a control over others, where the division of labour and differentiation of social functions and spheres of activity are little advanced (impossible, in fact, to distinguish here specific spheres of activity – economic, political, legal, religious, moral, scientific, philosophical, etc., that are clearly separated from one another), where the stability and durability of conditions to which actors are subject throughout their lives is maximal, where there are thus hardly any different, competing, contradictory models of socialization, and, on the other hand, *contemporary societies*, which are incomparably larger both spatially and demographically, with a strong differentiation of spheres of activity, institutions, cultural products and models of socialization, and with less stability in the conditions of socialization. Between the family, school, peer groups, various cultural institutions, the media, etc., that they are often led to frequent, the children of our social formations are increasingly confronted with heterogeneous and competing situations, which are sometimes indeed in contradiction with one another in terms of the principles of socialization that they develop.

I have noted above the difficulties that are encountered today by those total institutions that dream of a homogeneous world and a homogeneous socialization, in a social formation that is deeply differentiated and with heterogeneous principles of socialization. But there is another kind of social world, i.e. the world of work, especially when this involves a profession endowed with an *esprit de corps*, which – within very specific social and mental limits, since actors are never reducible to their existence at work – reproduces, even within differentiated societies, conditions of socialization that are relatively coherent and homogeneous. It is to Maurice Halbwachs that we owe the most penetrating sociological analyses of these corporate professional worlds. First of all, 'each individual who enters a profession must, when he learns to apply certain practical rules, open himself to this sensibility that may be called the corporate spirit, and which resembles the collective memory of the professional group.' This esprit de corps is explained by the long past of the function, by the fact that 'the people who exercise it are in frequent contact . . ., that they accomplish the same operations or in any case are engaged in operations of the same nature . . . [and] have the perennial feeling that their activities are combined with a view to a common undertaking'; but also because 'their function can be distinguished from other functions of the social body'; that it 'is important for them, and in the interest of their own profession, to emphasize these differences and make them clearly visible' (Halbwachs, 1992, p. 139). And Halbwachs grasps right away the fragility of such an enterprise in a differentiated society in which the 'spirit' of these 'professional bodies' can potentially be challenged by competing and heteronomous logics, all the more so in that the members of these groups do not belong exclusively to them, and that even in the context of their professional activity they live in permanent contact with outsiders who do not share the same values.

The members of such a body are thus obliged to create institutional separations if they do not wish to be penetrated by exogenous logics. Extended contact with these other logics takes place in the context of regulated and institutionalized exchanges that place the outsiders on the terrain of the professionals, and not in the context of encounters between equals, a course of interactions in which all points of view are valid. For example, a judge has to listen to external logics in the context of his own logic, rather than entering into a dialogue with this external logic:

> Given this situation, we may ask whether prolonged and often renewed contact with people dominated by other thoughts and feelings that differ from their own may not lead to the weakening and decline of the professional spirit among the people assigned to a function. In order to resist people who will most of the time oppose them in the name of collective beliefs and traditions, functionaries must rely on beliefs and traditions peculiar to their group. In other words, the judiciary, for example, is obliged to erect all sorts of barriers between its members and those of the other groups to whom they render justice, so as to resist external influences and the passions and prejudices of the plaintiffs. This is why their costume, the place they occupy in the court of justice, and all the apparatus of the tribunals indicate visually the distance that separates the group of judges from all others. It is also why communication between judges and plaintiffs does not take place in the form of a conversation – as it does in other groups – but through interrogations or in writing, following certain forms, or through the mediation of notaries and lawyers. (Halbwachs, 1992, p. 140)

There exist, in the same way, family worlds that are non-contradictory, made up of adults who are highly coherent among themselves, in which different principles of socialization do not interfere with one another, and that exercise their socializing effects on children in a regular, systematic and lasting fashion. But these family worlds, which objectively tend once again towards the model of the total institution, encounter almost the same social difficulties in persisting.

We can observe in research, for example, higher or less high levels of educational energy and coherence in terms of practices of reading and writing, stronger or less strong densities and coherences in educational work (Lahire, 1995d). There can be various encouragements to reading and writing: precocious initiation to reading and writing (sometimes with the purchase of reading methods), printed matter mobilized with the aim of extending family discussions, educational themes or cultural visits, subscription to various children's magazines that creates such a need in the child early on (certain parents describe waiting for such magazines at the end of the month as an exhilarating moment), books or magazines that are given for various important dates in the child's life (loss of a tooth, birthday, name day, good results, Christmas, etc.), visiting a public library to accustom the child to the place and world of printed culture, precocious formation of the child's own book collection, reading stories in the evening or at different times of day, frequent resort to the dictionary, gradual inculcation into exchanges of letters (from signature to the complete writing of letters or postcards), proposals to make drafts in order to check or have checked possible mistakes, gifts of address and phone-number books or diaries that call for reading, invitations to read short texts, to keep a notebook during the holidays, to write short words or take phone messages, etc.

According to the intensity and regularity of these encouragements, children are subject to matrices of socialization into writing that are more or less implacable. Certain parents are unflinching in their daily struggle for the acculturation of their children; others admit their abandonment of certain solicitations or vigilance (requests to write texts, taking them to the library, questions about certain difficult words or about reading, etc.), or they describe less tight networks of encouragement; still others are not in favourable conditions or lack the skills needed to encourage their children in any other way than disciplinary.

The educational investment in bourgeois milieus seems sometimes close to the academic and cultural overinvestment of intermediary milieus, even if the educational work carried out may be denied (the aspects of play or the shared emotion of time spent together are then emphasized). All the same, the educative work objectively realized shows very well that the 'inheritance of cultural capital' never takes place 'naturally', even in those families that are best endowed. It is striking to note the degree to which the 'transmission' of this capital requires constant and interminable daily work, sometimes painful for the children and parents alike.[15] For example, a child (eight years old, both parents doctors) 'groans' when his mother asks him to go and consult the dictionary, and she tells us that, even if he doesn't manage this very well, 'that is how you learn'. She does not hesitate to speak herself of the daily 'struggle' over homework repeated over the weekend, which cannot always be experienced as a childish joy. We could just as well mention the encouragement to writing letters or the demand to read when children, boys in particular, prefer for example to play football. One may even ask whether the dilettante attitude that is sometimes described in the sociology of education or culture is not an optical illusion, in which the sociologists share the illusion that the actors want to give, but also and above all that they give themselves. In fact, one need only objectify – in other words, describe with precision and systematically certain everyday situations – for the hidden educative work to become apparent, and even the subterranean educative discipline that is equally necessary to have children who are highly successful at school and have the taste for reading and writing.[16]

The strongest educative densities and coherences, which assume a constant presence and are most often realized when mothers have 'chosen' not to work in order to devote themselves entirely to their children's education, then lead to a kind of very tight control over the implicit and/or explicit programme of socialization (e.g. in respect to the inculcation of tastes and of reading and writing skills: keeping the child away from the television and video player or very strict control of programmes that are watched, restriction of children's propensity to read only comics, control of the choice of books read by the children – with respect to style as well as content – etc.). Despite this tight regulation of the family experience of socialization, which demands a real fighting spirit in daily life, the children experience social situations outside the family that make the task of these adults particularly difficult.

We could pose the theoretical and historical problem of the social foundations of singleness (or of homogeneity) by borrowing the insightful words of Roger Benoliel and Roger Establet: 'The production of homogeneous habitus in all spheres of life is a schoolteacher's dream. The cultural transfers that are intended or desired come up against many forms of resistance: social interests mobilized in opposing directions, indifferent audience, rebellious cultural material, competing sources of legitimacy. On the one hand the intentions of educational convicts, on the other social life in the open air' (1991, p. 29). And it is certainly not the state that is in a position, as is sometimes said in an abstract and superficial way,[17] to compensate for the multiplicity and heterogeneity of social worlds (and of social and socializing experiences) by a work of homogenization of the ensemble of national habitus.

The coherence of the habits or schemes of action (sensory-motor schemes, schemes of perception, appreciation, evaluation, etc.) that the actor has internalized thus depends on the coherence of the principles of socialization to which they have been subjected. Once an actor has been placed, simultaneously or successively, within a plurality of social worlds that are non-homogeneous, and sometimes even contradictory, or within social worlds that are relatively coherent but present contradictions in certain aspects, we are then dealing with an actor with a stock of schemes of action or habits that are non-homogeneous, non-unified, and with practices that are consequently heterogeneous (and even contradictory), varying according to the social context in which they are led to develop. I could sum up my thesis here by saying that every (individual) body plunged into a plurality of social worlds is subjected to heterogeneous and sometimes contradictory principles of socialization that they embody.

Rather than considering the coherence and homogeneity of the schemes that make up the stock of each individual actor as the typical situation, that which is most commonly observable in a differentiated society, it thus seems to me preferable to believe it is the most improbable situation, the most exceptional, and that it is far more usual to observe individual actors who are less unified and bear habits (schemes of action) that are heterogeneous and in some cases opposed and contradictory.

The plurality of social contexts and repertoires of habits

> We are all patchwork, and so shapeless and diverse in composition that each bit, each moment, plays its own game. And there is as much difference between us and ourselves as between us and others. *Consider it a great thing to play the part of one single man . . .*
> (Montaigne, *The Complete Essays*)

This heterogeneity of socializing experiences, which so many researchers are rediscovering today, was something that Maurice Halbwachs already placed at the heart of his reflections on memory. In fact, Halbwachs reminded us that 'each man is immersed successively or simultaneously in several groups' (1980, p. 78), and that the latter are themselves neither homogeneous nor immutable (ibid., p. 85).[18] These groups that constitute the social contexts of our memory are thus heterogeneous, and the individuals that go through them in the course of the same period of time or of different moments in their lives are thus the always variegated product of this heterogeneity of points of view, memories, types of experience: what we lived through with our parents, at primary and secondary school, with friends or colleagues from work, with members of the same political, religious or cultural association, cannot necessarily be cumulated and synthesized in an easy way . . . Without needing to postulate a logic of absolute discontinuity, by assuming that these contexts are radically different from one another and that actors jump every moment from one interaction to another, one situation to another, one social world to another, one domain of existence to another without any sense of continuity, we can believe all the same – and establish this empirically – that these experiences are not all systematically coherent, homogeneous or even totally compatible, despite our being indeed their bearers. Halbwachs thus already traced the lineaments of a dynamic vision, sensitive to the heterogeneity and plurality of experiences.[19]

To be sure, we know that the moments in the life of a human being when their different habits – or different repertoires of habits – are formed are not all equivalent. We can generally separate the period of 'primary' socialization (essentially in the family) from all those that follow, and that are called 'secondary' (school, peer group, work, etc.). If this distinction is important in reminding us that, at the first moments of socialization, the child embodies, in greatest socio-affective dependence towards the adults that surround it, '*the* world, the only existent and only conceivable world, the world *tout court*' (Berger and Luckmann, 1979, p. 154), and not a world perceived as relative and thus specific, it often leads to representing the individual trajectory as a passage from homogeneity (the family sub-world that forms the most fundamental mental structures) to heterogeneity (the multiple sub-worlds frequented by an actor already formed, who is then not fundamentally changed, or in any case not as profoundly as in their initial universe of reference). Various empirical facts, however, speak against this kind of simplistic representation. First of all, the homogeneity of the family universe is presupposed and never demonstrated. And yet, whether heterogeneity here is only relative, or leads to the most exacerbated family contradictions and conflicts (e.g. the case of family situations that lead to a kind of 'splitting of the self' in the child), it is always irreducibly present at the heart of the family configuration, which is never a perfect total institution.

But the primary–secondary succession or 'superposition' is frequently challenged by the very early socializing action (in certain cases, increasingly precocious) of social worlds or actors outside the family universe. This includes the experience of a nurse (a few days or weeks after birth), the crèche (just a few months after birth) or the infant school (from the age of two). It is impossible to act as if the implicit socialization programmes of these different social actors or worlds were necessarily and systematically harmonious with that of the family. How can we not see that the child placed in the crèche at a very early age learns in the first few months of its life that people do not expect the same things of it, and do not treat it identically, 'here' and 'there'? Peter Berger and Thomas Luckmann, describing the case of a nurse who came from a very different social world from that of the child's parents, even spoke of the possibility of an 'unsuccessful socialization', resulting from 'the mediation of acutely discrepant worlds by significant others during primary socialization' (1979, p. 188). Without introducing the (normative) notion of 'failure', we have to note that the experience of a plurality of worlds has every chance of being precocious in our ultra-differentiated societies. Finally, the secondary socializations, even when carried out in different socio-affective conditions, may profoundly put in question and compete with the family monopoly on the socialization of the child and the adolescent. The case of individuals 'upwardly declassed', which we shall describe further on, is a most flagrant example of this.

We therefore live (relatively)[20] simultaneously and successively in differentiated social contexts. There are on the one hand classic social institutions (around which sociology has organized some of its fields of research): the family, the school, the professional world, the church, the association, the sports club, the worlds of art, politics, sport, etc. But these different social worlds are not equivalent. For example, while the family context (in all its observable variations) remains, in our societies, among the most universally widespread socializing matrices, the church and the sports club are not just social worlds frequented only by a section of the actors of a society; they are places where certain actors exercise their principal social activity (the priest, the sports coach). In certain social worlds, it is possible to be a 'consumer', a spectator or an amateur, whereas others are rather producers and professionals. But this distinction makes no sense in the family world or in that of the workplace.

These worlds are sometimes – but not systematically – organized in the form of fields (of forces and struggles) in the sense that Pierre Bourdieu gave to this term. The historical process of differentiation of spheres of activity is not in every case reducible to the appearance of relatively autonomous 'social fields' as structured spaces of positions, with their specific stakes, rules of the game, interests, capitals and struggles (between the different dominant and dominated agents that seek to maintain their position, if not to improve it), where what is at stake is the (unequal) structure of distribution of capitals. The family universe, for example, does not in the strict sense form a field, any more than do the sporadic meetings of friends in a bar; the meetings of lovers or the holiday practices of windsurfing or climbing are not situations that can be assigned to a particular social field. Contrary to what the most general formulations may lead one to believe, not every social interaction or social situation can be classified in this way. Fields are essentially the domain of 'professional' (and 'public') activities, and above all those of 'agents' in struggle within these fields – i.e. producers (as opposed to consumers, spectators or persons participating in the field but not being particularly engaged in struggles within it: lower administrative staff, service personnel, workers, etc.).

Field of power, political, administrative or journalistic field, field of publishing, literary and theatrical field, field of the comic book, of painting, of fashion, philosophical and scientific field, social science field, university and college field, field of agents of geriatric management . . . it is notable that certain fields are sub-fields of others (the sociological field is a sub-field of the social science field, which is in turn a sub-field of the scientific and/or university field, which is again a sub-field of the field of cultural production, itself a sub-field of the field of power, which is itself a section of social space). Besides, certain fields are scientific constructions of reality which do not totally coincide with the divisions made to constitute other fields (e.g. the legal and medical fields each include sections of what otherwise forms the university field, as well as other extra-university elements). We can also note that certain practices or objects belong to several fields at the same time (e.g. a novel belongs to the literary field but also to that of publishing), and that the same physical person may belong to several fields at the same time (political and scientific fields, philosophical, literary and theatre fields . . .). But, above all, a large number of actors are outside any of these fields, drowned in a great 'social space' that has as its structuring axis only the volume and structure of capital possessed (cultural and economic). A good deal of scholarly energy has gone into explaining the great stages of power, but little into understanding those who build the sets and move the backdrops, sweep the floors and corridors, photocopy documents or type letters, etc., and who sometimes attend shows or consume the products of the producers (read novels, philosophical essays, works of social science, comic books, newspapers, etc., go to a theatre or museum, vote and watch politicians on television, move into retirement homes or move their parents there, play sport or appear in court, go to church and send their children to catechism or follow Koranic instruction, view fashion shows on television or photographs of models in magazines, etc.); there is little interest, therefore, in understanding life offstage or outside the field of the producers of the field.

It is quite revealing, given this exclusion of 'time outside the field' and 'actors outside the field', that this sociology not only focuses on the situation of those who are 'born in the field' or 'born in the game' (children of university teachers who follow the same profession themselves . . .), but that it sometimes misleadingly generalizes this model of the actor: 'The *illusio* is a kind of knowledge that is based on the fact of being *born in the game*, belonging to it by birth: to say that I know the game in this way means that I have it inside my skin, in my body, that it acts in me without my doing anything; as when my body responds to a knock without my even having perceived it as such' (Bourdieu, 1989, p. 44). Or again: 'Why is it important to conceive the field as a site in which one is born and not as an arbitrarily established game?' (ibid., p. 49).

The theory of fields resolves a whole series of sociological problems, but generates its own in so far as (1) it ignores the ceaseless transitions made by agents belonging to a field between the field in which they are producers, the fields in which they are mere consumer-spectators and the many situations that cannot be related to a field, reducing actors to their being-as-member-of-a-field; (2) it overlooks the situation of those who are socially defined (and mentally constituted) outside of any activity in a determinate field (which is still the case with many housewives without professional or public employment);[21] and (3) it considers what is outside-the-field, 'other rank', on the basis of standards of measurement that are social standards for measuring powers (educational qualifications, income level . . .), defining their 'habitus' by their dispossession, destitution and situation as dominated.[22] For all these reasons, the theory of fields (it would be better always to speak of the theory of *fields of power*) can certainly not constitute a general and universal theory, but represents only a regional theory of the social world.[23]

If habitus in particular, as systems of dispositions, are specific to fields, one may legitimately wonder what takes shape outside these fields – cognitively, affectively and culturally. If we aim to grasp the cognitive and social operations embodied in singular bodies, actors cannot be reduced to their field habitus, in so far as their social experiences overflow those that they can live within the context of a field (especially when they are outside these fields!). When we describe, for example, the literary habitus of a novelist, we can ask to what extent the latter imports this system of dispositions into a whole series of social situations (family ones in particular) situated outside the field. Is the ensemble of this individual's social behaviours – whatever the domain of existence under consideration – reducible to the application of this system of dispositions? Observation of actual behaviour shows that an assumption of this kind is far from being either self-evident or empirically confirmed.

Taking up our zoom lens or our microscope, we can thus distinguish, within these institutional and spatial spaces that are separate, relatively enclosed and apparently homogeneous, major internal differences in the types of interaction that take place there, in the social situations that are lived (a discussion around the coffee machine between colleagues is not an official meeting, nor is it individual or collective working-time). For example, far from constituting homogeneous realities, working-class family configurations, which I studied in their relationship to the educational world, displayed more than one case of heterogeneity (Lahire, 1995a). The child may be surrounded by persons that represent very different and even opposing principles of socialization and types of orientation towards school. An opposition or contradiction may arise, according to the particular case, between very strict moral control and indulgence, between 'amusement' and 'educational effort', between a very great sensitivity and a lesser sensitivity towards everything to do with the school, between a taste for reading and an absence of practices and tastes, etc.

Whatever the detail, it is rather rare to find family configurations that are absolutely homogeneous, either culturally or morally. There are few cases that make it possible to speak of a coherent family habitus, producing general dispositions completely oriented in the same direction. Many children live concretely within a family space of socialization with variable demands and characteristics, where examples and counter-examples jostle against one another (an illiterate father and a sister at university, brothers and sisters some of whom are 'successful' at school while others have 'failed', etc.), a family space in which contradictory principles of socialization intersect. Vis-à-vis the ensemble of their family members they are often faced with a wide spectrum of possible positions and possible systems of tastes and behaviours. And there is all the greater chance of finding contradictory elements if one examines large families in which several generations of children live under the same roof or that include, for various reasons, uncles, aunts, cousins and grandparents of the child in question.

Because we do not occupy identical or similar positions in such social contexts (we can be and have variously been 'son or daughter', 'school pupil', 'schoolfriend', 'father or mother', 'husband or wife', 'lover or mistress', 'colleague at work', 'goalkeeper', 'member of an association', 'attendant at church', 'worker', and so on), we live experiences that are varied, different and sometimes contradictory. A plural actor is thus the product of an – often precocious – experience of socialization in the course of their trajectory, or simultaneously in the course of the same period of time in a number of social worlds and occupying different positions.

We can therefore propose the hypothesis of the embodiment by each actor of a multiplicity of schemes of action (sensory-motor, perception, language, movement, etc.) and habits (of thinking, language, movement . . .), organized around so many repertoires and the pertinent social contexts that they learn to distinguish – and often to name – via the ensemble of their previous socialization experiences. If we take up the metaphor of a 'stock',[24] we can say that this stock (like the set of commodities available on a market or in a shop, and a site for keeping products in preparation) is distinguished from a mere 'heap' or 'stack' in that it turns out to be organized in the form of social repertoires (since there exist grammatical or logical repertoires that classify elements according to a grammatical or logical principle, we can use the metaphor of a sociological repertoire) of schemes, repertoires that are distinct from one another, but interconnected and certainly containing common elements. The repertoires of schemes of action (habits) are ensembles of summaries of social experiences, which have been constructed and embodied in the course of previous socialization in social contexts that are well defined, and that each actor gradually acquires more or less completely; there are as many habits as the sense of (relative) contextual relevance of their application. People learn and understand that what is said and done in one context is not said or done in another. This sense of situations is more or less 'correctly' embodied (depending on the variety of contexts that the actor encounters in their trajectory, and that earlier or later sanctions – positive or negative – address to them as indication of the limits, often vague, not to be crossed). To take the metaphor of a stock somewhat further, one could say that this is made up of products (schemes of action) that are not all necessary at each moment and in every context. Deposited (Latin: *deponere*) in the stock, they are available to the actor to the extent that they are disposable (*disponere*). The uses of these products (of socialization) are often deferred, so that they are kept temporarily or permanently in reserve, waiting for the triggers that will mobilize them. Finally, the transfers and transpositions (by analogy) of schemes of action rarely extend across the entirety of social contexts, but are made within the – vague – limits of each particular context (and therefore of each reservoir).

The Proustian model of the plural actor

In the criticism he made of the 'Saint-Beuve method', Marcel Proust sketched out a theory of the plural actor – implicit and only partial, but highly suggestive – i.e. of actors who show themselves to be plural and different according to the domains of existence in which they are led to develop socially. Proust defines the 'Saint-Beuve method' by maintaining that this consists in 'not separating the man from the work'. Presenting the issue involved in this way, Proust not only turns his back on a good part of the social and human sciences (the history and sociology of art in particular), which precisely seek not to separate the work from the man, but the criticism that he develops cannot fail to appear, in the eyes of these very sciences, as a typical case of artistic idealism and unrealism (the reaction of a man of letters who does not tolerate the conditions of production of the literary work being recalled).

Fundamentally, however, this is not what is involved. As against the manner in which Proust presents it, the method he discusses assumes that the literary quality of a work can be judged by what the public (or social) behaviour of its author can reveal (a 'man of quality' can only write literature of quality). Arguing against this, Proust is led to develop the idea of a plurality of 'selves' operating in differentiated practices: 'Such a method fails to recognize what any more than merely superficial acquaintance with ourselves teaches us: that a book is the product of a self other than that which we display in our habits, in company, in our vices' (Proust, 1988, p. 12). The situation of someone writing a literary text is altogether different from the situation that brings them into relationship with their friends, their publisher, their social calls . . ., and, fundamentally, it is not at all the same person that is acting in these different cases. If Sainte-Beuve is deeply mistaken, it is because he holds it possible to judge a 'self' on the basis of observation of these other 'selves':

> And not having seen the gulf that separates the writer from the society man, not having understood that the writer's self shows itself only in his books, that he only shows society men (even those society men that other writers are, when in society, who only become writers again once on their own) a society man like themselves, he was to launch that famous method which, according to Taine, Bourget and so many others, is his claim to fame, and which consists, in order to understand a poet or writer, in questioning avidly those who knew him, who frequented him, who may be able to tell us how he behaved in the matter of women, etc., that is, on all those very points where the poet's true self is not involved. (Ibid., p. 16)

Proust, of course, placing literary creation as he does above all else, at the top of the hierarchy of existence, has his own illusion about the writer's 'real self', to be found in a kind of 'genuine' dialogue between one self and another ('the true sound of our heart'). The 'self' that produces literary works is not any more 'deep', 'authentic' or 'true' than the 'self' that acts and interacts outside the hours of writing. Besides, focused on the difference to be made between 'literature' ('the sphere in which one writes') and 'outside-literature', Proust develops a particularly strong acuteness for everything in the former domain but remains blind to the internal differences within 'outside-literature', doubtless conceding this ground to his opponent (Sainte-Beuve). Instead of speaking of the 'outward self' (taken as a solid and undifferentiated block), he should rather (though this was not his main concern) distinguish 'the selves' that express themselves in the different domains of extra-literary existence. But once his hierarchical conception is abandoned, along with the dichotomic tendency that perceives only the differences between the literary self and the 'outward self', Proust's analysis proves to be a little theoretical gem for grasping the internal plurality of social actors.

'The self that produces works is obscured by the other self, which may be very inferior to the outward self of many other men' (Proust, 1988, p. 13). How then, in these conditions, can one correctly judge the literary work of Stendhal, Baudelaire or Balzac on the basis of what is known of them in terms of the relationships that they had with certain of their contemporaries? As opposed to Sainte-Beuve, one has to ask what is the specifically literary domain in which the writer places himself each time he writes:

> At no time does Sainte-Beuve seem to have grasped what is peculiar to inspiration or the activity of writing, and what marks it off totally from the occupations of other men and the other occupations of the writer. He drew no dividing line between the occupation of writing, in which, in solitude and suppressing those words which belong as much to others as to ourselves, and with which, even when alone, we judge things without being ourselves, we come face to face once more with our selves, and seek to hear and to render the true sound of our hearts – and conversation! (Ibid., pp. 14–15)

The case of Baudelaire, which Proust takes by way of example, shows a great fineness of analysis in this respect. Baudelaire, Proust recalls, wrote extremely deferential and ingratiating letters to Saint-Beuve in the hope of obtaining a good review. Whatever interpretation one might put on such actions (sincerity or a policy of cynicism), Proust says that they show the difference between what Baudelaire wrote and the type of behaviour he could display towards an influential critic of his day:

All this bears out what I was saying to you, that the man who lives in the same body with any great genius has little connection with him, but he it is whom his intimates know, so it is absurd to judge the poet by the man, as Sainte-Beuve does, or by the hearsay of his friends. As for the man himself, he is only a man and may be utterly ignorant of what the poet who dwells in him wants. (Proust, 1988, p. 39)

Proust then develops in a few lines the outline of a theory of the plural individual, made up of 'several persons superimposed':

Like the heaven of Catholic theology, which is made up of several heavens superimposed, our person, in the appearance given to it by our body, with its head, which circumscribes our thoughts inside a little ball, our moral person is made up of several persons superimposed. This is perhaps even more noticeable with poets, who have an additional heaven, intermediate between the heaven of their genius and that of their everyday intelligence, kindness and delicacy, which is their prose. (1988, p. 40)

And so we are plural, different in the different situations of ordinary life, foreign to other parts of ourselves when we are engaged in this or that domain of social existence. Attentive as he is to the differences within situations of writing, Proust even takes his analytical lens to distinguish, in the poet, the self-who-writes-in-verse (Musset writing his *Ballade à la lune*) from the 'self-who-writes-in-prose' (Musset composing his critical essays or speeches to the Académie). But if the poet who writes in prose is already very different from what he is when he writes in verse, *a fortiori* '[n]othing of this remains in the man, the man of real life, of dinner parties and ambition, yet it is to him that Sainte-Beuve claims to look for the essence of the other, of whom he has preserved nothing' (ibid., p. 40). This theoretical intuition of the plurality of 'persons' or 'selves' (or of the fractioning of the personality) – we would say summaries of embodied experiences – within one and the same biological person often leads Proust the novelist to distinguish between different facets of a character, describing 'the Swann of Buckingham Palace' or 'Albertine in waterproofs on rainy days' (Nicole, 1981), and to display the errors of judgement that his different characters commit towards one another (only grasping what of their personality they display in particular contexts) so as the better to bring out their relative inward heterogeneity.[25]

Splitting of the self and mental conflict: crossings of social space

> We see each milieu by the light of the other (or others) as well as its own and so gain an impression of resisting it. Certainly each of these influences ought to emerge more sharply from their comparison and contrast. Instead, the confrontation of these milieus gives us a feeling of no longer being involved in any of them. What becomes paramount is the 'strangeness' of our situation, absorbing individual thought.
> (Maurice Halbwachs, *On Collective Memory*)

> In my case, I made gestures without any thought to them, and as soon as I crossed the threshold, once outside I condemn my own behaviour but do not know how to conduct myself.
> (Annie Ernaux, *Les Armoires vides*)

The sole exception to the rule that the tradition that generally preaches the singleness of the actor is ready to accept is that which can be considered in a sense as arising – to a greater or lesser degree – from a form of mental pathology or disturbance of identity. Referring cases of internal plurality to the model of a 'divided self'[26] and of 'mental conflict', it seeks assurance in a certain sense by telling (itself) implicitly that the 'normal' (in the sense of the most common), and thus the 'law', is indeed on the side of singleness.

Freud, in fact, used the term 'splitting of the ego' to denote the idea of the 'coexistence at the heart of the ego of two psychical attitudes towards external reality' that 'know absolutely nothing of the other' (Laplanche and Pontalis, 2006, p. 427).[27] The subject thus experiences an internal conflict between two impulses, desires and feelings towards the situations that they live. This perpetual friction[28] is lived with inescapable suffering, which can even lead in certain cases to the verge of schizophrenia.

This type of plurality, while quite essential to understand, cannot, however, be taken as the general model of internal plurality of the actor. It is a particular case of the model of the plural actor as we conceive this. The first limitation of the idea of splitting, in fact, is precisely that the multiple is squeezed into the figure of the double and binary opposition (duplication of the personality, double bind, double consciousness, double game ...). But the plural actor is not necessary a *double agent*. He or she has embodied several repertoires of schemes of action (habits)[29] that do not necessarily produce (major) suffering, in so far as they can quite well coexist peacefully when expressed in social contexts that are different and separate from one another, or lead only to limited and partial conflicts in one or other particular context or domain of existence (many women, for example, are caught between the desire or necessity of work outside the home and the desire or necessity of domestic investment, thus living in these two spaces different 'forms of oppression' (McCall, 1992).

But if there is a doubling, if as a result there is just one single central conflict, and if this internal mental conflict provokes suffering, it is because the internal plurality of schemes of action (or habits) has ended up making the unitary illusion of identity impossible and raised in the actor a problem of mental coherence.[30] Everything happens as if the multiple repertoires that arrange the stock of embodied schemes of action were all cut into two parts, making the actualization of contradictory schemes of action possible in any context at any time. The heterogeneity of the stock of schemes of action embodied by the actor does not systematically lead to mental divisions and conflicts of identity of this kind. It is most often compatible with the – well-founded – illusion of personal coherence and identity with oneself.

In order for an actor no longer to be able to give themselves an illusion of unity of self, so that the main contradiction appears in the form of a double identity, 'an inward conversation between different segments of the Self' (Berger and Luckmann 1979), it is generally necessary to have had unusual experiences of socialization. In general, the actor will have undergone, at a very early age, systematically contradictory socialization experiences. The situation may be within a particular world (e.g. a double bind exerted at the heart of the family, and not necessarily represented by father and mother), or it may display two major social worlds in contradiction (e.g. the working-class family and the school, in the case of 'scholars' who become 'class *transfuges*').

In the case of those who, according to their situation, are described as 'class *transfuges*', 'upwardly declassed', 'uprooted', 'autodidacts', 'scholars' or 'the saved', and who rose from the social conditions of their origin by the path of education,[31] we have a clear opposition between two major and contradictory matrices of socialization (the family and the school), with symbolic values that are socially different in the context of a hierarchical society (prestigious/undervalued; high/low; dominant/dominated . . .), thus generating a heterogeneity of habits and embodied schemes of action that are organized in the form of a splitting of the ego, a central internal conflict that organizes (and embarrasses) every moment of existence. And yet, even in a case like this, the internal conflict can be appeased and does not always lead to major mental dissociations and more serious mental torments (that depends on the particular history of each actor). Richard Hoggart thus describes some people who are 'upwardly declassed' but do not experience their social trajectory with that much suffering, certain administrators or high officials, or a certain young man who is able 'to smile at his father with his whole face and to respect his flighty young sister and his slower brother' (Hoggart, 1998, p. 225).

Pierre Naville, who defined the individual personality as the more or less coordinated set of systems of habits that we have embodied within different social groups and in various social contexts, also laid the foundations for an understanding of cases of *'transfuges'*. As distinct from the actor 'whose integration and adaptation is satisfactory for the moment' and whose 'situation brings about . . . the predominance of a certain system of habits' ('we say that the man is "in his element". *Age quod agis!*'), other actors see 'one of several systems of habits' dominate 'according to the situation and its demands', even entering into conflict in certain cases ('now appeased and overcome, now again exacerbated'). In this latter case, we can note 'interferences' between the two contradictory systems of habits: 'a given stimulus may provoke, even partially, two kinds of antagonistic reaction' and produce 'hesitation, trembling, indecision, inaction' (Naville, 1942, p. 221)[32] – a wonderful analysis of the paralysis or discomfort occasioned by the competition of schemes of action among those who have embodied contradictory schemes within the same repertoires. When every social situation is perceived, assessed, judged and evaluated on the basis of two opposing and competing points of view, this ambivalence is a cause of suffering. If the opposing schemes of action could always correspond to distinct social contexts closed off from each other, if they systematically involved social practices and domains of affectivity that were very clearly distinct, we would not see a kind of constant competition and oscillation, but rather a genuine peaceful doubling (between 'here' and 'there'). For example, socially diversified cultural tastes apply also to objects or categories of object (furniture, clothing, interior decoration, etc.) that are identical between one social group (that of origin) and another (that of destination), and not only to different domains of practice. Socialized successively but in part also simultaneously in worlds in which habits of taste are different and even socially opposed, these 'class *transfuges*' oscillate constantly – and sometimes in a mentally exhausting manner – between two habits and two points of view.

The *transfuges*, in fact, in their crossing of social space, constantly pass from a situation of peaceful coexistence of embodied habits to a situation of conflict. Annie Ernaux,[33] in *Les Armoires vides*, describes the period of her childhood as one of calm cohabitation: 'This was a good time, between eight and twelve years old; I swung between two worlds, crossing from one to the other without even noticing. It was enough not to make a mistake; no coarse words or noisy expletives away from home, bound up as they were with the grey-green corners of the rooms, with the burned cassoulet that I scraped from the bottom of the pan' (1974, p. 71). This is the time when the child learns, without too much trouble, to apply different schemes of action according to context, and thus exert a kind of self-control. 'A nice balance for a few years. Until I was twelve this doubling was easy work ... The two worlds side by side without too much worry' (ibid., p. 73). On the one hand the family, on the other the school. More subtly still, on the one hand speech that is bound up mainly with the family world and not yet engaged too much at school, and on the other hand writing which is linked only with the educational context and more readily enables the formation of new ways of speaking and new linguistic habits (Bernstein, 1974):

> I used my new words only for writing, I gave them the only form that was possible for me. I couldn't put them into my mouth. Clumsy verbal expression despite good results, wrote the teachers on my class reports.... I carried two languages inside me, the little black characters of books, those delightful crazy insects, alongside the fat and coarse words so well rooted in the stomach, in the head, which made me cry at the top of the stairs on biscuit boxes, or joke under the counter... (Ernaux, 1974, p. 77)

As Richard Hoggart expresses the same condition: the scholarship boy 'is between two worlds, the worlds of school and home; and they meet at few points. Once at the grammar-school, he quickly learns to make use of a pair of different accents, perhaps even two different apparent characters and differing standards of value' (1998, p. 228).

The educational situation is indeed foreign, when seen, perceived and felt via repertoires of schemes of action that are essentially formed in the socializing context of the family:

> There was something strange and indescribable, a complete change of scenery. Nothing at all like the Lesur café and grocery, my parents and my friends in the yard.... Not even the same language. The teacher spoke slowly, in very long words, she was never in a hurry, she liked to chat, and not like my mother. 'Hang your clothes on the coathanger.' My mother, when I came in from playing, would cry out: 'Don't just throw your coat down like that, who's going to put it away? Your

> socks are all screwed up!' There was a world between the two. . . . This unease, this shock, everything the teachers said or did about anything, I listened to and watched, it was light, formless, calm, always to the point. Real language was what I heard at home: booze, victuals, get screwed, old meat. Everything was immediate there, shouts and grimaces, overturned bottles. The teacher spoke and spoke, but things didn't exist. . . . The school was acting as if things were funny, interesting, all right. The teacher gave her own radio broadcast, reading stories while she twisted her mouth and rolled marbles to play the big bad wolf. Everyone laughed, even I forced myself to laugh. Talking animals didn't interest me that much. I thought she was making fun of us by telling us these stupid things. She jumped up on her chair so well that I took her to be a bit backward and stupid for telling us these stories of dogs and sheep. (Ernaux, 1974, pp. 53–4)

But the question of a 'choice' between one world and another was not yet raised.

Then, as educational success confirms, the world of school takes the upper hand and becomes the 'point of reference': 'Now there was only books and school; the rest I began no longer to see' (Ernaux, 1974, pp. 85–6).

> At the moment of that solemn communion, the transition to secondary school, this odd feeling began to grow, of not being at ease anywhere except with my homework, an essay, a book in the corner of the courtyard, under the bedcovers on Thursday and Sunday, hidden at the top of the stairs. . . . I began not to notice anything. To ignore it all. The shop, the café, the customers, and even my parents. I wasn't there, I was in my homework, in my books, as they say. 'Don't you get a headache with all that?' I spoke less and less, it upset me. (Ibid., p. 91)

It is hard not to be upset by one's parents when one gradually comes to see them through the eyes of another world, on the basis of other ways of speaking, looking, acting and feeling. But it is hard as well to forget the ineradicable family and emotional tie that joins parents and children. Because parents are within a child, through all the habits it has constructed in its relationships with them, to despise them is to despise oneself: 'It is me that I hate. I rebel against their slaving away at the counter, and despise them. . . . Perhaps it is me who prevented them from buying a nice grocery' (ibid., p. 164). The *transfuge* or 'scholarship boy' thus feels 'cut in two', 'between two stools' (ibid., p. 181), belonging to 'both the worlds of school and home' at once (Hoggart, 1998, p. 227).[34]

To return to the start of my argument – i.e. the impossibility of making cases of 'splitting of the ego' a general paradigm for an approach to the plurality of the actor – I can note the fact that, like any actor, the 'class *transfuges*' are familiar with many other inward contradictions or differentiations – in terms of schemes of action and repertoires of these. They focus, however, on the main contradiction that occupies the foreground – i.e. their consciousness. To forget other differences that do not appear so clearly and consciously to the eyes of the actor, those that only reveal themselves in the close analysis of long interviews[35] or in the wake of direct and systematic observation of behaviours in varying social contexts, that reveal unknown to the person being studied their manifold little contradictions, their behavioural heterogeneity – this would be placing too much emphasis on the conscious subjectivity of the actor and the socially maintained illusion of the coherence and singleness of the self.

── Scene 2 ──

THE WELLSPRINGS OF ACTION

Presence of the past, present of action

Two further major tendencies can be distinguished among theories of action and the actor. On the one hand there are those models that confer a determining and decisive weight on the actor's past, and more particularly on the very earliest experiences (most often presumed to be homogeneous) undergone in the course of infancy (e.g. the various psychological or neuropsychological theories, psychoanalytic theory,[1] the theory of habitus);[2] and, on the other hand, there are models that describe and analyse moments of an action or an interaction, or a given state of a system of action, without concern for the past of the actors (rational-choice theory, methodological individualism, symbolic interactionism, ethnomethodology). In the first case, past experiences lie at the root of all future actions; in the second case, the actors are beings deprived of a past, constrained only by the logic of the present situation: interaction, system of action, organization, market, etc. In the former, study of the 'order of interaction' is very commonly neglected, likewise the singular and complex characteristics of the immediate pragmatic context of action; while, in the latter, what is neglected, whether deliberately or not, is everything in the present action that depends on the past embodied by the actors.

If the models of the actor 'fully complete in interaction' or 'in the situation of the moment' that define him or her by place, role and position exclusively in this present moment undoubtedly produce knowledge of the social world, it is not within this sociological tradition that my own research work and theoretical reflection is located. These sociologies of the actor without a past remain quite formal and empty from the perspective of an analysis of actors, and their concern is essentially less with the actor who acts than with the action *per se* (its contexts, course, modalities, grammar), no matter what the past of the actor effecting it. A sociology relieved of any theory of memory, habit and embodied past, a sociology of anti-Proustian inspiration, you could say. But it is just as legitimate that other literature can inspire other sociologies. My intention is therefore to take up theoretically the question of the embodied past, of earlier socializing experiences, while by no means neglecting or denying the role of the present (of the situation) by pretending that our whole past acts 'like a single person' at each moment of our action, or by claiming that what we are and are engaged in at each moment is the *synthesis* of everything we have previously experienced, so that it is this synthesis, this unifying principle, this (magic) formula generating all our practices, that has to be reconstructed.

In fact, the question of the relative weight of past experiences and the present situation in accounting for actions is fundamentally bound up with that of the internal plurality of the actor, which is itself correlative with that of the plurality of the logics of action in which actors are inscribed or are led to inscribe themselves. If the actor is the product of a homogeneous and unambiguous family configuration X and encounters in the course of their life only situations identical or analogous to X, then past and present are one and the same thing. There is no longer any difference between what the actor knew previously and what she knows now, and one can then observe, in an expression of Pierre Bourdieu's drawn from phenomenology, a profound relationship of ontological complicity between mental structures and the objective structures of the social situation, a complicity that is at bottom that of the *illusio* – i.e. the enchanted relationship to the situation: the actor lives the situation in his element. But then there is no longer either past or present (which is precisely a formula like: '[h]abitus spontaneously orchestrated among themselves and pre-adjusted to the situations in which they operate and of which they are the product' (Bourdieu, 2000, p. 145), since the actor has lived and continues to live in a homogeneous social space that is never transformed. In a formula of the kind: 'a present past that tends to perpetuate itself into the future by reactivation in similarly structured practices' (Bourdieu, 1990a, p. 54), the homogeneity and singleness of the past is presupposed, and the problem of the encounter between an 'embodied past' and a 'present' that are different and contradictory is prematurely closed.

The articulation of past and present, therefore, acquires its full sense only when (embodied) 'past' and (contextual) 'present' are themselves fundamentally plural and heterogeneous. If the present situation cannot be ignored, this is, on the one hand, because there is a historicity implying that what has been embodied is not necessarily identical to or in harmonious relationship with what the present situation requires, and, on the other hand, because those involved are not 'One' – i.e. not reducible to a single formula that would generate their practices, a single internal law or internal *nomos*.

If practices 'cannot be deduced either from the present conditions which may seem to have provoked them or from the past conditions which have produced the *habitus*, the durable principle of their production' (Bourdieu, 1990a, p. 56), a perfectly balanced formula which it is hard not to accept, the theoretical model most commonly applied implies a relative primacy of past experiences, in as much as these are not simply the 'principle' for understanding subsequent experiences, but also for selecting these (accepting, rejecting or avoiding them):

> Unlike scientific estimations, which are corrected after each experiment, according to rigorous rules of calculation, the anticipations of the *habitus*, practical hypotheses based on past experience, give disproportionate weight to early experiences. Through the economic and social necessity that they bring to bear on the relatively autonomous world of the domestic economy and family relations, or more precisely, through the specifically familial manifestations of this external necessity (forms of the division of labour between the sexes, household objects, modes of consumption, parent–child relations, etc.), the structures characterizing a determinate class of conditions of existence produce the structures of the *habitus*, which in their turn are the basis of the perception and appreciation of all subsequent experiences. (Ibid., p. 54)

Or again:

> Early experiences have particular weight because the *habitus* tends to ensure its own constancy and its defence against change through the selection it makes within new information by rejecting information capable of calling into question its accumulated information, if exposed to it accidentally or by force, and especially by avoiding exposure to such information . . . [Bourdieu gives here the example of homogamy.] Through the systematic 'choices' it makes among the places, events and people that might be frequented, the *habitus* tends to protect itself from crises and critical challenges by providing itself with a milieu to which it is as pre-adapted as possible, that is, a relatively constant universe of situations tending to reinforce its dispositions by offering the market most favourable to its products. (Ibid., pp. 60–1)

The many occasions for maladjustment and crisis

If Bourdieu is right to emphasize the propensity of actors to try to avoid major crises – i.e. situations that would go too forcibly or permanently against their embodied programme of socialization – not only does he confuse propensity (or desires) and real situations (which do not always permit such avoidance and do not really leave the choice to the actors), he forgets the existence of the many polymorphous crises that beset actors in their everyday lives. In point of fact, by privileging major crises bound up with important transformations of social position in social space ('In the absence of any major upheaval (a change of position, for example), the conditions of its formation are also the conditions of its realization'; Bourdieu, 2000, p. 150), one ends up neglecting all the minor or medium-level crises that actors are led to experience in a differentiated society. By considering certain major shifts in social space only in terms of the volume and structure of distribution of capital possessed (cases of social decline or great upward social mobility), one ends up forgetting that there are also shifts and/or changes in the world of the family (becoming a parent, divorcing after being married . . .), the world of friends, etc., as well as those of a socio-professional order (losing one's job, changing employers, moving from one kind of work or employment to another).

Privileging in this way the case of 'happy' situations, those in which, as Naville puts it, someone is 'in their element', the model of magic adjustment of embodied habits to situations (with which the actor is confronted),[3] Bourdieu remains blind to their multiple occasions of maladjustment, uncoupling, that produce crises and reflections – which should clearly not be systematically understood as scholarly or metaphysical reflections – on action, on others, and on oneself. Crises of adaptation, crises of the tie of ontological complicity or connivance between what is embodied and the new situation – such situations are numerous, multiform, and characteristic of the human condition in complex, plural societies undergoing transformation. The model of happy actors 'in their element', feeling 'like fish in water' since they are made for the water and the water made for them, actors not pulled or laboured by other impulses, embodied habits or tendencies, but complete in their action – this model basically corresponds more to what one might imagine as the life of an animal in its natural element than to that of a man.

By way of summary, we offer a list here – undoubtedly not an exhaustive one – of the cases of discrepancy, uncoupling or maladjustment that observation of the social world allows us to distinguish:

1 situations of enforced cultural contradiction in which the actors cannot do otherwise than live in a situation of permanent cultural contradiction to what they had previously embodied (e.g. the case of many pupils forced to go regularly to school even when this brings them into real crisis – 'educational failure' and its various manifestations being one such situation of crisis [Lahire, 1993a] – or the situation of indigenous people in Mexico between the sixteenth and eighteenth century, on whom the Spanish imposed Western cultural and religious forms [Gruzinski, 1988]);
2 more or less enforced individual or collective transplanting from one social world to another (e.g. long-term hospitalization, military service, imprisonment, migration, movement of populations . . .);
3 major biographical ruptures or transformations in individual trajectories (e.g. sudden social decline or upward *déclassement*, forming a couple, marriage, divorce or separation,[4] the birth of the first child, retirement, loss of employment . . .);[5]
4 discrepancies between certain social properties of the actor and those of his or her social environment, reminding actors of the absence of 'ontological complicity' between a part of their dispositions and the situation in which they live (e.g. being the only black lawyer in a major New York office; a woman occupying a profession considered socially as masculine, or vice versa;[6] coming from a particular religious or ethnic community and frequenting members of a different community after a mixed marriage,[7] etc.);
5 being pulled between competing habits (tendencies) that lead a person to live permanently out of phase and with a bad conscience (e.g. the case of women divided between their housekeeping and their professional role, or the related but rather different case of fathers engaged in their professional sphere who experience bad conscience about their absence from home and their children's education, but who conversely think of their work – which is not getting done – when they devote time to their family);
6 the many small discrepancies (that provoke mini-states of crisis: loss of temper, feeling of unease, anger, boredom, escape, inattention, etc.) between embodied past experiences and new situations; these situations do not necessarily amount to deep questioning of the socialization situations experienced previously, but neither do they ever confirm them completely, presupposing therefore supplementary embodiments that are heterogeneous but not contradictory;
7 the minimal adaptations without conviction (at a distance from the role) made possible by the fact that the stock of embodied schemes

is not completely homogeneous and thus enables actors to draw on a part of them to 'tolerate', temporarily or permanently, a situation and adapt to it without too much suffering (especially if the other embodied schemes turn out to be actualized in other contexts and other social situations).

These discrepancies and situations of crisis are rarely isolated, and may combine any which way, increasing troubles and multiplying minor or major sufferings, questionings and self-examination, and making existence heavy or burdensome.

It is consequently impossible to say – other than very approximately, very abstractly and very simplistically – that 'the same history inhabits both habitus and habitat, both dispositions and position, the king and his court, the employer and his firm, the bishop and his see', and that 'history in a certain sense communicates with itself, is reflected in its own image' (Bourdieu, 1981, p. 306). This would mean, for example, that the employer was reducible to his business activity and that nothing occurs to disturb this miraculous adjustment between his habitus as employer and his business. He would have in a certain sense to have been 'born' (and raised) in the business. If the formula of adjustment and correspondence between dispositions and position (or at least dispositions and conditions of existence) is theoretically interesting, it is, however, never completely verifiable empirically[8] or historically, for the simple reason that an actor's dispositions are not constituted in a single social situation, a single social world, a single social 'position'. An actor (and his or her dispositions) can thus never be defined by one single 'situation' or even by a series of social coordinates.

The plurality of the actor and the openings of the present

That man whom you saw so adventurous yesterday, do not think it strange to find him just as cowardly today: either anger, or necessity, or company, or wine, or the sound of a trumpet, had put his heart in his belly. His was a courage formed not by reason, but by one of these circumstances; it is no wonder if he has now been made different by other, contrary circumstances.

(Montaigne, *The Complete Essays*)

The 'present' thus has all the more weight in explaining behaviour, practice or conduct, the more the actors are plural. When these have been socialized in particularly homogeneous and coherent conditions, their reaction to the new situations may be very predictable. Conversely, the more such actors are the product of heterogeneous or even contradictory social forms of life, the more the logic of the present situation plays a central role in the reactivation of a part of the experiences embodied in the past. The past is thus differently 'open' according to the nature and configuration of the present situation.

Rather than assuming the systematic influence of the past on the present – in other words, rather than imagining that all our past, like a block or a homogeneous synthesis, weighs at each moment on all our lived situations (statistical and probabilistic approaches teach us that the past of an actor opens – and closes – their field of present possibilities but can in no case describe the relationship between past and present in terms of causality, for example) – the field of investigation proposed here opens up the question of the modalities of the triggering of embodied schemes of action (produced in the course of the whole set of past experiences) by the elements or configuration of the present situation – i.e. the question of the ways in which a part – but only a part – of the embodied past experiences is mobilized, summoned up and reawakened by the present situation.

This scientific interest, if we examine it more closely, is already present in those statistically based sociological arguments which, rather than the routine and lazy practice of always using the classic list of independent variables (socio-professional category, level of education, sex, age, etc.), seek to determine the most pertinent variables as a function of the specificity of their object. The question is, on each occasion, on the one hand to find those variables that are most pertinent in terms of the object studied – i.e. those that best summarize the particular and specific series of summaries of experiences (or schemes) activated in the very particular case being studied (cultural practice, diet, family behaviour ...) and generate the maximum in the way of differences within the population under research – while on the other hand determining the most adequate indicator of the contexts that are favourable or unfavourable to the activation and triggering of the schemes in question.[9] And even when the classic variables continue to 'function' well, the sociologist must always ask what it is in such and such a variable that happens to explain the differences established in this or that particular domain. Unless they are (more or less) systematically discriminatory, synthetic variables end up telling us nothing new about the operation of the social world.

For example, historical research tends to show the absence of a direct relationship between literacy (or ability to write) and practices of correspondence. Everything happens, in effect, as if 'mastery of a skill [that of writing] is not sufficient in itself to arouse its mobilization in a practical sense. Other reasons are needed. Economic and social emancipation, which multiplies the circumstances in which writing a letter is a necessity and opens up spaces that were long closed in on themselves, making long-distance relationships necessary, is one of these' (Chartier, 1991, p. 12). A favourable institutional context (such as a nearby post office) is not by itself a sufficient trigger ('the high density of the former does not always offer strong indications of correspondence'; ibid., p. 19). In the same way, in contemporary France, I have been able to show that women with the equivalent of degree-level education write more in the home situation than do men, developing their skills more by their position in the family than by formal schooling (Lahire, 1993d, 1995b, 1997b). In parallel with this, there are similarly confused effects of educational skills in relation to practices of reading: students who obtain good marks in French are not necessarily heavy readers, a section of them that is far from negligible even being quite weak (Singly, 1993a). According to the particular case (objects, domains of practice, etc.), the variables that make it possible to account most pertinently for differences in practices will vary. As the American sociologist Anselm L. Strauss rightly says, these social conditions (social class, sex . . .) 'can be major or insignificant conditions, depending on the specific contexts of social life that they may or may not much affect' (Strauss, 1993, p. 211).[10]

If the present situation certainly does not explain anything by itself, it is this that opens or leaves closed, awakens or leaves in reserve, mobilizes or silences the habits embodied by the agents.[11] Negatively (by what they leave 'unexpressed' or 'unactualized') as well as positively (by what they allow to be 'expressed' or 'actualized'), the elements and configuration of the present situation have a quite fundamental weight in the generation of practices. And this is indeed confirmed by Freudian psychoanalysis, with its finding that 'a memory may be reactualized in one associative context while, in another, it will remain inaccessible to consciousness' (Laplanche and Pontalis, 2006, p. 248).

It is paradoxically from Henri Bergson, generally viewed as an antisociological author, that we can draw the elements of a sociological analysis of the relationship between present and past. By slightly transforming certain formulas of this philosopher (as well as setting aside another part of these),[12] we can thus assert that the present (the present situation) has the ability to 'supplant the past' and allow only those memories or habits that can 'fit' into the 'present attitude' ('that which resembles the present perception from the point of view of the action to be accomplished'). This same 'present attitude' ('the necessities of the present action') also possesses the negative 'power to inhibit' that part of the embodied past which cannot find a way of activation in the context in question. As Bergson writes, 'it is from the present that comes the appeal to which memory [or we could say 'habit'] responds' (1912, pp. 114, 220, 199, 197).

It is also quite surprising to see how the sociological tradition that emphasizes the 'weight of the past' is basically able to neglect the role of the present situation, even though it is this that often 'decides' what of the past is allowed to resurface and act within the present action. This is the case when Bourdieu evokes the analysis that Erich Auerbach offers of a passage in Virginia Woolf's *To the Lighthouse*, to argue for the importance of the past in everyday actions and reactions (Bourdieu and Wacquant, 1992, p. 124), even though this very example equally reveals the importance of the triggering event (i.e. trying on a stocking). We need only think of those schemes of action that, because of radical social transformation or more or less enforced individual transplantation from one social universe to another (e.g. imprisonment, long-term hospitalization, migration, war, sudden social decline or lightning social ascent, etc.), no longer find the conditions of their happy and harmonious actualization to remind or convince ourselves of the importance of the present situation.

Conditional dispositions

> The essential characteristic of the dispositional term, its conditionality – if s_i then b_j most of the time becomes degraded into an *unconditional* 'act'.
>
> (J. Van Heerden and A. J. Smolenaars, 'On traits as dispositions: an alleged truism')

> Failing to understand that dispositions result from this continuous exercise of activity is the act of a completely foolish mind.
>
> (Aristotle, *The Nicomachean Ethics*)

Like physical 'dispositions' (e.g. fragility, inflammability, elasticity, solubility . . .), social ones (the dispositions to act, feel, evaluate, think, appreciate in such and such a way) are never directly observed by the researcher. They are unobservable as such (as empiricist logicians like Quine have not failed to note; Crane, 1996, p. 1), yet they are supposed to be 'at the root' of observable practices. The researcher must reconstruct them on the basis of (1) the description (or reconstruction) of practices, (2) the description (or reconstruction) of situations in which these practices are deployed, (3) the reconstruction of elements deemed important in the history (itinerary, biography, trajectory, etc.) of the practitioner.

Is it useful, then, to continue speaking of 'dispositions' if it turns out that this term is more serviceable to theoretical rhetoric than to the understanding and explanation of social practices? Are we faced here with an empirically useful concept, without which research work and accounts of it would not be what they are, or rather with what Michel de Certeau had no hesitation in calling a 'mystical reality', a 'supplementary category' (between structures and practices) that sociologists need to close their theory (Certeau, 1984, pp. 57–9)?

Contemporary philosophers do not give sociology much support on this question, since as many arguments against the notion of disposition are to be found as those in its favour. Jacques Bouveresse, for example, following here Hilary Putnam, notes that, for certain practical aptitudes, such as knowing how to use a language, 'a description of the practical knowledge that makes the practice in question possible risks being in the end not very different from a description taken from the practice itself' (1995, p. 582). In point of fact, what extra have we said when we speak of 'linguistic competence' (or 'dispositions' to produce linguistic utterances) in order to 'explain' the 'linguistic performances' of speaking subjects? We are not far removed here from the *'virtus dormitiva'* of opium. Bouveresse, however, develops this line of argument and enables us to illuminate the problem, or at least present it in better terms:

> Explanations in terms of 'disposition' or 'habitus', when these cannot be the object of a sufficiently independent characterization of the simple description of the kind of behavioural regularities to which they give rise, can evidently be suspected of remaining essentially verbal. As Quine has remarked, a dispositional explanation resembles the recognition of a debt that one hopes to be able to repay one day by producing the description of a property of corresponding structure, as chemists have done for such dispositional predicates as 'soluble in water'. (Ibid., pp. 592–3)

The example of chemistry strikes me as particularly enlightening, and one can put it to good use in order to draw a series of conclusions. Imagine the following (very) modest experimental procedure: take a piece of sugar and a glass filled with water; place the sugar in the water and it will be seen to dissolve. Can the result of this experiment be summed up by saying that the 'quality' or 'property' of sugar is to be soluble in water? Can we say that sugar 'has' this property ('solubility') in the sense of a 'potentiality already there', a 'disposition' that exists before any contact with water, taking up therefore the Aristotelian distinction between 'disposition' and 'action' ('*hexis* and *energeia*')? That the 'disposition to be soluble' (solubility) is revealed by water? Or again that the 'solubility' of the sugar is 'actualized' in contact with water? Is water simply a ground of actualization, a site of 'revelation' of a property 'in itself', a substantial property? Or is the water itself a co-producer of this 'solubility', which belongs neither to the water nor to the sugar, but to the point of their encounter?

Water does not have the power to dissolve any product; sugar does not dissolve in air. And so there is no property-in-itself that is lodged somewhere in the sugar, and it may even appear desirable, from a heuristic point of view, to avoid speaking of the 'solubility' of sugar, so as not to reify the product of an interaction. Instead we can describe, as we began by doing, the act of dissolution of the sugar in the water. The property or the disposition in question is a 'relational property', a 'property of interaction', and it sometimes seems preferable to keep to the description of actions rather than to assume a 'potential' that 'actualizes' itself on the occasion of the encounter (in the 'accident' that this 'occasion' constitutes). In all cases, to attribute a 'disposition' to an object, a substance or an actor is to wager (though in some cases, such as the physical and chemical sciences, the wager is a sure bet, whereas in others we remain in probabilistic reasoning) on the propensity or tendency of the object, substance or actor to act (or react) in a certain fashion in determinate circumstances.

In the order of social behaviour, it would be far too naive to play with (or on) words by rhetorically distinguishing what is only the occasional 'trigger' of these behaviours (the event or the context) from their 'real determinant' (the embodied disposition). In point of fact, neither the 'triggering' event nor the disposition embodied by the actors can be designated as the real 'determinant' of practices (which would assume a quite improbable model of human action). The reality here is in fact relational (or interdependent); the behaviour or the action is the product of an encounter in which each element is neither more nor less 'determinant' than the other.[13] By positing the triggering event or the context as simply the 'occasion' for liberating the virtual power or potential of schemes or dispositions, we would surreptitiously draw on the Saussurian model of speech as simple actualization (exemplification or illustration) of language (code or system) – a model which we well know prevented in its day the study of practices of language and contexts of utterance. Besides, by proceeding in this way, we completely avoid the fact that the absence of the triggering or contextual events in question (or the presence of other types of trigger) has the negative power of leaving dormant (or silencing), or at least inhibiting, according to the particular case, memories, skills, dispositions, attitudes, habits, and schemes of action. As J. Van Heerden and A. J. Smolenaars emphasize: 'It is imaginable that an object or person has a certain disposition that never or rarely reveals itself because its manifestation is blocked by other factors' (1990, p. 299).

A first limit to the comparison between the lump of sugar and the actor on the one hand, the water and the present situation on the other, lies in the fact that the sugar has no 'past' and reacts in exactly the same fashion no matter what particular water (H_2O) is involved. The sugar has not constituted its 'disposition to dissolve' by way of a history of past contacts with water, whereas the actor is the product of his or her multiple past experiences, multiple acquisitions – more or less complete – made in the course of situations that have been lived previously.[14] There is thus a profound complicity between actors and social situations, a kind of natural communion, the actor being the product of the embodiment of multiple situations. The question raised is therefore that of the mode of accumulation and restructuring of lived experiences and the actualization of this capital of experiences (embodied in the form of schemes) as a function of the situations encountered.

A second limitation follows from the fact that, if dispositions – whether physical or social – are manifested only in particular conditions or circumstances (e.g. the solubility of sugar in water; a social situation S), the result of the encounter is more ambiguous with social dispositions and conditions. There is always an uncertainty here, as to (1) what actor A will 'retain' in the situation S, and (2) what in actor A will be triggered by the situation S. It is hardly possible to find 'social conditions' and 'actors' of whom it would be possible to predict with certainty the manifestation of a singular disposition equivalent to the dissolving of sugar in water. Sociological determinism is never as unambiguous as physical or chemical determinism (Becker, 1994). The behaviour of an actor may well be completely socially determined, but it is impossible to predict as easily as in the case of the chemical experiment the appearance of this behaviour. That depends on the social complexity of the situation (never reducible by the sociologist to a limited series of parameters, contrary to the reduction of the situation to a formula of the kind 'H_2O'), which is also never totally identical to those that the actor has lived previously (as distinct from the water, which remains identical to itself), as well as the internal complexity of an actor whose stock of habits (schemes) is more or less heterogeneous. Apart from these differences, the example of the sugar and the water pinpoints the tendency to verbalism and reification that lies in wait for anyone who speaks too rapidly the language of 'dispositions' and substantializes the realities of interactions.

There is always a great risk of (1) forgetting the conditional (circumstantial, contextual) dimension of dispositions and (2) ignoring their scientifically constructed[15] nature, or (3) increasingly disassociating the potential from the acts that have socio-genetically constituted it. The cases of abuse of language (in Wittgenstein's sense) are thus very numerous among adepts of dispositional explanation in the social sciences.

For example, in everyday life (and sometimes also in science) we face the temptation of reifying into personality traits the behaviours or attitudes of an actor that are the product of past socialization and the situation in which the embodied past is actualized. Then a person is said to be 'calm', 'anxious', 'scornful', aggressive', etc., whereas these 'dispositions' are not properties inscribed in them but rather relational realities (of interactions) that are observed only in the encounter between this person and something or someone else. To convert into dispositional language (solubility, aggressiveness, etc.) what can be described more simply as a situated behaviour (it dissolves in water, he was aggressive towards his classmate . . .) does not increase our knowledge of the social world. In effect, if an actor's disposition can be seen only in moments of action, in various practices, one may wonder whether the distinction between 'dispositions' and 'practices' is really useful. In such a case, it is always preferable to privilege the precise description of the action in its context (Lahire, 1998b). But one could even say that, if dispositional language sometimes does not add a great deal to the circumstantial description of an action, it can also say too much, in so far as it transforms a disposition under certain conditions into a general and transposable disposition. From aggressiveness towards a classmate, we move – by excessive generalization – to a general aggressive disposition towards other people.

Once the slippage is made from 'conditional' dispositions to permanent dispositions, generalizable and transposable to any situation whatever – in other words, once the clause 'under certain conditions' is dropped – the role of the context is seriously diminished – and sometimes even eliminated. For example, omitting the fact that social dispositions are indissociable from the actions on the basis of which they can be scientifically constructed, but also by way of which they are developed and constituted in the socialized body, one ends up imagining the existence of dispositions which may always remain 'in a virtual state'[16] without ever being actualized. If chemical or physical analysis of the properties of certain materials can indeed maintain that a substance is soluble even if it has never been put in water, or that a glass vessel is breakable without its ever having been broken, because these properties (not acquired) are stable and identical, what should be said of a sociological proposition that consists in maintaining that a person is logical, without their ever having been seen to realize a logical solution of a problem or without indirect evidence having been received that affirms the existence of such situations? There is even a tendency to make embodied dispositions into (internal) motors of action, self-propelled and self-sufficient: the disposition then seems to dictate its law, its *nomos*, outside of any particular context, in the form of a strong injunction, a compulsive 'it's stronger than me'.

From the (reconstructed) potential to the act (observed and on the basis of which the potential in question is reconstructed), it seems that one ends up forgetting what the words we have chosen – or that others have chosen for us – mean, and the ties between the two terms (potentiality/manifestation, cause/effect, assumed/observed) remain problematic.[17]

It is never totally possible to avoid dispositional explanation if one wants to take into account the past experiences embodied by each actor, but this should be used with caution, avoiding excessive generalization, and always looking out for manifestations and counter-manifestations of these dispositions, circumscribing their fields of activation and their fields of inhibition. Sometimes, even, the notion of disposition is useful in order to show what these micro-practices have in common.[18] But this should never give researchers the right to generalize the force of the disposition they believe they can reveal as being the origin of certain practices, beyond the field of practices concerned.

Is it possible, none the less, after having observed the diversity of practices of one and the same actor in very different situations, to reconstruct 'general dispositions' that would account, beyond visible differences, for a profound unity of attitude, orientation, relationship to the world and to others, behind the purely phenomenal motley of behaviours? The perfectly legitimate theoretical ambition hidden behind this desire to grasp the fundamental wellspring of action, the one 'principle' of all practices, etc., leads us back, however, to our initial question as to the singleness or plurality of the actor.

The negative power of the context: inhibition and latency

The present thus defines and delimits what of the embodied past can be actualized. By approaching things the other way round, as is commonly done, one can say that the present is seen, perceived and interpreted by way of our summaries of past experience (appropriation of a situation in terms of perception schemes already constituted), but this is to deny the active role of the present situation (of its elements and/or its overall structure) as a structure of selection, as a filter that offers the possibility for certain schemes to be activated ('expressed', 'opened up'), but at the same time closing any other possibility for the 'expression' or 'actualization' of other schemes. This means very specifically – one could almost say politically – that the social situations in which we live (from the most formal and institutional through to the most informal) represent genuine 'activators' of the summaries of embodied experiences that are our schemes of action (in the broad sense of the term) or our habits, and that we are thus strongly dependent on these social contexts (institutional or not) that 'draw' from us certain experiences and leave others in a state of gestation or latency. A change of context (professional, conjugal, familial, friendly, religious, political . . .) is a change in the forces that act on us.

And if these forces sometimes require of us things that we are unable to give, then we generally have no other choice but to find a different way of continuing our life – the least bad possible – in the same context (minimal adaptation), changing the context (escape), or radically transforming it to make it more liveable (reform or revolution). The nature of the contexts that we are led to pass through determines the degree of inhibition or repression of a smaller or greater part of our reserve of competences, skills, knowledge and know-how, ways of speaking and doing of which we are bearers (e.g. the cases of children with unlikely educational success, class *transfuges*, and children in educational difficulty who are forced to repress their everyday verbal skills when they are placed in a situation of academic speech reveal from this point of view a high degree of repression or inhibition).

In what sociology has been able to observe of these phenomena, despite a rather unfavourable theoretical context, we have all possible cases of competences, habits, dispositions and schemes . . . inert, torpid, asleep, that are made temporarily or more permanently latent (for 'their time') or suspended. Bringing them back to activity may depend on the social micro-situation (e.g. interaction with a particular actor, a certain situation, permitting schemes or habits to be actualized that are inhibited in some other type of interaction and/or with some other actor), on the domain of practices (e.g. applying in relation to food consumption different cultural schemes from those applied in relation to cultural consumption), on the social universe (e.g. doing in the family or leisure world what one cannot do in the professional world), on the social group (e.g. doing in a certain social group what one would not do in some other social group),[19] or again on the moment in the life cycle (e.g. habits embodied unconsciously in childhood or during the period of adolescence[20] reappear – after a longer or shorter interval of dormancy – at a different moment in the life cycle: establishing themselves outside the family home or the first work situation, forming a couple, embarking on parenthood, their own children leaving home, retirement . . .). In the final case, the actors may thus be bearers of habits (schemes of action) embodied in childhood but which become active and effective only in adult life. These schemes are then, as it were, products in waiting (for releasers, triggers, demands, external solicitations, favourable contexts), products (of socialization) with deferred uses.

We can observe, for example, the dual and ambivalent behaviour of women in a working-class milieu who, on the one hand, work in their capacity of 'wives' to maintain their husband in the home territory by struggling against his propensity to flee the domestic space in order to occupy various external spaces (the garage, the bar, places of hunting and fishing, etc.), and, on the other hand, are the first, in their capacity of 'mothers', to develop in their sons (but not in their daughters) the desire to 'go out' (Schwartz, 1990, p. 208). The behaviours, attitudes or practices (as you like) around one and the same event thus appear different according to the identity (of wife or mother) engaged in the situation.

In the same way, we know that forming a couple or establishing a family with the birth of the first child (as particular moments in the life cycle) can transform certain women in a quite surprising way (particularly for those around them – i.e. those who knew the woman in question before she entered a relationship, in a single situation, but also for herself). This is the case, for example, with those women

OUTLINE OF A THEORY OF THE PLURAL ACTOR

who seem to have broken with the model of housewife as represented by their mother, and who, once they form a relationship, whether for the first or a subsequent time, often find themselves back in this traditional role whose habits they had embodied in the course of their childhood and adolescence, often without even having realized it.[21] The same person thus reveals herself to be bearing at least two heterogeneous domestic schemes of action, and, depending on the mode of interaction established with her partner (expecting a woman attached to the domestic space or one more attracted by a professional career), one of the two schemes is activated and the other put in reserve (Kaufmann, 1994, p. 307). According to the particular case, different identities or embodied habits, different and sometimes even contradictory internalized schemes of action, find their terrain of expression either in other sites than that of the domestic space (in the mode of compensation) or at particular moments in the life of the couple, whether in a conflictual or a pacified mode.[22]

In the course of my own research on educational behaviour in primary school (Lahire, 1995d), I was able to establish major variations in behaviour as a function of the scene in question, thus indicating the activation of different social dispositions and schemes of action according to context. In a kind of game proposed to class teachers for the third year of primary school, who were asked to position each of their pupils systematically from the standpoint of perceived educational categories,[23] I obtained contradictory responses on many occasions, provoked by kinds of micro-conflicts of evaluation that arose from taking into account different educational contexts. Those teachers who tacitly anchored their evaluations or appreciations in the context of the classroom and the time spent strictly teaching did not have any particular problem in carrying out this task. On the other hand, when a certain variety of educational micro-contexts or types of educational interaction were taken into account by the teachers, the difficulty of classification could become insurmountable. A pupil could thus prove 'good' in one context (the class) and 'bad' in another one (the playground).

For example, in the list of pairs of adjectives proposed, a woman teacher (private Catholic school in Lyon) judged one of her pupils, Anne-Sophie, on the positive side: calm, polite, active (but ineffective), having sufficient desire to work if she was in good conditions (only if she had excellent emotional surroundings), participative, disciplined, stable, not really disorganized, having a good memory, quite rigorous and stubborn; and, on the negative side: fearful, anxious, emotional, not very reflexive, rather babyish, lacking self-confidence, often asking for explanations but especially for affection, not autonomous at work, laborious from the standpoint of comprehension, irregular in work effort, not very logical, not very cultivated, not particularly curious, not particularly gifted, 'pedestrian', not very careful and influenced by her schoolfriends. She also assessed her as kind and agreeable in interaction with adults but very aggressive and disagreeable with her schoolfriends, reserved with adults but talkative with schoolfriends. Above all, the teacher emphasized Anne-Sophie's radical change of behaviour between class and playground. 'She is completely different in recreation with other children. She always rushes in with the boys; she is very boyish, she wants to play football with the boys, and I'd say she had a very masculine side to her.' According to the situation in question, the adjectives used for her could often be opposed: 'One could almost have put down the opposite.'

The same type of situation was found in a completely different educational context (state school in a Lyon suburb). Akim was a pupil with some educational difficulty, but posed no problem to his teacher in the classroom. Contrary to many pupils who were very weak academically, 'got nothing out of working in a group' and 'remained passive', Akim had good relations with his classmates in the groups: 'He is quite able to join in with the group; he can take his place and even has things to say.' But the particular reason he is assessed as 'special' is that his behaviour in class is quite the opposite of his behaviour in the playground. 'Although he's just a child, when you see him in the playground you say: "He must be horrible", and it's true that he behaves hatefully, he defies the teachers and people whom he doesn't know. When he's in class, he gets down to work.' Though the teachers are horrified by his behaviour in the playground ('I saw him there again early in the afternoon. He approached a pupil with his "little ruffian" side and began to threaten him . . .'), he turns out to be very disciplined in the classroom: 'Whereas in class, apart from asking me questions, I'm hardly aware that he's there. I don't have to do anything. Not a thing!' His teacher reacts very clearly to the list of adjectives shown her: 'Careful about this one, he's completely different in class and in the playground. There's nothing in common at all. In class I hardly hear him', (whereas in the playground) 'he kicks up a racket, he's aggressive, a leader, everything that he isn't in class!' Akim seems to have made a division of his habits according to the situation (classroom or playground), disciplining himself in class and letting his more aggressive dispositions run riot in the playground ('a horror').

An important question, therefore, already raised by the work of Pierre Bourdieu and Abdelmalek Sayad on the situation of the Algerian peasants, remains that of knowing whether the different schemes of action or different habits embodied by the actors in the course of their past experience can be reactualized within the same social contexts (e.g. in the couple for spouses), or whether their heterogeneity and their contradictory character are such that they can only tolerate lives separated into types of interaction, social situations, social groups or social worlds that are dispersed and relatively closed off from one another with different persons and in different spaces and times (e.g. the peasant who evaluates his agricultural production in money when it is sold to dealers, but remains in a pre-capitalist logic when he is within the family or community).[24] In the second type of case, only one part of social being is 'realized' in the couple, another part in the sphere of work, a further part in the exercise of cultural activity, and so on – the nightmare then being, both literally and figuratively, finding all these persons in one and the same situation.[25] In fact, contrary to the proverb that maintains that 'the friends of my friends are my friends', condensing a whole vision of interpersonal involvement as always identical to itself, the friends of my friends are precisely not necessarily my friends. In point of fact it is not 'entire' actors with homogeneous habitus that spend time with one another, but actors who adapt or agree among themselves sometimes on precise points and in well-defined situations. This simple fact accounts for the many cases of social intransivity (if x is on good terms with y who is on good terms with z, this does not mean that x is on good terms with z).

'Code switching' and 'code mixing' within the same context

If we had to cite just one field of research that had finely worked through the question of the plurality of habits and their circumstantial triggers within the same context, we would have to refer to several works of North American sociolinguistics. Working in multicultural contexts (from the standpoint of socio-economic position, but also ethnic origin in their subjects), on the terrain that they have adopted (practices of language), these sociolinguists have studied in depth the phenomena of heterogeneity of embodied linguistic and language habits. Thus John Gumperz noted that minority groups, in fact, pass a large part of their days in sites where the dominant norms prevail.... This juxtaposition, symbolized by a permanent to and fro between modes of action and expression that are internal to the group and others that are external, produces considerable effects on everyday behaviour.... Those who belong to majority groups and have never lived this disjunction between public and private behaviour often find it hard to appreciate its effects. (1989, p. 80)

What is particularly to be observed with such actors is the change of language between one 'sentence' and another ('code switching'), and even in the course of the same 'sentence' (a mixture of languages or 'code mixing'). These changes are never the result of chance or an incoherence due simply to repeated cultural contacts with a tongue different from the maternal one. The subject of conversation associated with the world of the mother tongue (Spanish, for example) can suddenly trigger a shift into this language.[26] When the theme of discussion becomes more formal, or the relationship between the two interlocutors is less warm and friendly, the bilingual subject may pass from his or her mother tongue to English – in the same way as one moves in French from the familiar to the polite form of address. And similar facts are observed within the same language, between different styles of speech (in a social hierarchy from the more prestigious to the more stigmatized), as William Labov notes in his account of a case of sudden triggering of language habits that were kept carefully inhibited up until then thanks to a great self-control (hyper-correction):

> I interviewed a foreman on the railroads in Atlanta, and my wife, who is a sociologist, interviewed his wife. The wife had an educational level and social origin that was lower than her present position. What was surprising, given the social characteristics of this subject, is that no double negative – a form highly stigmatized in English – appeared in her discourse. Up to the moment that my wife asked her a question about cooking: 'Do you measure the quantities?' Spontaneously, she replied: 'Honey, I don't measure nothin'.' The researcher here touched on a key theme of symbolism in cooking. A good cook does not measure. Measurement is bound up with a superficial knowledge drawn from recipe books. The symbolic of vernacular cooking implies use of the vernacular language, in particular the double negative. (Labov, 1983, p. 71)

But it is David Efron's (1941) anticipatory analysis that offers the prototype of all sociolinguistic studies. Efron studied gestural behaviour, starting with the provisional hypothesis that this varied culturally from one group to another. To test his hypotheses, he undertook primarily in New York, and secondarily in the Adirondacks, the

Catskills and the town of Saratoga, a series of direct observations (and in a 'natural' situation, with subjects who did not know they were being observed, in houses, streets, parks, markets, theatres, religious buildings, restaurants, hotels, at public political meetings, in schools, colleges and universities, summer resorts . . .) of the gestural habits of several socio-cultural groups. These were Eastern Jews of Lithuanian origin and Southern Italians hailing from the Naples area and Sicily, each group divided in turn into two categories – i.e. 'traditional' (preserving the habits of their country of origin, or that of their parents) and 'assimilated' (more or less removed from the customs of their group of origin, adopting North American habits, with the feeling of being well integrated). If one of the lessons of this study is certainly the empirical finding that gesture is in no way innate but varies culturally, Efron considered all the same that one of the most significant aspects of the gestural behaviour of Americanized Italians and Jews consisted in the combination of gestures issuing from the groups or communities of origin with gestures specific to Americans of Anglo-Saxon origin. He called this kind of combination 'hybrid gesture' or 'gestural bilingualism'.[27] The cases that Efron mentions show very well how what triggers the use of this or that gestural register can vary according to the situation: use of language (using Italian gestures when speaking Italian), the interlocutor (whose cultural origin spontaneously triggers the use of associated gestural habits), the style of the utterance (use of North American gestures in argumentative reasoning and gestures from the Jewish community in a moment of impassioned emphasis). Efron even indicated the possibility of actors embodying the gestural habits of more than two groups.

Actors uncertainly swinging

University students, for the first time in their educational progress, have to face up to a fundamental problem in their studies. This problem, which is resolved right away by institutions with strong educational support (lycées, the preparatory classes for the grandes écoles, departments for higher technicians, university technology institutes . . .), consists in organizing and arranging one's daily, weekly and annual time.[28] Leaving students 'free' to organize and occupy a large part of their time, the university institution leaves them objectively free to fail in the practical (cultural) resolution of this problem. If those students (who are then still more like pupils) with the strongest educational support experience long sequences of unambiguous activities, constrained to an educational mono-activity for a relatively long period, university students on the other hand confront a difficulty (new in their educational trajectory) of establishing a context of educational study most often in a non-academic domestic world.[29] They must set up for themselves specific places of study, and especially specific times, within space-times that are most often multifunctional, in which several activities can compete within the same temporal sequence. Why get up at seven or eight in the morning if classes don't begin until two in the afternoon? Why not watch television, chat with one's parents, brothers and sisters or friends, when writing up course notes or preparing for the end-of-year exams can wait a while – or at least appear to wait?

When the separation of the educational context from the non-educational context and the fluctuations between them are no longer objectified and institutionalized (as was the case in the context of the lycée), they become 'personal' problems that each student must seek to resolve. As Erving Goffman writes, if a 'collectively organized social activity' is 'often marked off from the ongoing flow of surrounding events by a special set of boundary markers or brackets of a conventionalized kind', and these conventional parentheses 'occur before and after the activity in time and may be circumscriptive in space' (Goffman, 1974, pp. 251–2), university students must then invent markers of this kind so as to work in the absence of any external and coercive imposition of particular moments of work:

> We become so used to measuring time in order to use it fully that we no longer know what to do with those portions of duration not so measured, when we are on our own and outside the current of external social life, as it were. These could become so many cases where we momentarily forget time but rediscover ourselves. Quite to the contrary, we are aware of what are really empty intervals, and our problem is knowing how to pass the time. (Halbwachs, 1980, p. 90)

University students, particularly in the less supported faculties, are differentiated among themselves from the standpoint of the degree of self-discipline, self-government and asceticism they are able to display as a function of their family socialization and earlier education. Very often, however, for some of them it is a question of repressing or inhibiting hedonistic dispositions, which they are well aware act against a part of themselves that desires to work.

Recent research in cognitive psychology tends to show that the human being – child, adolescent and adult – is endowed with a composite mental structure, in which heterogeneous and even contradictory schemes of perception, representation and action coexist. In the context of tasks to realize, the inhibition of 'dangerous' or 'disturbing' schemes (from the standpoint of the nature of the task), which coexist with pertinent schemes, enables individuals not to fall back into the trap that is held out to them. Thus we do not have, in the context of mental development, a simple linear progression from inadequate schemes towards more adequate ones, but rather the coexistence of heterogeneous and logically contradictory schemes (from the most 'rational' to the most 'irrational'). Success in the task thus presupposes the activation of the pertinent schemes, but also necessitates the inhibition of competing schemes which, if they were triggered, would lead towards an error of perception and/or a failure of realization (Houdé, 1995; Pascual-Leone, 1988; Pascual-Leone and Baillargeon, 1994). One could thus say that success here lies, for a large section of students, in their ability to inhibit social dispositions that are inadequate (in relation to the objective of success in their studies). We thus observe a real struggle by these students, and sometimes a very conscious one, against a part of themselves that they do everything to keep dormant. There is only one thing they can draw on for this: the work context. This is then chosen consciously and conscientiously – which is otherwise a rather uncommon situation – with a view to arranging the most favourable conditions, those most propitious to establishing ascetic and educational dispositions and, conversely, avoiding dangerous temptations.

Choosing to study on the university premises (in the library or a study room) is sometimes a deliberate way of avoiding the domestic space, site of all (bad) temptations and 'bad habits', which concentrates the greatest number of triggers of anti-scholastic dispositions or pretexts not to work (TV or hifi almost instinctively switched on, family members demanding attention and breaking the continuity of school work, musical instruments that silently invite students to close their books, a fridge that invites constant nibbling . . .). The university location makes it possible to place oneself in optimal conditions for establishing ascetic schemes. For all that, the university library can also be the site of informal discussion with friends, which stops work from advancing. It is also necessary to choose partners in one's work or else isolate oneself in individual study cubicles. Certain students are aware of the conditions in which they can draw best advantage from themselves ('I know myself . . .') and deliberately act ('This forces me . . .') on the work context: the choice of work site and the arrangement of the work situation constitute a kind of technique of self-control.

Besides, often being on both sides of the opposition between ascetic and hedonistic dispositions, students can, in the light of changing encounters from one year to another (depending on whether the fellow students they hang about with are hard-working or rather bohemian), acquire the taste for extra-curricular pleasures (going out in the evenings, group sociability, relaxing, love affairs . . .) and give expression to hedonistic dispositions that were previously repressed or postponed or, on the contrary, reinforce their studious dispositions (mutual aid between students, motivating educational discussions . . .).[30]

— Scene 3 —

ANALOGY AND TRANSFER

Practical analogy and the triggers of action and memory

> Our daily life is spent among objects whose very presence invites us to play a part: in this the familiarity of their aspect consists.
> (Henri Bergson, *Matter and Memory*)

Action (practice, behaviour, etc.) is thus always the meeting point of individual past experiences that have been embodied in the form of schemes of action (sensory-motor schemes, schemes of perception, evaluation, appreciation . . .), of habits, of manners (of seeing, feeling, saying and doing) and of a present social situation. In the face of each 'new' situation that presents itself, the actor will act by 'mobilizing' (without necessarily being conscious of this mobilization) embodied schemes that the situation calls forth.

In this opening up of the embodied past by the present, in this mobilization of the embodied schemes of past experience, the role of *practical analogy* seems especially important. It is in the capacity to find – practically and globally, and not intentionally and analytically – a resemblance (what Wittgenstein called an 'air of resemblance') between the present situation and the past experiences embodied in the form of summaries of experience that actors can mobilize the 'competences' which enable them to act in a more or less pertinent manner. (Social life is indeed not poor in misunderstandings, in 'errors' of diagnosis on the part of the actors; Gumperz, 1989).

Practical reasoning of the type 'this resembles that', which rarely needs to be made explicit, is a reasoning that is generally approximate and variable. It can both neglect certain features of the situation under way in order to retain only a general relational scheme (the man–woman relationship, that of mother–daughter, of hierarchical superior to inferior, etc.) and attach itself to a detail totally de-contextualized from the situation as a whole (a gesture, a smell, a taste, a word, a voice, a noise, an object, a place – house, landscape, quarter – a photograph, etc.).[1] Since the analogy or resemblance is most often not thought of as such by the actors, the latter can even, in certain cases, have an impression of *déjà vu* or *déjà vécu* – i.e. an intuition of having experienced the same situation, felt the same sensations, feelings, etc. – in short, of having played the same scene or seen it played in a more or less distant past.

What it is in the order of memory that can lead someone to say 'this reminds me of' (seeing this, hearing that, smelling a certain perfume . . .) is more rarely explicitly manifest in the order of action, where what is involved is rather 'this makes me act in this or that way', the 'this or that' here being ways of acting that were earlier acquired, and are more or less nuanced and modulated according to the demands of the new situation. We are dealing here with a kind of (weakly instrumented) jurisprudential comparison between the present 'case' and 'cases' already experienced (which form 'precedents'), which reopens the past in order to resolve a problem (more or less new for the actor) that the present situation generates, or, more simply, in order to react adequately to this situation. The legal metaphor – though limited by the infinitely weaker degree of objectification, formality and reflexive consciousness in more everyday and less institutional situations – makes it possible none the less, on the one hand, to avoid an overly formal recourse to theories of action that invoke norms or rules by which actors orient their action[2] and, on the other hand, to insist on the importance of the present in the mobilization of the *embodied archives* of the past: if there were no new cases to 'deal with', the past would not be mobilized in terms of the specific logical characteristics of these new cases. If it is possible to insist on the operation of the 'reactivat[ion of] the sense objectified in institutions' (Bourdieu, 1990a, p. 57) by the habitus as practical sense, one should not neglect the converse operation of the reactivation of the embodied past by institutions. By appropriating an object, a situation, an institution or a place, actors give life to what went unheeded, but, conversely, it is because they find themselves in the presence of the object, situation, institution, place, etc., that this arouses what would otherwise have remained temporarily or more permanently in a latent state.

Studies of the relationships of interdependence within family configurations, for example, reveal the fact that certain types of conflict within couples (husband–wife) arouse and reactivate daughter–father conflicts.[3] In other cases, the daughter–father relationship is explicitly mentioned by the female interviewee in order to be able to talk about the husband–wife relationship: if the former relationship could make the second possible (the commonplace idea of the daughter who finds in her partner physical attitudes or characteristics that 'remind' her of her father), the second in fact reopens the first more or less consciously. Sometimes, however, the same couple that can on occasion, in certain circumstances, reactivate the daughter–father relationship instead reactivates more the mother–son one (the woman being to her husband what the mother was to her son).[4] In the same way, in family interrelationships, certain practical convergences or associations of two 'empirically' different individuals lead to a relationship with one being lived in a way that may be bound up with the history of the relationship with the other: this was the case with one of my female subjects, whose interview described the rancour she feels towards her sister-in-law (her brother's wife) and who also developed an aggressiveness towards the wife of her husband's cousin, whom she seemed spontaneously to perceive as analogous in some way to her sister-in-law. Almost unknown to herself, therefore, she could play scenes with the second individual that she habitually played with her sister-in-law, and the sociological interview in such a case was the moment when this became conscious.

But the analogy between situations can be still more complex, and bring into play both characters in an interaction. Thus the account by one interviewee enabled me to reconstruct a relationship that had been experienced a few years before. The two protagonists in this scene were both academics: the first was a young Moroccan man, not yet thirty, who had come to France to attend a conference; the other was a French woman of about fifty, one of the conference organizers. During the man's stay, a friendly relationship was established (the origin of which we can well imagine), the second individual invited the first for dinner, and they gradually revealed their respective life stories: the man was the son of divorced parents, and had basically lived with his mother, with whom he maintained a very strong tie; the woman had been divorced about ten years earlier, and lived alone with her son of fifteen. The interview with the first individual told of how he experienced a feeling of deep affinity with this woman whom he had only known for a few days. The woman who invited him – still according to the account that he gave – seems to have experienced the same almost magical feeling. Everything happened as if these two people, unknown to one another, university colleagues for the time of this conference, had played out a mother–child scene, given that both shared a common situation in the family positions that they occupied. One could say that the charm or magic of the situation here lay in the fact that they were sufficiently conscious to 'tell the difference' ('He is not my son', 'She is not my mother'), yet without being able to do otherwise than operate practical convergences, analogies and tacit associations that led them to relate to one another in the context of a quasi mother–son relationship. These two individuals were still in regular touch with each other three years after their first meeting.

Involuntary action and memory

And soon, mechanically, dispirited after a dreary day with the prospect of a depressing tomorrow, I raised to my lips a spoonful of tea in which I had soaked a portion of the madeleine.
(Marcel Proust, *The Way by Swann's*)

Thus is gradually formed an experience of an entirely different order, which accumulates within the body, a series of mechanisms wound up and ready, with reactions to external stimuli ever more numerous and various, and answers ready prepared to an ever growing number of possible solicitations. We become conscious of these mechanisms as they come into play; and this consciousness of a whole past of efforts stored up in the present is indeed also a memory, but a memory profoundly different from the first, always bent upon action, seated in the present and looking only to the future.
(Henri Bergson, *Matter and Memory*)

Maurice Halbwachs explained 'forgetting' by the disappearance of the social contexts of memory that allow us constantly to mobilize and reactivate our recollections: if the groups, institutions, individuals, objects, etc., that sustain our memory disappear, this puts in question a whole part of our mnemonic capacity, not because this has disappeared, but because it no longer finds in the experienced present the triggering elements capable of recalling to consciousness what then seems definitively and desperately forgotten (Halbwachs, 1992, p. 172).

Simply noticing something familiar in an everyday surrounding (landscape, urban space, apartment ...), the sight of a detail (a gesture, an object, a piece of clothing ...), an auditory stimulation (a voice, a laugh, a noise ...) or one of taste or smell (whether natural or artificial) can trigger a memory (and in this way provoke great emotion), reopen a whole piece of the past that one believes forgotten ('that reminds me of ...'), or impel to action by provoking the operation of a scheme of action or a habit ('this makes me act like . . .'). As Maurice Halbwachs writes on the subject of the child who has 'left one society in order to pass into another', and who seems to 'have lost the ability to remember in the second society all that he did and all that impressed him, which he used to recall without difficulty, in the first. In order to retrieve some of these uncertain and incomplete memories it is necessary that the child, in the new society of which he is part, at least be shown images reconstructing for a moment the group and the milieu from which the child had been torn' (ibid., pp. 37–8).

One can thus conjure up, in the manner of Proust, the experiences of involuntary action and involuntary memory that are an everyday part of our relationship to social situations. By involuntary memory Proust understands memory that is the product not of a conscious intellectual effort, but rather of a 'spontaneous' trigger, often mysterious for the person who experiences it, of fragments of the embodied past. Without this being done voluntarily or intentionally, consciously sought, actors are invaded by a past that imposes itself on them under the effect of minute external stimuli.[5] An evocative little nothing, a minuscule and seemingly anodyne event (the taste of tea or a madeleine, the scent of hawthorns, the smell of a bungalow, stumbling on the uneven paving of a courtyard, the marbled pink of a pond, etc.) can thus activate a past sensation, and along with it the whole context or set of experiences that are associated with it. The famous episode of the softened madeleine dunked in tea gives us the very paradigm of this involuntary memory: a smell and a taste suddenly trigger the memory of analogous sensations in the past[6] or reawaken these sensations by bringing 'the whole of Combray' to consciousness – i.e. the whole context of the time with which these sensations are irrevocably bound up. More realistic and correct than those realist novelists who organize their story chronologically at the cost of destroying the multiple links between the present action and the remobilized past, neglecting the constant provocation of the past by the present, Proust deemed real life to be 'very little chronological, with so many anachronisms intervening in the passage of days' (cited in Raimond and Fraisse, 1989, p. 108).

The model of involuntary action can be conceived along similar lines: instead of and in the place of memory, we then have a scheme of action (a habit) that is triggered by continuous contact with elements of the context that surrounds the actor.[7] It is this type of action that Bergson was seeking to describe[8] when he spoke of 'an *instantaneous* recognition, of which the body is capable by itself, without the help of any explicit memory-image' (1912, p. 109). This certainly does not mean that we let ourselves be guided, in the course of our action, by the different sensory stimuli that we find along our way. Such a specimen of actor – a kind of permanent *flâneur* – would not get anywhere, and never achieve any goal. Thus, in the example that Bergson gives after the above definition ('I take a walk in a town seen then for the first time. At every street corner I hesitate, uncertain where I am going. I am in doubt; and I mean by this that alternatives are offered to my body, that my movement as a whole is discontinuous, that there is nothing which foretells and prepares future attitudes. Later, after prolonged sojourn in the town, I shall go about it mechanically, without having any distinct perception of the objects which I am passing'; ibid, p. 110), it seems clear that the actor may well have intentionally decided, for example, to go to his place of work. But the practical knowledge of the route, acquired by regularly following it, means that this can be realized in the mode of involuntary action. Though decided intentionally (which again does not mean 'freely'), the route that takes me to work does not consist in a series of voluntary, intentional and conscious acts.

Rather than 'remembering' things from the past – i.e. 'representing' the past and maintaining a mnemonic relationship with it – actors 'see' their past (embodied in the form of schemes of action and habits) activated and triggered for action. We must make clear, however, that this 'action' is not restricted to 'bodily' or 'gestural' action. The habit that we have of viewing action (as in 'action' novels or films where things 'move' – i.e. where spectacular physical events constantly recur) as necessarily 'active' (rather than 'passive') often leads us to neglect the action of thinking, imagining, daydreaming, speaking, writing, etc. The word 'action' thus has to be understood in the broad sense of the term: speaking and responding, thinking or mentally imagining a 'thing' or a situation, making a gesture, running, walking, lying down, turning, pivoting, jumping ... The analytic dividing line between memory and action simply indicates consciousness of the past in the one case and the absence of consciousness in the other.[9] In remembering, the actor locates in the past images that arise and impose themselves under the effect of a particular trigger. By acting (speaking, thinking, moving ...), the past comes to 'expire' (Bergson's word) in their action, but it does not appear as such; it is acted or replayed rather than being newly presented or memorized. In these triggers of schemes of action (habits of thought, language, movement ...) the past is at the same time so present and so totally invisible, so perfectly imperceptible as such, that, as distinct from memory, it is confused with perception, appreciation or gesture. 'Habit rather than memory, it acts our past experience but does not call up its image' (Bergson, 1912, p. 195).

The role of habits

> Man is a creature who can get used to anything, and I believe that is the very best way of defining him.
> (Fyodor Dostoevsky, *Memoirs from the House of the Dead*)

From a historical inquiry into the concept of 'habit' in sociology, Charles Camic concludes that it is the institutional struggles of sociology (dominated) against psychology (dominant, particularly – in the United States – in its behaviourist version) that largely explain the marginal place that this concept has occupied in sociology (Camic, 1986). The concept has been in some ways the victim of the desire for autonomy and legitimacy on the part of the sociological discipline and its revolt against behaviourism. By abandoning to psychology the study of 'habit', sociologists have in a certain sense – for reasons of scientific strategy – lost a battle in order to win the war (recognition and institutionalization of their discipline); they have sacrificed a part of what could have been their territory in order to ensure the success of their legitimate claim for autonomy. It is sometimes better to lose part of one's territory and ensure one's independence than to fight on all fronts and risk losing everything. It is in this way that the notion of 'habit' was dismissed and reduced to the idea of a 'mechanical reaction to determinate stimuli', deprived of reflexivity and self-generated.

In the minds of many American sociologists of the first half of the last century, the term 'habit' was necessarily tied to the reductionist notions of behaviourism in the study of human action. Habits and other conditioned reflexes were unable to win the favour of sociologists, for whom reflective action was of principal importance. From W. I. Thomas and F. Znaniecki, via R. E. Park and E. W. Burgess to Talcott Parsons, the primacy and central place of consciousness, reflection, the intellectual elements of action, rules consciously followed, etc., was regularly emphasized – i.e. those dimensions that ultimately differentiate us from the animal realm and the physiological register. Rather than 'habit', the preferred term was 'attitude'. Why then go back[10] to a notion that seemed to have been definitively buried?

First of all, for the converse of the reasons that led to its abandonment. Today sociology is in a position to renew its ties with psychology (in its various forms: from experimental psychology through clinical psychology to cultural psychology). We could even say that it must do so if it does not want to continue living with an outmoded conception of psychology, embedded in its theories of action, emotion and cognition. Also because, as distinct from the notion of habitus, which alone in contemporary sociology – along with that of 'routine' used by certain North American interactionists (Strauss, 1993) – refers centrally to embodied habits, the notion of habit makes it possible to avoid a fatal confusion in social science – i.e. between habit as a modality of action, involuntary and unintentional, and the kind of habit (reflective or non-reflective – e.g. having the habit of kicking a football rather than that of taking a grammatical look at language). Thus habit can be a habit of theoretical thinking, a habit of reflection, of planning, conceptualization, etc., and is in no way at all reducible to pre-reflective behaviours. An intellectual and scholarly habit, which presupposes the highest degree of reflexivity, is not any the less applied pre-reflectively in the everyday reasonings of researchers. Scientists may make use of the specific habits of reflexivity without being aware of it, without having to think of it, without any particular need for reflexivity – and it is this that enables them to proceed very quickly in their reasoning. Being reflective (about a point, in the face of a situation, a piece of work, an object, a proposition . . .) does not mean putting one's reflexivity to work *reflectively*, since this reflexivity comes from habits that are contracted (embodied) in protracted scholarly activity, family or social conversation, the reading of scientific or philosophical works, etc. Thus the pre-reflective kind of habit is not the only one possible. As against a very widespread usage in the social sciences, we will not oppose 'habit' or 'routine' and 'reflectivity' or 'consciousness', but rather speak of bodily, gestural, sensory-motor, etc., habits, and of reflective, deliberative, rational or calculatory ones. The latter kind of habits are not any less constructed socially in formal or informal repetition and training.[11]

Habit, as a scheme of action, lies at the root of all involuntary action (similar to involuntary memory). It is bound up with a whole socializing past that has gradually constituted it, from the first steps, the first hesitant and clumsy stumblings, painful and slow, through to virtuosic practices that may be in the register of gesture, speech, perception, evaluation, etc.). For habits and schemes of action to exist, therefore, there has to be repetition. 'It is by working as a blacksmith that one becomes a blacksmith' – Aristotle's expression in *The Nicomachean Ethics*, which has become a popular proverb, says the essential thing about the mode of constitution of habits. Only accumulation and repetition (voluntary or otherwise, organized pedagogically or drawn from social experience) of behaviours and practices that are relatively analogous can constitute these 'summaries of experience' – as Piaget happily called them – that are schemes of action or habits. These are often so well internalized and naturalized that one could even believe they were their own motor, forgetting in this way the infinitesimal triggers that activate them.[12]

When they are triggered and brought into action, those gestural or bodily habits that are sufficiently constituted[13] can leave the field of consciousness free for habits of reflection, internal conversation and daydream, just as the automatic pilot of a plane relieves the pilots of part of their vigilant attention. It is possible to set gestures under way in a quite natural fashion, without any need to instruct the body to do them, without any conscious calculation intervening to guide them. We can thus drive a car while reflecting on our worries at work or in the family,[14] cook while thinking of what we are going to do next weekend, organize our files while mentally preparing a letter we have to write, etc. Habit of a non-reflective kind, however, is constantly rectified, corrected and controlled by the trigger of habits of reflection, at the same time as practice is under way, for the circumstances of action rarely permit consciousness and reflection to absent themselves completely. Something unforeseen, a difficulty that arises, etc., leads non-reflective habit to be coordinated and coupled with more reflective habits of behaviour. Far from overloading action, slowing it down or even paralysing it, reflection and reflective decision then supervene to facilitate it and permit it to resume its normal course.

From analytic transfer to the interview relationship

We find congruent remarks on the way in which memory and action are triggered in psychoanalytic discussions of the question of 'analytic transfer', enabling past situations (conflictual and often repressed) to be reproduced, replayed (action) or re-evoked (memory) by analogical transfer in the context of the relationship between analyst and patient (Laplanche and Pontalis, 2006; Bakhtin, 1987). The specific structure of this relationship thus constitutes the context that provokes the 'awakening' and reactualization of sedimented past experiences. By modifying the configuration of the analyst–patient relationship, other elements of this past can be aroused, and we see clearly here how the relationship between past and present is not simply deductive, with the present 'arising' naturally, purely and simply from the past.

Freud posited a difference between the revival of memory and transferential repetition. In the first case, the analytic relationship, which must be conducted in a kind of analytical neutrality (in which the psychoanalyst particularly seeks to suspend any normative judgement – moral, religious or cultural – towards the patient), provokes the awakening of memories either by the technique of free association on the basis of a given trigger (word, image, etc.) or by the very relationship that is established between the two protagonists of the analytic scene. In the second case, instead of remembering, the patient replays in the relationship to the psychoanalyst a (conflictual) relationship they have had with their father, mother or any other key figure from their past. They thus treat the analyst, by practical analogy, as a quasi-father, quasi-mother, etc., and reproduce (never quite identically) the relationship that they had with the latter. The opening up of the past by trigger elements or by the form of relationship established between psychoanalyst and patient inevitably has cathartic effects for the latter.

But one can just as well consider the situation, more commonplace for sociologists and yet rarely conceived as such, of the sociological interview: at bottom, subjects always recount their 'life' (their practices, opinions, tastes, emotions, etc.) through the structure of an interaction between interviewer and interviewee. The research situation thus plays an important role in the determination of what, out of the ensemble of past experiences, will be effectively mobilized. It plays a powerful role of selection, implying that a part of these experiences remains buried, non-activated, and sometimes even consciously silent (Singly, 1982); such experiences may reappear on other occasions if the new situation permits this.[15]

The interview situation is like a particular social framework in which part of the 'memory' of the interviewee (their experiences, practices, etc.) can be actualized. Academic routine tends to consider the interview as a situation in which information (opinions, representations) is extracted that pre-exists the interview relationship, like an object contained in the head of the interviewee. The sociologist is then to the words of the interviewee what the fisher is to fish: with a good technique, the fisher can catch in their net fish that pre-exist the act of fishing. And yet words are not waiting there (in the head or the mouth of the interviewee) for a sociologist to come and 'catch' them. They are the product of the encounter with an interviewee endowed with schemes of perception, appreciation, evaluation, etc., that have been constructed in the course of the various earlier social experiences and with a singular social situation that is defined both by its major characteristic properties (which distinguish it from other forms of social relationship, and in particular from other schemes of verbal interaction such as the police interrogation, the administrative interview, the employment interview, the journalistic interview, the oral examination, the religious confession, the analytic cure, the social conversation, the exchange of ritual insults . . .), and by various other properties – far from secondary – bound up with the circumstances of the interview, its location, the way in which researchers present themselves and conduct the interview, etc. When sociologists fix the objective of grasping the experiences of the interviewees, they must consequently seek to constitute a mechanism that triggers these experiences, whether this arises from a situation of trust or is based on the most material elements of the situation. For example, when I conducted interviews about commonplace educational practices of schoolteachers in working-class milieus, I made an effort to orient the interviews towards class situations, class practices, descriptions of the procedure of lessons, etc., most often asking teachers to give examples. They cited these 'from memory', but just as frequently got up in the middle of the interview to look for students' exercise books, a textbook, or their preparatory notes, to show exercises that had been done or 'mistakes', and to read extracts from students' writings, etc. The quasi-totality of the interviews took place in the classroom, where the teachers questioned in their professional context visibly felt still caught up in the 'worries' of the day, surrounded by all the exercise books, preparatory notes, textbooks and different pedagogic materials which had been used that very day or in the course of the week. They were invested in their status of teacher, the classroom attesting to what they were saying and imperceptibly supporting them at each moment (Lahire, 1993a).

The experiences mentioned by the interviewee, the manner in which these are related, the experiences intentionally left silent as well as the unconscious ones unable to appear – all this depends on the particular form that the social relationship of the interview takes, which thus constitutes a kind of 'deciding' filter between what can and what cannot be said, favouring the utterance of certain events and constituting a powerful obstacle to the evocation of others, etc. Elements as evident as the gender of the interviewer, their age, ethnic or social origin, thus exert a very strong influence on the type of discourse that the interviewee is able to conduct.[16]

A relative transferability

> There is some justification for basing a judgment of a man on the most ordinary facts of his life; but in view of the natural instability of our conduct and emotions, it has often seemed to me that even good authors are wrong to insist on fashioning a consistent and solid fabric out of us.
> (Montaigne, *The Complete Essays*)

Sociology has lived for too long on the unquestioned self-evidence of necessary transferability (transposability) and the similarly 'generalizable' character of cultural schemes or dispositions. To the extent that sociologists have borrowed here once again – without too explicit a reference – from the scientific findings of a particular historic state of psychological research (essentially the school of Piaget), it may be useful to reopen the doors of past and contemporary psychology in order to put in question what formerly functioned, at best, as a theoretical academic routine making it possible, despite everything, to study the links and transitions from one domain of activity or existence to another, and, at worst, as simply a kind of tic (bad habit) of language, with no consequence at all in terms of the construction of objects for research and the production of knowledge about the social world.

A return to the repressed (psychology) makes it possible not only to locate the origin of the problems raised by the notions of transfer or transposition, but also to stress the growing distrust of many contemporary psychologists towards these notions – concerned as they are to escape from the laboratory and the logic of experiment to work 'outdoors' in varied and contrasting social contexts.

The fundamental problem that the notions of 'transferability', 'transposability' or 'generalizability' present could be called one of 'excessive or premature generalization' (or, alternatively, 'lack of theoretical modesty'). What makes for this problem, in fact, is a subtle and scarcely detectable slippage from the *potentially* transferable and generalizable to the *empirically observed and attested* generalization. It is not scientifically questionable that a scheme or a disposition is 'disposed' to be activated in contexts different from – but analogous to – those in which it was acquired, constructed and constituted. What is more questionable is the idea that these schemes or dispositions are all transferable and generalizable on every occasion.[17] This simple semantic slippage leads to a series of errors of interpretation and a great deal of laziness on part of researchers. Passing directly to the 'presumed transferable and generalizable', they thus short-circuit the normal investigative procedure and avoid the tiresome comparison of practices between one domain of activity and another, or even one situation and another, which alone makes it possible to say whether there has indeed been a transfer or generalization (empirical laziness). Moreover, researchers then deduce too hastily – from analysis of the behaviour, actions and practices of an actor or a series of actors in one particular domain of activity, social context or micro-situation – schemes or general dispositions, in short, habitus, that operate similarly everywhere else, in other places and in other circumstances (error of interpretation). It would be impossible to list all the books and articles in the social sciences that authorize deducing, from an interview or observation of an actor in a particular type of context, dispositions that are supposedly general and transposable. Whatever may be said, the social sciences then do no better than common sense does with a notion like that of 'character'. With the mere difference that disposition is explicitly considered as socially constituted through conditions of existence, the sociologist generalizes and reifies – into constant, permanent and transposable dispositional traits – attitudes, types of reaction and action, etc., that are drawn from direct observation of behaviour in a restricted context – or, more frequently still, from its reconstruction on the basis of interviews. There are few works that seek to follow the same actor (let alone a series of actors) in very different domains or situations of practice. How can the claim be made, in such conditions, to grasp a general habitus (a system of dispositions) on the basis of examination of behaviour observable in very particular and limited circumstances?

The differences in observable behaviour between one context and another are then seen simply as the product of a refraction of the same habitus (the same system of dispositions) in different contexts.[18] The generalized transfer regime thus prevents conceiving (or observing) the existence of schemes with a very local application (specific to particular social situations or domains of activity), partial modes of categorization, perception, appreciation, evaluation or sensory-motor action that are attached to specific objects or domains. By this abusive generalization, the notions of transfer and generalization lose their imaginative power (which attracts the researcher's attention to analogical connections between one domain of practices and another) and become theoretical obstacles to knowledge of part of the processes observable in the social world.

The origin of French sociological conceptions of transfer is essentially to be found in the psychological work of Jean Piaget, who defined 'schemes of action' in the following way:

We shall apply the term 'action schemata' to whatever, in an action, can thus be transposed, generalized, or differentiated from one situation to another: in other words, whatever there is in common between various repetitions or superpositions of the same action. For example, we shall apply the term 'reunion schemata' to behaviour such as that of a baby piling up bricks or an older child assembling objects in an attempt to classify them; and we shall find this schemata repeated time and time again, right up to logical operations such as the linking of two classes of things ('fathers' plus 'mothers' = 'parents'). In the same way, 'order schemata' will be recognized in widely different kinds of behaviour, such as making use of certain means 'before' achieving a goal, arranging bricks in order of size, constructing a mathematical series, and so forth. Other action schemata are much less general, and their completion does not involve such abstract interiorized operations: for example, the schemata involved in swinging a suspended object, in pulling something on wheels, in sighting an object, and so forth. (Piaget 1971, p. 7)

One can recognize in this text the main source of the more 'technical' – i.e. more precise – definition of habitus given by Pierre Bourdieu. This definition particularly deserves the contemporary reader's attention, since it contains both what Bourdieu took over from his reading of Piaget (in the first part of the quotation) and what he left out (the second part).

As regards the first part of the quotation, we find the definition of schemes as what in an action is generalizable and transposable from one action to another, but we also find the same certainty as regards the transposability of schemes of action from one situation or domain of activity to another. There seems to be no doubt for Piaget (as also for his prestigious successor) that the 'combination scheme' that the baby applies in piling up bricks is actualized later on in connection with 'logical operations such as the linking of two classes of things'.[19] As a psychologist, Piaget developed an ideal and linear conception of child development. For him, in fact, 'the sensorimotor schema is applied to new situations and thus dilates to embrace a larger realm' (Piaget, 1952, p. 139). By way of its multiple experiences, the child comes to 'generalize the schema' by applying it to other objects, other situations and other problems (by sucking the mother's breast, objects placed in its mouth, its thumb, tongue, bottle, etc., the child establishes the 'sucking' scheme a bit more on each occasion). A balanced process of assimilation of situations to embodied schemes is thus developed, and of accommodation (correction) of schemes earlier acquired to variations and changes in the situation. In this model, no place is left for anything of the order of a cognitive or sensory-motor crisis in the child deprived of schemes enabling it to deal with the situation. A 'correction of schemes that is always more active' makes it possible to understand 'how the good forms take the place of the less satisfactory ones through a gradual accommodation of the structures to experience and to each other' (ibid., p. 393). The 'new' (the present situation) is forcibly assimilated to the 'old' (the scheme acquired earlier), and the 'difference' that the 'new' brings only leads the old scheme by accommodation to a greater degree of generalization: 'To the extent that the new objective resembles the old one, there is recognition and, to the extent that it differs from it, there is generalization of the schema and accommodation' (ibid., p. 411). We are even justified in wondering how new schemata can be established in such a model of development, which privileges the reproduction and adaptation of schemes already present very early on in the child's development, and which, from correction to recognition, from accommodation to generalization, from adaptation to assimilation, the child, adolescent and adult follows from the first games and manipulations of infancy to the most rational and complex structures of logic and contemporary science. The idea according to which accommodation consists in a 'progressive extension of the total schema that enriched itself while remaining organized' (ibid., p. 133), and that, for its part, the 'reproductive assimilation' that 'constitutes the schemata' is nothing but 'the tendency of every behaviour pattern or of every psychic state to conserve itself and, toward this end, to take its functional alimentation from the external environment' (ibid., p. 411), could be reduced to a formula of the kind 'how to make old into new' or, better, 'how to continue doing the old on the basis of the new'. *Mutatis mutandis*, almost the same terms reoccur in Bourdieu's arguments: 'As for the principle of this minimum coherence, it cannot be anything other than analogical practice founded on the *transfer of schemes*, which takes place on the basis of acquired equivalences facilitating the substitutability and the substitution of one behaviour for another and making it possible, through a kind of practical generalization, to master all problems of similar form capable of arising in new situations' (Bourdieu, 2000, p. 57).

But what if, instead of expanding, these schemes were simply inhibited or disactivated to make way for the formation or activation of other schemes?[20] If there were situations that could not be readily assimilated by the child or adult because the schemes acquired earlier are unable to accommodate them? Piaget seems to have seen 'gradual accommodations' only in the context of a fairly simple hierarchy from less satisfactory schemes to more satisfactory ones, or from more effective or adapted to less so. But the sociologist's problem lies in the fact that it is socially difficult to conceive such a hierarchy and homogeneity of schemes: what is adequate for the actor as father (*vis-à-vis* his son), for example, is not so for the son (towards his father); what is satisfactory or pertinent in one social world (e.g. professional or educational) is no longer so in a different one (e.g. that of the family). Which schemes are socially pertinent depends on the social contexts of their application (social micro-situation or configuration, specific social world, field, etc.). Instead of expanding and generalizing, they may be no more than specific social schemes with a well-circumscribed domain of validity. The same actor learns to develop different schemes of action (sensory-motor schemes, schemes of perception, appreciation, evaluation, etc.) in different social contexts: he is not necessarily quite the same as father, as office worker with his colleagues (different again in the same professional situation but in the presence of his hierarchical superiors), as son, or as member of a voluntary organization or religious community.

Each social context can trigger specific schemes (and this is a question that theory cannot and should not settle *a priori*). But the same goes for the most basic sensory-motor schemes. If normally 'the sight of stairs suffices to set in motion appropriate movements of the legs and feet in the subject accustomed to climbing a staircase' (Piaget, 1952, p. 129), whereas the sight of a hand stretched out in front of me spontaneously triggers the movement of my own arm and hand, which stretches out in return, we can imagine what would happen in a psychologically more rigid world in which only the scheme 'shaking hands' was acquired, and constituted the sole response to any confrontation with external 'obstacles': before a staircase one would then observe individuals improbably stretching out their hands ... But it occasionally happens in the social world that certain actors lift their leg when you stretch out your hand towards them! From temporary distraction or a more lasting lack of social adaptation, actors may activate schemes that are (deemed) totally unadapted to the situation and produce behaviour that provokes laughter (e.g. many characters in novels who are permanently out of phase with the situations they are led to live),[21] annoyance (e.g. class *transfuges* or 'school failures' who frequently offer answers that are 'not with it', apparently absurd, and whose conversations with the teachers are a dialogue of the deaf) or fright (e.g. cases of 'madness' or 'delinquency'). Cognitive-social rigidities of this kind have often been pointed out even in the world of science – for example, the case of the monomaniac customs of a research method denounced by the authors of *The Craft of Sociology* (Bourdieu, Chamboredon and Passeron, 1991, pp. 48–9).

The working-class 'school failures' that I have studied are sometimes led to experience situations so disturbing that assimilation and accommodation become quite problematic. They can swing between different characteristic cases: (1) they deal with situations at school according to their own logic but experience negative sanctions for this reappropriation – i.e. rejection of their homework and educational injunctions (Lahire, 1993a);[22] (2) they clumsily try to grasp the new logic and then experience fairly negative sanctions (if less severe than in the first case); (3) a number of them manage in a more or less fragile way, more or less painfully, to construct specific cultural schemes for school that are in total or partial dissonance with the schemes previously acquired within the family world (they then draw on their family configurations and begin to make sense of the double life that is constructed) (Lahire, 1995a).

Finally, with respect to the second part of the Piaget quotation, we cannot help noting Bourdieu's forgetting the possibility that Piaget opens of understanding less general and more specific schemes that correspond to limited situations. Piaget himself, however, rarely recalls the case of these less abstract and general schemes in his definitions of the scheme: 'By sensory-motor schemes we mean the sensory-motor organizations susceptible of application to an ensemble of analogous situations, which thus attest to assimilations of reproduction (repetition of the same activities), of recognition (recognizing objects by attributing to them a significance in terms of the scheme), and generalization (with differentiations as a function of new situations' (Piaget, cited in Dolle, 1988, p. 61).

From general to partial schemes

Contemporary psychological work is far from supporting the idea of a generalized process of transfer. Jean Lave, for example, shows that learning transfer across time, and from one situation to another, is far from being an obvious fact, even when the research findings of theorists of cognitive transfer are taken into account (Judd, 1908; Thorndike, 1913; Simon, 1980). In many studies, for example, subjects who pass experimental tests in which they have to resolve problems of analogy (set up as such by the researchers) do not manage to transfer the mode of resolution from one problem to another unless their attention is explicitly drawn to the connection between the two problems (Lave,

1988, p. 27). But if many studies cast doubt on the evidence of cognitive transfer from one experimental situation to another in the case of resolving a problem – even when these situations are homogeneous contextually (they are always tests) and cognitively (the same type of task: a problem to resolve), and are conceived so as to maximize the probability of a transfer appearing (distinct formal problems proposed immediately after one another, with the explicit indication of a possible transfer)[23] – transfer is still more debatable when we are faced with the transition from experimental or educational situations to those of everyday life, or from one situation of everyday life to another. For example, rather than a transfer of arithmetical skills acquired through education to other situations of everyday life that require an activity of calculation (such as purchases in a supermarket), we observe different practices of arithmetic in different situations (ibid., p. 63; Carraher, Carraher and Schliemann, 1985).

The issue of the generalizable character of schemes as well as of their transferability has been particularly well raised and dealt with at length by researchers seeking to show the 'cognitive effects' of practices of writing. One of the key points in the work of Sylvia Scribner and Michael Cole (1981) has precisely been to cast light on the existence of partial schemes that are contextualized, bound up with very specific contexts, and whose effect is not 'felt' (or 'measured') beyond these contexts ('Instead of generalized changes in cognitive ability, we found localized changes in cognitive abilities'; ibid., p. 234).[24] In the debate between psychologists, historians and anthropologists, these authors have contributed to demonstrating the fact that the presence of 'writing' in certain societies can in no case be taken as an indicator of the existence of general (meta-)cognitive competences or faculties (ibid., p. 229).

Among the Vai peoples of Liberia whom they studied, the use of a syllabic type of writing (and without space between the words) is occasional, brief and belated (towards the age of twenty). It is taught sporadically in the course of special occasions or encounters (the need to send a letter, for example, and the presence of a friend able to write letters and willing to show how to proceed). Instead of being taught for their own sake in a formal and institutional relationship of apprenticeship,[25] reading and writing are learned through interpersonal relationships, and inscribed in particular social practices (a particular 'need' to write) and in forms of particular discursive genres (you don't learn to read and write a wide variety of texts, but to read or write a letter, a list of donors and gifts drawn up on the occasion of a funeral, plans, records of financial transactions, of family work, of goods or customers . . .). Moreover, social life is organized, in several fields of practice, without any recourse to the practices of writing and written skills. The greater part of the processes of embodiment are thus effected without the mediation of writing (no body of knowledge objectivized in writing, no practices of writing and reading associated with this knowledge, etc.). As a consequence, the social contexts of the use of writing remain relatively marginal and occasional, and contribute only little to producing and reproducing the different domains of social life. The absence of a specific place and time for apprenticeship in writing, moreover, is readily understandable.[26] From the fact of this objective social situation, the cognitive effects tested by Sylvia Scribner and Michael Cole display more in the way of partial schemes, particular knowledges limited to particular situations, than of general schemes that are durable and transposable (general capacities to generalize, abstract, define, formalize, deduce . . .). When the uses of writing are limited in this way, the schemes acquired by way of these uses can be transferred only to a reduced number of contexts or highly circumscribed domains of activity. Conversely, when the contexts of use are uncoupled, the occasions for schemes to be transferred proliferate.

But what is then clearly apparent to the eyes of the researchers is the fact that the presumed 'general capacities' measured by psychologists (along the lines of those elaborated by Binet and Simon) for logical or psychological tests are capacities just as limited as any others, but more highly valued socially – i.e. capacities that are learned through formal education. The unschooled Vai people do not get good results in these tests when they require the definition of words, distinguishing an object from its name, applying syllogistic reasoning or explaining what is wrong in the case of ungrammatical utterances – all these being skills acquired through the school system. Children or adults who have attended school are regularly trained in this kind of exercise, and pass the tests successfully in as much as they immediately recognize in the situations and problems proposed the tacit educational injunctions that are lodged in them. As a result, there is certainly in such cases an analogical transfer of educational skills into the test situation. But the latter are, from the point of view of their main contextual and cognitive properties, quasi-educational situations. For example, if the school attenders manage better than others to formulate explanations verbally on the reasons for their replies, this is quite simply because 'such skills are demanded by typical teacher–pupil dialogue in classrooms . . . Teachers often require students to respond to questions such as "Why did you give that answer?" or "Go to the blackboard and explain what you did"' (Cole, 1996, p. 234). Michael Cole concludes, ironically but quite correctly, that the reality that the psychologists make into a 'dependent variable' (the battery of tests) stands in an intimate and even incestuous relationship with that referred to as the 'independent variable' (education).

What can we conclude as to the generalization of schemes or the strength of processes of transfer? The evidence shows (though routine has eventually made us forget it) that schemes prove that much more general when they find a greater number of social situations to which they can be applied or in which they can be usefully and adequately mobilized. Their degree of transferability or the power of their generalizable character thus does not depend on themselves (on their quality or their intrinsic property as Piaget defined these), but rather on the objective forms of organization of social life that decide on the scope of their transversality (transposability). A scheme of action (sensory-motor, of perception, evaluation, appreciation, etc.) is general when it finds a multitude of social situations propitious for its deployment (its transfer); it is partial and local when it can be activated only in situations of social space that are limited, particular and relatively uncommon. The general (or partial) character of a scheme thus depends directly on the degree of social and historical generalization of the contexts in which it is susceptible of being actualized.[27] And the question of knowing the extent to which a scheme that is observed and reconstructed in a given context can be considered as a central cognitive, sensory-motor or affective characteristic of the actor, which is applied in a whole series of other contexts, should be posed by the researcher and not presupposed. When it is impossible to reply to such a question, the latter should at all events seek to avoid excessive generalization of findings of knowledge that are indeed limited, but contextually pertinent.

The fact that schemes of action (sensory-motor, schemes of motivation, appreciation or perception) are always, to one degree or another, partial schemes attached to a finite and limited – however important – context of mobilization or activation can appear to be self-evident if we take, for example, the case of motor skills. Learning to ski or learning rock-climbing implies setting a series of particular sensory-motor schemes. In everyday life these motor skills (sense of balance and of position, suppleness, particular muscle strengths ...) do not generally find the opportunity to be actualized (except in the ensemble of professional or quasi-professional activities that require such capacities: Alpine chasseurs, mountain rescuers, fire-fighters

...). Only exceptional situations can mobilize them (for example, in the case of climbing, going up a tree to retrieve a ball caught in the branches or a scared cat). These genuinely are specific skills bound up with specific contexts and domains of practice, like those that Piaget discusses – swinging a hanging object, pulling a cart or aiming at a target. The idea of conceiving them as general schemes of action that are transposable to any situation should not arise here. And even the direction of the effort, training or asceticism acquired in regular sports training is not necessarily transferable to other social contexts (e.g. professional, educational or domestic). Sometimes a part of the sensory-motor schemes originally established in the repeated experience of climbing or skiing – but only a part – can be transferred at the price of some adaptation to the new situation: a move, for example, from mountain skiing to water-skiing, from sailboarding to surfing, from Formula 1 to rally driving, from the manual dexterity acquired by learning to sew to that required in certain industries for the assembly of electronic apparatus, etc.

Some psychologists now refuse, as a general rule, to deal with cognitive problems (memory, attention, perception, reasoning, categorization, etc.) 'in general', but prefer to view them as processes bound up with 'contents' – i.e. domains of skill or activity that are always specific (Shweder, 1991; Loarer et al., 1995). For example, rather than speaking of 'memory' or 'mnemonic capacity', researchers discuss 'specialized forms of memory' appropriate to specific activities. According to the domain in question, actors will have 'more or less' good mnemonic performance, and can never be ascribed a (good or bad) memory 'in general'.[28]

From generalized transfer to limited and conditional transfer

I do not agree with the judgment given in favour of Sophocles, on the strength of seeing one of his tragedies, that it proved him competent to manage his domestic affairs, against the accusation of his son. Nor do I think that the conjecture of the Parians sent to reform the Milesians was sufficient ground for the conclusions they drew. Visiting the island, they noticed the best-cultivated lands and the best-run country houses, and noted down the names of their owners. Then they assembled the citizens in the town and appointed these owners the new governors and magistrates, judging that they, who were careful of their private affairs, would be careful of those of the public.

(Montaigne, *The Complete Essays*)

Coming back to my starting point, it appears presumptuous, therefore, to act as if every scheme were generalizable, of systematic and universal application, whatever the domain of practice in question:

> The habitus . . . is a general, transposable disposition which carries out a systematic, universal application – beyond the limits of what has been directly learnt – of the necessity inherent in the learning conditions. That is why an agent's whole set of practices (or those of a whole set of agents produced by similar conditions) are both systematic, inasmuch as they are the product of identical (or interchangeable) schemes, and systematically distinct from the practices constituting another life-style . . . [from] different habitus – systems of generative schemes applicable, by simple transfer, to the most varied areas of practice. (Bourdieu, 1984, p. 170)

When sociologists postulate the existence of such socio-cognitive processes, they dangerously short-circuit the whole series of precautionary and fastidious empirical analyses (still under way, need we recall?) that, as we have seen, cast on each term employed (scheme, transfer, systematic transposition, general disposition, systematic and universal application, etc.) the shadow of doubt and of contextualized questioning. By universalizing the findings of a state (not completely outdated, that goes without saying) of contemporary psychology (that of Piaget), psychological concepts are imported into sociology in a reified manner, undiscussed and unchanged for two decades, concepts that – like any scientific concept – are no more than a kind of résumé of the state of psychological research that was among the most advanced on this question at that time.

We need only take the example of 'writing' that Bourdieu gives (1984, p. 193), following Merleau-Ponty,[29] to illustrate 'the transfers from one field to another of the same scheme of action' in order to realize the limitation of the model of generalized transfer. The manner of graphically tracing letters keeps its coherence through changes of medium or of writing instrument. But can we go as far as saying that the same dispositions at work in handwriting are to be found in a whole series of other social behaviours (personality, style, character . . .)? This hypothesis of graphology is extremely debatable scientifically.

If there may well be dispositions or schemes that are general and transposable, that 'colour' almost every moment of our existence, that run through every domain and constitute the foundation of what is commonly called 'personality' (accent, speech, ways of carrying oneself or of laughing . . .), not only can this situation never be taken for granted and must be empirically attested by the systematic observation of behaviour, but it should not constitute an obstacle to the study of more partial schemes, 'local' or contextualized.

The process of analogical transfer remains, as we have seen, one of the principal means for sociologists to account for the cognitive, sensory-motor, appreciative, emotional, etc., functioning of actors, but this transfer is never effected irrespective of the domain of activity or situation in question (regime of generalized transfer). There is rather a limited and conditional transfer (conditioned by social situations).

Scene 4

LITERARY EXPERIENCE: READING, DAYDREAMS AND PARAPRAXES

> For it seemed to me that they would not be 'my' readers but the readers of their own selves, my book being merely a sort of magnifying glass like those which the optician at Combray used to offer his customers – it would be my book, but with its help I would furnish them with the means of reading what lay inside themselves.
>
> (Marcel Proust, *Time Regained*)

When I began to work on reading, and more precisely on working-class modes of appropriation of texts, I was broadly guided by a philosophical and sociological interpretative scheme, that of the opposition between aesthetic and ethical-practical dispositions. This dichotomy, in various forms, can also be found in Mikhail Bakhtin's analysis of aesthetic criticism and in Pierre Bourdieu's sociology of cultural production and consumption. The aesthetic disposition assumes that the artistic form (style, manner, representation, etc.) is privileged in relation to the content or its function, and is thereby opposed to the ethical-practical disposition that rejects the disassociation between form and function, form and content, mode of representation and represented content, etc. Bakhtin described the ethical-practical intent as the viewpoint of those whose orientation in the social world is by way of 'ethical and practical cognitive categories (those of the good, the true, and those of practical goals)' (Bakhtin, 1984, p. 109), and who, by that fact, prefer to *live* stories (heard, read or produced) rather than entering into a aesthetic relationship in the strict sense. Thus the child who plays with his friends at being

> the leader of the highwaymen, lives his highwayman life from inside. It is through the eyes of the highwayman that he sees a second kid run past

a third, who for his part is the traveller.... The relationship that each of them maintains with the event in life they have decided to play – the attack on the stagecoach – is nothing more than the desire to take part in the event, the desire to live this life in the capacity of participant.... This relationship to life that is expressed in the desire to live it in one's own person is not an aesthetic relationship to life; in this sense, the game is similar in kind to daydream or the naïve reading of a novel, in which one identifies with the principal character in order to live, in the category of the self, their reality and their interesting life, in other words dreaming precisely under the direction of an author, but this has nothing in common with the artistic event. (Ibid., p. 89)[1]

Though my own work on modes of reading in working-class milieus was inspired by Bourdieu's comment that this was a gap in research (Bourdieu, 1984, pp. 32–3), what I actually found was something else. In fact, there was no sociological study comparable to my own on 'middle-class' modes of reading; on the one hand, therefore, I had the results of an empirical study on ways of reading in a working-class milieu and, on the other, *supposedly* cultivated readings that engaged an 'aesthetic disposition'. As I was expecting, those readers with poor educational qualifications invested in their various readings of printed matter a desire for these texts to be anchored in a different reality from simply the textual one: in a practical configuration (books and practical magazines designed for practical application), in a space that was already known and experienced (local papers, lists of births, deaths and marriages, 'human interest' stories ...), in the natural and physical world (popular science books and magazines), or in contexts and schemes of past or present experience (novels, biographies and autobiographies ...). Their mode of reading literary texts seemed to reveal clearly this ethical-practical disposition, presupposing a participation and identification, an anchoring of the text in elements of past or present everyday experience. This anchoring of reading in a different reality from just the literary one explained the fact that the theme, the subject and the reality effects produced by the style and/or the context (e.g. the author of the novel or autobiography being familiar from television) were far more often emphasized than were the author or the style, and what was never mentioned, in connection with novels, were literary tendencies or publishing houses. A pragmatically anchored reading, which all evidence shows is quite contrary to forms of reading with a literary anchoring, which obtain their meaning in relation to other readings, in the functioning of relatively autonomous literary references ... (Lahire, 1993b, pp. 101–27; 1993c; 1995c).

And yet, as soon as we leave the terrain of the assumed 'aesthetic disposition' for that of empirical study of the reading of readers with higher educational qualifications, the theorist is greatly disappointed. Those readers with a more academic culture act just like our readers from working-class milieus: they immerse themselves in situations, identify with the characters, love them or hate them, anticipate what will happen next or imagine what they would do themselves, appreciate or disapprove the moral of the story, feel emotional frissons, laugh or cry as they read the novel ... Strictly aesthetic reading is not absent from their discourse (and even working-class readers can mention the 'beautiful style' or 'fine writing'), and they may enjoy comparing authors or literary tendencies, but this is certainly not what holds them and retains their interest in the stories that they read.

This reference reading or stylistic reading certainly exists, but in actual fact it characterizes mainly professional readers: reader-producers, and particularly those belonging to the literary avant-gardes,[2] whose sociological characteristic is to place style above all else, and reader-critics, who ritually repeat that 'the story matters little, as long as there's style'. The opposition that I was basing myself on here, therefore, was not what I believed. It was rather one that divided lay readers, external to the issues of the literary field, simple consumers and spectators (ignored, as I previously remarked, in the theory of fields of cultural production) from professional readers, who were agents involved in the competitive struggles of the field (writers, critics, cultural journalists, etc.).

On the other hand, lay readers are very obviously divided among themselves according to the types of social experience to which they are sensitive. Not living the same lives, the same social conditions of existence, not having had the same trajectories in education, family, love, work, etc., readers do not all have the taste for the same types of story. When our working-class readers insist on rejecting what they call 'fictitious', stories 'without rhyme or reason', they often designate themes or subjects that are too far removed from themselves (from their own experience) to really interest them. How can one appreciate presentations of grown-up people perpetually in search of themselves, posing themselves a thousand metaphysical questions on the meaning of existence, feeling the absurdity of life, etc., when one actually belongs to a social milieu in which these scenes are not part of everyday life? How can one put up with narratives of endless to-ing and fro-ing in bourgeois and petit-bourgeois love life, when one does not have the same view of love or married life? This is where the real differences among lay readers of literature are to be found – apart from differences bound up with mastery of different lexical or syntactical registers according to level of studies. The taste for stories that are 'true', 'real', 'down to earth' – or at least written *as if* they were true or real[3] – is a relatively universal taste among non-specialists (even if not expressed in this way in all social milieus). On the working-class side, the loss of a baby, drugs, life with a disabled child, the period of German occupation, the struggles a woman waged to get back her child ... in short, all the themes that could make possible, by cultural and social proximity, a positive or negative participation and identification with the story, and thus make it possible to apply in imaginative mode the schemes of one's own experience, all these are the themes that delight readers.

And so it is not just working-class readers, as I started off believing, who engage this type of reading of literary texts. Narratives of this kind enable all readers to read in them situational models, models of behaviour, solutions (reactions, behaviours ...) to happy, difficult or problematic situations. For all of them, the novel (or, more rarely, theatre) supplies typical situations, roles, possible trains of events, schemes of action (sensory-motor, schemes of perception, evaluation, appreciation, etc.). For all of them, it can be read as a manual or a practical guide, through which one tries out, in a kind of jurisprudential comparison between situations experienced (past or present) and the written situations, new roles and new situations (possible, conceivable or inaccessible). With everyone, the novel can play a restorative and therapeutic role, in the wake of dramas of existence ('it's an enormous help at difficult moments', a woman reader said), making it possible to work through a painful experience so as the better to accept it, to try to make sense of what appears senseless and intolerable (e.g. the death of a loved one, a painful separation ...).[4]

On the basis of present-day knowledge about investment in literary reading, we can even put forward the hypothesis that the situations of maladjustment and disconnection that are provoked by crises of different strength[5] are particularly propitious occasions for this kind of symbolic work. Moments of rupture in personal biography and identity (divorce, separation, the death of a loved one, etc.), certain major moments in the life cycle (adolescence, 'apprenticeship' in the role of mother or father, retirement) are favourable circumstances for the appearance of reading of this type.[6] At a time of crisis (e.g. adolescents reading novels that present situations analogous to those that they live or believe themselves living) or after the event (e.g. reading by uprooted individuals of novels that recall their region or country of origin that they left many years ago), reading makes it possible to (re)develop schemes of experience and identities.

But not all novels can fulfil this function for all readers, both on account of the linguistic and stylistic mastery that they assume on the part of the reader (this is the first barrier of access to books, by linguistic code, which depends on the time spent at school in reading texts that are lexically and syntactically complex) and on account of the themes that they develop, the experiences they recount (this is the second barrier, which depends on the stock of schemes embodied by different readers as a function of previous social experience). It is obvious that both types of obstacle are sometimes combined, but not systematically (and the problem is posed more acutely for less educated readers than for others, to the extent that the first type of obstacle prevents them right away from appreciating the 'story', whereas more educated readers can read certain texts without experiencing any linguistic difficulty, but aware of their lack of sensitivity to their 'content').

The 'sensitivity' of various readers to different texts essentially depends not on a one-to-one correspondence (e.g. that workers would like novels that describe the working-class situation, women would like novels speaking of women, Catholics or Jews books with Catholic or Jewish characters . . .) between written and lived situations, but rather on the possibility for the reader to enter – by some imaginary modifications or transformations – into the world of the text (Ricoeur, 1984-8, vol. 2, pp. 228–63). A simple analogy – even very distant and vague – between situations facilitates this work of imagination on the part of the reader: whether a love affair between a woman and a man takes place in medieval England or late twenty-first-century New York does not prevent a young Frenchman of our own day from 'seeing himself' in it. A taste for this or that literary work, therefore, does not presuppose a simple similarity between the world of the reader and the world of the text: the most approximate, distant and vague analogy is amply sufficient to produce the literary emotion. We could even say that this literary emotion is produced at the confluence of the near and the distant, the same and the other, the similar and the different: the charm of the literary text, interesting because it 'recalls' a lived situation, always lies in the gap that separates it from this same situation. One 'finds oneself' at the same time as one discovers other worlds, one finds the familiar through discovery of unfamiliar characters, places and situations.

The meaning of reading or, better, the experiences that readers live through books is a question that sociologists have almost totally ignored. The sociology of reading has remained, until now, marked very largely by a sociology of cultural consumption.[7] Texts are often reduced to the names of their authors, to their titles or to the generic categories to which they are deemed to belong (romantic novel, detective story, classical literature . . .), and this information functions as an index of their lesser or greater cultural legitimacy. This reduction of the reality of texts makes it possible to relate these first indicators to other socio-demographic indicators (socio-professional categories, educational level, age, class, sex, etc.). It is not surprising, then, that surveys[8] should establish that reading increases as we move towards those socio-professional categories that presuppose high cultural capital (though business leaders share the most distinctive practices of those most weakly endowed with cultural capital). They show the specific effect of educational level still more clearly when they measure statistically, on this basis, the frequency of practices of reading: rising up through the hierarchy of qualification we find an increasing number of heavy or very heavy readers, people who exchange books, often buy them, go to the library at least once a week, and read books in connection with their work. None of this is at all surprising, given that reading (the basics of reading as well as certain specific modes of appropriation of texts)[9] is taught at school, and that school remains the fundamental matrix of socialization to books.

But the taste for reading a particular kind of literary work can in no way be simply deduced from a cultural (aesthetic or ethical) disposition, and therefore from a certain volume of cultural capital (lesser or greater). No more can it be assigned to a single social criterion of specification – i.e. position in social space. This literary taste or sensibility, which can vary individually according to the point in the reader's social trajectory, their social situation at the time of reading (child, adolescent, adult, senior; single, cohabiting, divorced, etc.),[10] their gender, social experiences that have left a lasting mark on them or that preoccupy them during the period of reading – all this can in no way be reduced to a simple effect of legitimacy (so that legitimate readers would read legitimate books . . .), but rather depends, as I have said, on the stock of embodied summaries of experience. Reading as a social experience is thus not reading as viewed by a sociology of cultural consumption. It fits completely into the framework of a theory of action such as I conceive this.

The appreciations expressed about books or literary genres 'in general' often indicate a very different logic from that applied to an individual book. The task of the sociologist studying singular literary experience thus appears indispensable, in order to get beyond the very flimsy kind of 'party game' that investigations of cultural practices often propose to their subjects: What do you think of so and so? Which do you prefer? Classify these books in a decreasing order of preference ... With this procedure, there is every chance of grasping only the connection between more or less legitimate books and readerships endowed with more or less educational capital (given that questions are asked only rarely about the nature of this capital – scientific or literary, for example). But this tells us nothing about the actual practices and receptions, whose contents and forms clearly are less readily explained as the effects of educational socialization. Besides, if literary experience were reducible to questions of cultural legitimacy, nothing would enable us to distinguish between religious, scientific, magical, sporting or culinary experience. By reducing everything (the social reality of the readers as well as the literary content) to differences in cultural legitimacy, and thus to spaces of positions organized into a hierarchy (market in symbolic goods, social space), nothing is grasped of the contents of experience, which are just as much socially determined, and the semiotic nature of the work (pictorial, textual, musical, theatrical, etc.) may be completely ignored. Structural equivalents (in terms of position in their respective aesthetic fields) are grouped together without even asking whether this does not amount to a fantastic abstraction, a tremendous de-realization from the standpoint of the experiences undergone with these works. Taken seriously, the experiences people have with books show on the contrary that a text is not a picture, which is not a film, which in turn is not a work of music; and, more precisely still, that a Manet is not a Picasso, a novel by Proust is not a novel by Balzac ... This line of questioning does not lead to a flat positivism, but forces sociologists to reconfigure the objects they construct if they want to grasp even a little of what people do with works of art, what their actual relationship is to these, what is the real reception of such works (and not that intended or dreamed up by critics, cultural producers, authors or editors).

Anselm L. Strauss began his career by conducting a study of the daydreams of his students (1993, p. 6). These imaginary scenes, projected in moments of inactivity or distraction (in relation to a main action), or accompanying gestures that are made without the need for much conscious attention, divide into two categories: 'anticipatory daydreams', in which the authors construct little scenarios in which they try out or practise future roles (certain, probable or hoped for), imagining that they might act or react in this or that manner in a particular circumstance, and 'retrospective daydreams', in which the actors replay scenes that they experienced and that disturbed or upset them, imagining how things might have turned out differently. We can expand Strauss's thesis by considering that retrospective daydreams can just as well concern pleasant and agreeable themes which the actor constantly replays 'in the mind' – like a scene from a film that you particularly enjoy, except here with possible modifications. Now, these beginnings of a sociology of daydreams – which Strauss subsequently abandoned – could inspire a research programme for a sociology of literary experience. Works of literature, in fact, provide support for daydreams of this kind. Rather than creating their scenarios out of the whole cloth, or instead of drawing on past experience in order to 'replay' scenes experienced, actors can appropriate scenes, plots, characters and sequences of events that others have written for them, and continue to apply the schemes of their personal experiences.

Literary texts are thus triggers of daydreams that make it possible to return to an action, to continue it, support it or prepare it. Far from being a passive activity disconnected from courses of action, reading is part and parcel of the action. Readers sometimes seek out books with the desire to 'apply' this or that type of experience (e.g. the case of mothers looking for stories that present problems of adolescence, or divorced women who appreciate stories of marital conflict . . .), but they can always emerge from their reading with other past situations that they had stopped thinking about having been reactivated, with other possible scenarios that enable them to reawaken and test certain impulses of theirs that remain unsatisfied, to 'try out'[11] roles that are highly improbable, or else ones that can be envisaged in a near or more distant future. One draws from books the resources needed to 'escape' from or give meaning to (and sometimes sublimate) the monotonous, boring and painful reality, as well as to prepare oneself to confront the most problematic, embarrassing, sombre or painful situations. The 'world of texts' is so intimately mingled with the experiences of the reader that the latter may sometimes no longer be able to distinguish a personal memory from an analogous literary scene, as Maurice Halbwachs remarks:

> First of all, I have since read a number of factual and fictional accounts describing impressions of a child who is entering a class for the first time. It may very well be that, when I read them, the personal remembrance that I had kept of similar impressions became intertwined with the book's description. I can recall these narratives. Perhaps in time I have preserved and can retrieve, without being certain as to what is what, my own transposed impressions. (1980, p. 70)

The first steps of a (North American) sociology of dreams and daydreams broadly confirm the closeness of the situations of reading and dream (especially of daydreams). In both cases – literary and dream experience – actors project (or project themselves into) scenes or situations that concern them very deeply. For instance, the sociologist Delores F. Wunder (1993) asked the brothers and sisters of disabled people for tales of night-time and daytime dreams that they might have had about such people. The dreams revolved around various themes – anticipations of certain scenes of everyday life with the disabled person, presentations of the dreamer as rescuer, winning respect for having come to the aid of a disabled person, construction of scenes in which the disabled person made a miraculous return to normality, feelings of guilt for being able oneself while the other person was disabled, scene in which the disabled person dies[12] – and all show the constant symbolic work done to make it possible to tolerate, and sometimes help to resolve, a difficult situation. Statistical analysis of thousands of dreams similarly reveals that, no matter how strange certain of them appear, they are always bound up with places, characters, actions and emotions that constitute everyday and familiar elements of the waking world.[13]

The reading situation is one social framework and context among others, but not quite 'like' others. As in daydreams and play (which constitute 'make-believe' *par excellence*; Goffman, 1974, p. 52), it makes it possible to try out roles, to manipulate (replay, modify, invent) scenes, without risk or immediate social consequence. And one may well ask what the confrontation with the text triggers in the reader's past, from their personal social experiences, to give them sometimes the impression of 'knowing themselves better' or feeling 'revealed to themselves' through books (Tralongo, 1996).

We can put forward the hypothesis here that, as in dreams and daydreams, embodied summaries of experience or schemes of action (whether these concern impulses, motivations, dispositions . . .) that do not find a way to actualize themselves in the various forms of social life in which the actor participates can find expression in the literary experience. As I have already noted, the plural actor can activate various schemes of action (dispositions), sometimes even contradictory ones, in different social contexts. It is possible therefore for the researcher to discover, through a sociology of literary experience and sensitivity, dimensions and aspects of the subjects that they do not necessarily display in current social situations.

For a better comparison with the themes tackled by psychoanalysis, and a better grasp of the specificity of my object, I could say that, as distinct from the reading of a literary text or a dream, certain categories of parapraxes can be sociologically interpreted as the surfacing of behaviours or intentions (and thus the activation of schemes of action) in a social situation that should properly – for reasons of social norms – forbid their presence (e.g. declare a meeting closed when one was supposed to declare it open, forget to bring home one's homework ...).[14] Parapraxis consists in the infiltration into a social context of an 'intention', an 'attitude', a 'sentiment' or a 'sensation' that could generally be expressed (because of social norms) only in other social contexts (and often more behind the scenes, in Goffman's sense,[15] than on the official stage). Forgetting, misreading, lapse, mislaying an object, a clumsy action, and so on, often indicates that the actor is beset in this kind of social situation by various desires, orientations, inclinations, injunctions and schemes of action. Freud defined parapraxis in terms of 'the interference of two intentions'.

As a singular social situation, a particular context for triggering a portion of the reader's schemes of action, the situation of reading literary texts turns out – apart from a few differences – to be very much like that of daydreaming. This proximity thus brings the sociology of literary sensibilities close to a sociology of daydreams, and ultimately also to a sociology of action.[16]

Act II

Reflexivities and Logics of Action

— Scene 1 —

SCHOOL, ACTION AND LANGUAGE

The scholastic break with practical sense

Man possesses the ability to construct languages capable of expressing every sense, without having any idea how each word has meaning or what its meaning is – just as people speak without knowing how the individual sounds are produced.
(Ludwig Wittgenstein, *Tractatus logico-philosophicus*)

Of all the major socializing worlds, it is that of the school where the break with linguistic practical sense is made most systematically and lastingly. This is a truism, experienced by a whole population, and yet not considered in its specificity, its historic originality and, ultimately, its radical strangeness. For what happens at school, right from the primary level (and often even earlier), is weird and astonishing, to say the least. At all events, this is how we need to view the school if we are to have any chance of understanding it.

Everyone knows that primary school is the place where language is taught. The phrase 'teaching language' is a commonplace today, self-evident, though it should really be surprising. 'Teaching language' does not mean 'learning to speak'. What the school designates by this expression is a specific activity that consists in bringing children into a structured linguistic world, with letters, words, sentences, texts, rules of composition for words, grammatical rules, rules of spelling and textual constraints (narratives, descriptions, arguments, etc.). There is nothing comparable with the gradual and unnoticeable first entry into linguistic exchange, in forms of social life that are always particular, nothing in common with the internalization by the child of schemes of verbal interaction or social functions of speech by way of example and practice, by hearing and saying. The situation of teaching at school is quite contrary to that which phenomenology describes in respect to language: 'I begin to understand the meaning of words through their place in a context of action, and by taking part in a communal life' (Merleau-Ponty, 1962, p. 179), or again:

> As for the meaning of the word, I learn it as I learn to use a tool, by seeing it used in the context of a certain situation . . . [Subjectivity] does [not] constitute the word, but speaks as we sing when we are happy; nor again the meaning of the word, which instantaneously emerges for it in its dealing with the world and other men living in it, being at the intersection of many lines of behaviour, and being, even once 'acquired', as precise and yet as indefinable as the significance of a gesture. (Ibid., pp. 403–4)

School aims first and foremost – even before correcting expression – at a particular relationship to language: a relationship that is reflexive and distanced, that makes it possible to deal with language like an object, to dissect and analyse it, to manipulate it in every possible sense and discover the rules of its internal structuring. To objectify language means subjecting it to a radical ontological transformation: the child was *in* its language, she now holds this *in front of* her and observes it, divides it, emphasizes it, classifies it and arranges it in categories. The child previously used language to say or do things, and could almost ignore its existence, given how its presence was indissociable from situations, objects denoted, other people, intentions, emotions, actions. She is now made to become conscious of language as such, in its materiality and its specific operation, and not really taught to make use of it in the context of particular usages, but rather to discover its specific laws of operation, to see *how* it serves its purpose. 'Talking well' is not enough to be a good student; you have to be able to show that you know what you have done and how you have done it. Just as Plato criticized the *mimesis* of the oral poets, since it was not enough, according to him, just to relive experience, you have to know how to analyse and examine it, to think what you say instead of just saying it, separate yourself from the discourse by becoming a 'subject' who remains outside the 'object' in order to reconsider and evaluate it (Havelock, 1963), so the school is not content with a talking subject who 'plunges into speech' (Merleau-Ponty, 1962, p. 403) instead of making speech an object of study and questioning, and it refuses to acknowledge as 'mastery' what is mastered pre-reflexively. If, as Roman Jacobson writes, 'Peirce gives an incisive definition of the principal structural mechanism of language when he shows that every sign can be translated by another sign in which it is more completely developed' (1981, p. 41), we have to add that the semiotician was describing above all the written-scholastic operation of language, as embodied by the dictionary, and not a universal language 'mechanism'.

To be rigorous, one should speak in relation to school of 'tongue' and not 'language'. A 'tongue' is a system of signs constituting 'an abstraction, arrived with a good deal of trouble and with a definite cognitive and practical focus of attention' (Bakhtin, 1973, p. 67); this is exactly what children are confronted with at school. This tongue is objectified and materialized in dictionaries, books of spelling, grammar, reading, etc. It is the fruit of a long historical work that has made it possible, and above all the result of the slow invention of the written alphabet. But once again here, school deploys an instrument that is no longer perceived as a rather curious cultural product but simply as a natural everyday object. The written alphabet? A perfect duplicate of speech. Yet it required erudition, analysis, and many inventions to reach this system of alphabetic signs. The first writing – in Mesopotamia and Egypt around 3000 BC – began as what are variously known as pictograms, ideograms or logo-syllabics. These graphic representations, writings and quasi-paintings of things, were gradually schematized, de-themed (the profile of a mountain was no longer recognizable in the sign for mountain), and steadily undertook a slow progression towards phoneticization without ever becoming totally and systematically phonetic. It was from these systems of writing that the Sumerians and Egyptians acquired the means for analysing language. They established its first objectification: writing breaks up the chain of sound, the continuous flux of oral utterances, into discontinuous signs, leading to an awareness of the reality known as the 'word', which did not pre-exist its discovery by writing. It is because our habit of writing (with the convention of leaving a space between words) gives us the feeling that we speak with 'words' that we cannot see anything extraordinary in this logographic invention of the 'word' unit. But by thinking in this way we reverse (in everyday as well as scientific usage)[1] the real course of history; we now conceive speech in terms of the categories that writing has enabled us to construct. Before writing there were no words, no syllables, no sentences – just varied linguistic usages that did not give a handle on language as such. The means disappears in favour of the (diverse) ends that it fulfils.

When scribes wrote lists (semantic or graphic) of words, they detached what had previously existed in contexts of specific statements and extracted the 'words' from the utterances in which they were generally found. Hence a double abstraction: from the context of statement (and the speaking subjects) and from the context of the specific utterance. And it is this double abstraction that constitutes what can be called a 'tongue'. Once objectified, language can undergo treatments that were not previously conceivable, and we have the start of that great work of ordering, classification, etc., that represents the first steps towards a science of language.[2] Far from being a duplicate, a fixative, a mere recording of 'speech', it is writing that made possible its symbolic and reflexive conquest and mastery.

Around the beginning of the eighth century BC, the Greeks made the transition from the syllable as graphic unit to the 'letter', which represented a tremendous abstraction (Havelock, 1976, pp. 49–50). As a genuine phonetic analysis of speech, alphabetic writing effected a clear distinction between meaning and sound, signs and their referents. From now on, language was the object of all kinds of reflection (grammatical, logical, rhetorical, etc.), which gradually formed bodies of knowledge about 'language' that were relatively autonomous, or rather – as these knowledges were not attached to a pre-existing tongue – that constructed this tongue in an increasingly differentiated manner. The system of language grew more complex, the number of possible classifications of the same linguistic sign increased. Lists and tables were drawn up, detailing analogies, contradictions, contrasts, differences. Phonological, morphological, semantic, logical, grammatical and rhetorical classifications could be made. And it was this scientific reality that we take today for a natural duplicate of speech.[3] It is this same reality that is the object of systematic instruction within the school system.

From the age of six (and steadily earlier) children are placed in situations akin to those in which scribes or 'scholars' (philosophers, grammarians, rhetoricians, logographers) lived several thousand years ago. They discover first of all the specifically phonological reality, learning to decompose and analyse the flow of sound. They work to separate words (Chervel, 1981, pp. 31–2) (and children's resistance to this lexical separation still recalls today how the notion of 'word' is something cultural; Lahire, 1993a, pp. 104–13), to classify them according to various principles, to combine letters to make words, to assemble words into 'sentences', those purely grammatical units that contain at least a subject and a verb, beginning with a capital and ending with a full stop.

Whether in relation to phonological or grammatical reality, pupils at school do not truly use language in everyday situations where it always has a social function, but manipulate, displace, transform, analyse and classify the elements of language, so as to experience the existence of a system of signs. They focus their attention, according to the particular case, either exclusively on the signifier (e.g. exercises in recognizing letters, syllables and sounds, in combining letters and syllables) or exclusively on the signified (e.g. to classify words according to a given semantic principle). They envisage different signs from the standpoint of their grammatical function (noun or verb?) or their role in the text (e.g. introduction–development–conclusion). The pupil enters, with greater or less ease according to whether or not his or her parents are already the product of a prolonged schooling, the complex world of the tongue, which is not that of everyday language, produced without even a thought in the multiple situations of everyday life.

Thus pupils do not learn to speak, they learn to construct, to deconstruct and to reconstruct, to combine (e.g. letters, words, groups of words, sentences . . .), to transform (e.g. give a sentence the form of a question, put it into the past tense, find the masculine or plural . . .), to order or recognize signs according to different principles of organization (e.g. put this word into the list of words beginning with 'p', the list of names of animals, the list of adjectives, adverbs, nouns or verbs), to compose sentences with the help of elements denoted by the name of the boxes into which they have already learned to order them (e.g. a noun + a verb + a complement of place), and so on. All these linguistic signs (even those without any meaning of their own, such as letters and a large portion of syllables) have a virtual place in various boxes in which they can be grouped according to the particular case. These boxes are lists or paradigms that make it possible to have a constant hold on the language-object by cutting it up in a thousand ways and defining its coordinates. A word may be recognized and classified on the basis of one or several of its letters, of its grammatical function, its word family, its homonyms, synonyms, etc. The word is not in contact with a situation, articulated to a gesture or a person, involved with an intention or an emotion; it is an element susceptible of being noted, named, distributed, transformed, displaced. The same goes for oral education and textual production, which are sometimes curiously known as 'oral expression' and 'written expression', but are in no way the spontaneous expression of feelings or experiences. To speak explicitly and in a grammatically complete and correct fashion (Lahire, 1991a), to introduce, conclude, spell out, punctuate, to be able to stick to the same guiding thread throughout a narrative, to privilege the coherence and autonomy of one's textual construction (Lahire, 1992) – all this pertains to a conscious game of construction and has little connection with the pre-reflexive language habits that are triggered in appropriate situations.

Basically, the school makes language the object of a particular attention, a conscious, voluntary and intentional manipulation (to follow Vygotsky, 1962). It develops a reflexive attitude towards objective language, keeping this at a distance and considering it as an object to be studied in and for itself on the basis of various perspectives. There is a radical difference between practical mastery of language in its various ordinary usages (linguistic practical sense) and the kind of symbolic mastery (there could indeed be other kinds) that the school proposes (historically, educationalists have often spoken of this second mastery, which orders and reasons what comes from simple habit and usage) in learning alphabetic reading and writing, in the teaching of grammar and orthography or in that of oral or textual production. Far more than merely becoming aware of a medium that usage tends to make us forget, or to confuse with intentions, emotions, objects, individuals, situations, etc., it involves the discovery of a system (with its units and rules) that is totally new to the child. As a world of written culture, the school is indeed the central place where the attempt is made, systematically and durably, to make children conscious of language, by multiplying the angles of attack on language per se through a constant work on it by means of exercises, questions and incessant reflexive correction – a place where the break is made with practices of language that are 'spontaneous' and 'everyday'.

Research that seeks to measure the cognitive effects of school always shows how schooled children or adults succeed better than others in those tasks that require verbal explanation (e.g. to explain why a sentence is grammatically correct or incorrect, and not simply judge whether it is so), that demand the production of explicit verbal instructions (e.g. concerning a game that is already mastered in practice) or that require sticking to the verbal message alone in the resolution of a problem (e.g. the case of syllogisms) (Scribner and Cole, 1981; Goody, 1987, p. 235). For example, in a study conducted on the Mayas and Mestizos of the Yucatan peninsula, D. Sharp, M. Cole and C. Lave show that those subjects with little or no schooling generally resolve syllogisms by referring to everyday information about the world, rather than by keeping simply to the information contained in the problem. To a syllogism of the type: 'If Juan and José drink a lot of beer, the mayor of the town gets angry. Juan and José are drinking a lot of beer now. Do you think the mayor is angry with them?', certain subjects would respond that so many men drink beer they don't see why the mayor should be angry (Cole, 1996, p. 83) . . .

I have myself shown in a series of observations conducted in classrooms over three years that the pupils with educational difficulty in primary school are those who are unable to take this distance from language, to view it as an object that can be studied per se: they have difficulty analysing the chain of sound right from their first introduction to reading and writing, for lack of the ability to maintain their attention on the phonological level, persistent collage or inadequate partition of 'words' (e.g. 'the safternoon' for 'this afternoon', etc.), comprehension problems in reading that are partly bound up with their inability to seek intra-textually the indications that make it possible to construe the meaning of the text, difficulties in the field of grammatical analysis and a pragmatic reappropriation of certain grammatical demands, poor meta-linguistic mastery of the words in a vocabulary that can also be mastered practically, frequent mistakes in orthography (especially grammatical mistakes) that signal an insufficient mastery of the paradigms and syntactical relationships that connect the elements of different paradigms (e.g. so as not to write '*Je les cueilles*' but '*Je les cueille*', you need to recognize the verb and its subject, and to know that the verb agrees with the subject), an oral expression in which the predominant aspects are implicit – i.e. gesture, mimicry, posture, intonation – and which thus appears 'poor' in the eyes of teachers who privilege the explicit (e.g. 'confusion of tenses', juxtaposition rather than textual organization of 'ideas', profusion of facts with no connection between them apart from that they happened in the same period of time . . .). All these manifestations of educational failure remind us – by the resistance that they show towards educational forms of apprenticeship and educational knowledge – of the originality and specificity of the world of school. By observing over a protracted period the reactions of pupils in crisis to the pedagogic desire to draw them into this system of signs that is language, one may end up doubting formalist and structural linguistic theories of the linguistic system. And we can be sure that one of the elements that explains why Ludwig Wittgenstein abandoned the 'speculative and hyper-theoretical attitude' of his *Tractatus logico-philosphicus* was his experience as a country schoolteacher in the years from 1920 to 1926 (Bouveresse, 1987, p. 569). It is certainly not accidental that, without initially knowing this biographical fact, I was able to use several philosophical remarks by this author to illustrate the behaviour of children in difficulty towards the exercises and demands of school.[4]

Saussure, or the pure theory of scholastic practices on language

I could summarize my argument here by saying that school is profoundly Saussurian[5] (and by the same token anti-pragmatic and anti-phenomenological), or conversely that Saussurian theory is the most scholastic of theories about linguistic facts. Indeed, the linguistic theory developed by Saussure describes quite precisely the way in which the educational system deals with language. It is Mikhail Bakhtin, a bitter critic of formalism in linguistics and champion of a pragmatic and dialogical conception of language practices, who comes to my assistance in showing the unsuspected connection between Saussure and the school. Bakhtin criticizes the 'abstract objectivism' of Saussure in studying 'units of language' and not 'units of verbal exchange'. The unit of language is the 'proposition':

> This is not bounded at its two ends by the alternation of speaking subjects, it is not in immediate contact with reality (with the trans-verbal situation) and no more does it have an immediate relationship with anyone else's utterances, it does not possess a full significance and is unsuited to arousing a responsive attitude on the part of the other speaker, i.e. to determining a response. The proposition as a unit of language is grammatical in nature and has limits, a completion, a unity, that derive from grammar. (Bakhtin, 1984, pp. 280–1)

Bakhtin's critique, therefore, amounts to saying that Saussure subjected the units of verbal exchange ('utterances') to a radical transformation that could be called 'grammaticalization'. This operation disconnects the utterance from any social situation and any speaker, converting it into an object that has neither a sender nor an addressee and does not arouse any particular verbal or non-verbal reaction ('the isolated monologic utterance'; Bakhtin, 1973, p. 78). A proposition of the kind 'the pope is dead' does not trigger any particular emotion or reaction, in as much as it is simply an example of grammar.[6] Linguistics, moreover, treats with the same neutralizing attitude the propositions: 'The pope is dead' and 'The pope is alive', which, if they were uttered in a particular social situation, would undoubtedly produce very different effects. For linguistics these are no more than simple actualizations or illustrations of one and the same grammatical structure: subject/verb/predicate. The opposite of the 'active responsive comprehension' that the utterance implies is 'passive comprehension' (Bakhtin, 1984, p. 289), suited to someone who treats the mother tongue as a 'dead language' – i.e. the object of various kinds of dissection.

But school proceeds no differently from the linguistics that Bakhtin criticizes here, and Saussurian linguistic theory is a marvellous instrument for describing the educational practices of teaching language. Pupils learn when they embark on alphabetic writing to distinguish between the signifier (the acoustic image), the signified (the concept) and the referent, to make a difference between units that are lacking in meaning (letters and a large number of syllables) and units of meaning (words); they learn to order the different elements of the linguistic system in lists and paradigms (paradigmatic relationships)[7] and to combine them (syntactical relationships);[8] they utilize a 'common treasury' of linguistic signs that the dictionary materializes very concretely, etc.

Dictionaries and textbooks of grammar, moreover, give a quite correct idea of Saussurian language as a system of signs. On the basis of a limited number of phonemes it is possible to produce an unlimited number of sound chains; on the basis of a limited number of words and (grammatical) rules for their combination it is possible to produce an endless number of acts of speech. And it is not accidental that the closure of a system of signs, in which only relations between the signs count, can make us think of a 'mathematical formula' (Bakhtin, 1973, p. 54), and that algebra has been seen as a kind of 'logical ideal' of grammar (Vendryes, 1959, p. 154). The Saussurian theory of language, however, cannot be considered as a universally pertinent theory, in as much as, once it emerges from the world of education (or the scientific world that is very close to education), it atrophies and immediately loses its descriptive power.

And yet Bakhtin does not draw all the theoretical consequences from the facts he establishes. Like other theorists attentive to the links between language and social activities, situations of statement, etc. (pragmatists, phenomenologists ...), he stops midway on the theoretical road on which he has embarked.[9] He is wrong to some extent in not seeing how Saussure was partially right, at least as far as the world of education is concerned. Language does indeed sometimes present itself to us as a kind of constraint, with its principles, rules and internal logics of operation. And this is indeed the experience that pupils have at primary school when they learn grammar and orthography, or more simply just to read and write. It is wrong to maintain that 'the speaker's subjective consciousness does not in the least operate with language as a system of normatively identical forms' (Bakhtin, 1973, p. 67), or that 'There is no analysis capable of making language crystal clear and arraying it before us as if it were an object' (Merleau-Ponty, 1962, p. 391), since this is what the school and Saussurian linguistics generally practise very rigorously. Saussure was certainly mistaken outside the walls of the school – and his critics are right to stress the limitations of his model – but he remains just as pertinent for understanding the quite surprising fashion in which the school tackles language.

Bakhtin rejects the Saussurian theory by arguing that 'the result of all this is a fundamentally erroneous theory of understanding' (1973, p. 73). Now, if we take Saussurian linguistics for what it is – i.e. a kind of pure theory of written educational practices, a kind of conceptual explanation of a series of educational practices of language and an educational (and written) relationship to language – we then have to admit its specific scientific interest. Bakhtin, blinded by his critique,[10] seems to have forgotten his own analyses of the relationship between linguistics, the daughter of philology, and the school:

> Monuments were made over from heuristic documents into a classical model of language for the lecture hall. This second basic task of linguistics – its creating the apparatus essential for instruction in a deciphered language, for codifying it, so to speak, in line with the aims of lecture hall transmission, made a substantial imprint on linguistic thinking. Phonetics, grammar, lexicon – the three branches of the system of language, the three organizing centres for linguistic categories – took shape within the channel of these two major tasks of linguistics: the heuristic and the pedagogical. (Bakhtin, 1973, pp. 73–4)

If linguistics is a response to educational demands, it is impossible to sweep it away with a wave of the hand by terming it a 'false theory of understanding'. The relative scientific 'error' of structural linguistics actually corresponds to a social reality: that of written educational work on language and of the written educational relationship to language.

The social conditions of departure from practical sense

The reflexive relationship to language that the school both constructs and demands is steadily developed by way of exercises, questions, situations and corrections, which all contribute to drawing the child's attention to the specific properties of the system of linguistic signs. It is prolonged socialization in this kind of social world that enables actors to acquire a series of reflexive habits in terms of linguistic practices. Not all pupils will become professional grammarians, linguists or philologists, they do not all succeed in appropriating these scholastic situations with such ease, but none the less they all undergo, for a long period (at least ten years, between the ages of six and sixteen), exercises that are the fruit of thousands of years of work by these communities of scholars. They will later handle writing, which always demands a minimum in the way of meta-linguistic awareness, whether in terms of construction (textual order), making a sentence (grammatical order) or simply spelling (lexical and orthographic order).

The distanced relationship to language, therefore, is not simply developed in any situation whatsoever, in any which way, by any kind of practice or exercise. It is precisely constituted by educational exercises based on a system of inscription and objectification of language (alphabetic writing) and on bodies of accumulated written knowledge (grammatical, orthographic, stylistic, alphabetic-phonetic . . .) that constitute specialized and relatively autonomous reflexive regards bearing on particular aspects or singular dimensions of language. Everything thus begins with alphabetic writing – which, as we have seen, is in no way a natural duplicate of speech, but rather an instrument of objectification of language and the basis of its symbolic mastery (and of apprenticeship to it). Specialist knowledge of language itself varies historically (e.g. grammar was first introduced at primary-school level in France in the mutual schools of the early nineteenth century) and could be other than it is. One could imagine, for example, that the primary school might partly replace the teaching of grammar (whose function is indissociable from the teaching of spelling; Chervel, 1981) by that of rhetoric. Such changes, while significant, would be secondary in relation to the reflexive attitude that it is intended to develop. These then are the indissociably social and intellectual conditions for the construction of a reflexive relationship to language.

If I emphasize here the concrete conditions for the social construction of such a relationship to language, this is because there is an alternative point of view on this question that places at the heart of the problem the suspension of temporal urgency and removal from economic necessity. To have free time and not to be subject to the practical demands of existence (conceived as economic necessity) are in this view the two major conditions for the formation of the reflexive and detached relationship to language, as likewise for the aesthetic disposition, the scholarly viewpoint, etc. This is the thesis that Pierre Bourdieu maintains, and which has been only rarely criticized, but which I believe is both abstract and imprecise.

For example, the aesthetic relationship to creative works that sees the form or the medium (iconic, verbal, written, etc.) as primary in relation to their function or their content, and assumes that language is the object of a specific attention, certainly does require time, being outside the 'pressure of temporal urgency ... which makes it impossible to linger over interesting problems, to approach them several times, to go back' (Bourdieu, 1990a, p. 287) and, as a result, disposing of favourable economic circumstances that free one from the immediate practical concerns of existence. But it also implies above all a specific work on language as such, a work that was historically made possible by the invention of writing and the multiple cognitive deployments of written knowledge. In point of fact, the 'withdrawal from economic necessity' or the 'objective and subjective distanc[ing] from practical urgencies' (Bourdieu, 1984, p. 54) are not enough to achieve this distanced relationship to the world – either theoretical, scholarly, distanced reason or the aesthetic disposition. If sociology is to understand what these dispositions are, it cannot dispense with analysing the practices of language by which these have taken form.

If we did not proceed in this way, we would fail to grasp how those in the social categories most removed from immediate economic necessity, but in some degree lacking in educational qualifications (leaders of business and industry), very often share the cultural judgements, tastes and practices of those fractions of the working class most lacking in economic (and educational) capital.[11] And yet the sociological interpretation of these educational dispositions continues to be based on a reduction of society to a ladder that is decreasingly subject to practical urgency as one moves up the scale:

> As one moves away from the lower regions of the social space, characterized by the extreme brutality of the economic constraints, the uncertainties diminish and the pressures of economic and social necessity relax. As a consequence, less strictly defined positions, which leave more scope for manoeuvre, offer the possibility of acquiring dispositions that are freer in respect of practical urgencies – problems to solve, opportunities to exploit – and seemingly preadjusted to the tactit demands of the scholastic universes. (Bourdieu, 2000, pp. 16–17)

It is not that this theoretical model is faulty as such, since it well describes a part of the social world as seen from an economic perspective. But it lacks the ability to account for such dispositions. Particularly missing is the distinction between the regular (intellectuals, scientists) and the secular[12] (e.g. top leaders of business and industry), the latter being still further removed from personal economic worries (their large economic capital enables them to 'take things as they come') but no less caught up in economic and social issues, in the most pressing secular action that leaves them hardly any leisure (or desire) to cultivate a reflexive relationship to language, an aesthetic disposition or a theoretical relationship to situations. Actors living in the greatest material comfort, but men of action involved in the business of the economic world.

From the standpoint of the educational experience that is compulsory for all, a certain suspension of the economic conditions of existence is shared by all children of a generation. Whether their origin is working class, petit bourgeois or bourgeois, all children and adolescents are protected for a lengthy period from the need to work and face up to the hazards of existence. On the other hand, they are very unequally prepared culturally by their socialization in the family to establish a reflexive relationship to language. When they manage this, however, despite the initial cultural obstacles, their social origin and the economic modesty of their conditions of life do not prevent them from developing their educational and scholarly skills (see Hoggart, 1988).[13] For adults, moreover, the reduction in weekly and annual working time for all employees makes it ever less plausible to assume a direct effect of time (devoted to earning a living, or removed from economic constraints) on cultural behaviour and attitudes. The 'free time, freed from the urgencies of the world, that allows a free and liberated relation to those urgencies and to the world' (Bourdieu, 2000, p. 1) is not enough to account for the emergence of educational perspectives. Time can also be devoted to leisure activities or occupations that are far removed from aesthetic, speculative or scholarly questions.

The basic problem, in an interpretative scheme of this kind, is that the school is viewed as an unreal place, socially – or more exactly economically – outside the game: 'The scholastic situation (of which the academic world represents the institutionalized form) is a site and a moment of social weightlessness' (Bourdieu, 2000, pp. 13–14). To say that the apprenticeship of schooling is in this way 'freed from the direct sanction of reality' (ibid., p. 17), or that it is distinguished from 'real situations', is to assume that on one side there is the 'real' and on the other something that is not real (ibid.), and we then have to ask what it is.[14] In this explanatory model, of course, it is the economy that fixes and defines the nature and quality of the 'real': 'Learning situations, and especially scholastic exercises in the sense of ludic, gratuitous work, performed in the "let's pretend" mode, without any real (economic) stake . . .' (ibid., p. 14). What is real, with social weight and immediate necessity, is economic, and outside of this we fall into weightlessness, inconsequence, make-believe, play, etc. But how then should we conceive a particular scholarly exercise, for example that presented by Austin as an example of what he calls the 'scholastic view' – i.e. 'the fact of enumerating or examining all the possible senses of a word, without any reference to the immediate context, instead of simply observing or using the sense of the word which is directly compatible with the situation' (ibid., p. 12), in relation to the immediate needs of economics? The economistic reduction of social reality makes it quite impossible to understand the transition from the non-reflexive and pragmatic relationship to language (as described by phenomenologists and pragmaticians) to the reflexive relationship to language.[15] To appeal to liberation from economic pressure in order to understand scholarly exercises of this kind ('the neutralization of practical urgencies and ends, and more precisely, the fact of being detached for a more or less long time from work and the world of work, from serious activity, sanctioned by monetary compensation . . .'; Bourdieu, 2000, p. 14) is like trying to collect water in a sieve. It is not denying the importance of economics to maintain that this has no direct effect on the type of relationship that one establishes with language, and that it is preferable to grasp the sociogenesis of knowledge and of the exercise techniques that produce a reflexive relationship to language rather than believe that one has analysed the essence of such scholastic exercises by describing them all as 'playful' and 'inconsequential', sparing oneself an observation of educational practices and the elaboration of a theory of these.

Finally, using the same expressions ('distanced, inconsequential, detached' or 'scholastic vision') to denote an exercise carried out at primary school, a question in an opinion poll, or the most avant-garde concepts in the literary or pictorial field ends up making these 'amorphic' expressions in Weber's sense. The theoretical satisfaction that one may experience in attacking such different furrows with the same plough is inversely proportional to the heuristic power of the concepts. We have therefore to return to the empirical analysis of singular practices and authorize only cautious and limited generalizations.

— Scene 2 —

THE EVERYDAY PRACTICES OF WRITING IN ACTION

Depend upon it there is nothing so unnatural as the commonplace.
(Arthur Conan Doyle, 'A case of identity')

What matters is not the subject but the eye. If there is an eye, a subject will be found; if there is no eye, if you are blind, you won't find anything in the subject.
(Fyodor Dostoyevsky, *A Writer's Diary*)

No one studies such everyday and seemingly insignificant objects as shopping lists, reminder notes, travel itineraries, jottings made in diaries, on calendars or on mere pieces of paper without some theoretical perspective in mind. We might wonder, indeed, what scientific legitimacy should be granted to such trivial objects of study. More than one sociologist – with their (good) sociological practical sense – will immediately detect a sociologically suspect object, without any social bearing, too tiny and too removed from the 'basic' theoretical debates of their discipline. Academic dignity prefers that the only objects studied should be those socially (symbolically) worthy of interest. Practices of writing thus appear to academic understanding as a 'bizarre' or 'insignificant' object, of no importance in relation to the 'big problems' or 'major themes' already established – a typical object for the ethnologist, in other words. This is the way of the *vita academica* and the flair of good researchers who seek out and find 'good objects', those resembling the 'really good objects' of the sociologist, which, because they correspond to these all too perfectly, reinforce interpretative laziness and rarely take sociological knowledge forward.

And yet one might still be inclined to think that the big theoretical problems could and should be posed on the basis of the study of objects that are apparently minor, and that the latter imply neither a quest for exoticism at home nor a systematic focus on the marginal. One may prefer, like Bourdieu, to 'expect a solution to such and such a canonic problem from case studies' (1996b, p. 178), rather than remaining enclosed for all time in the four walls of texts that already have been commented on to death. The theoretical insight that I have always kept in mind during my research on writing (whether in school, at work or in the home) is the question of practical sense. Little by little, from interview to interview, observation to observation, case study to case study,[1] it became clear to me that the everyday practices of writing basically constitute fantastic exceptions and tremendous counter-examples to what the theory of practice and practical sense describes. These practices represent real acts of rupture with practical sense, practical logic, and may be understood on the basis of the negative relationship that they have with the embodied practical memory of the habitus. They make possible the symbolic mastery of certain activities, as well as their rationalization.

Without this fundamental question of practical sense, at the heart of the theory of action, the researcher perceives only the most striking features of these practices and can only arrive at formal typologies that are rather weak, never seeing what they have in common. Among the many kinds of domestic writing, one can distinguish for example those that are (quasi-)compulsory (e.g. filling in administrative forms or writing various administrative documents) from those that relate to social habits. Among the latter, one can again separate 'family' practices (e.g. shopping lists, notes on a household calendar, mail orders, classification of administrative papers, writing or copying of kitchen recipes, labelling of food products . . .), and these in turn from more 'personal' practices (writing in a diary, crosswords), aesthetic practices (writing stories, poems or songs, keeping a personal journal), 'functional' or 'utilitarian' practices (e.g. calculations of family accounts, keeping a 'log book' for the car . . .), regular practices (e.g. family correspondence, little notes from one family member to another, written memos, lists of things to do . . .), occasional practices (e.g. list of things to take on holiday, travel itinerary, notes in a photo album . . .).

But it is more by asking what the indissociably social and mental dispositions (relationship to time, to space, to language, to self and others) are that these make possible, and to a large extent that they establish, that it is possible to grasp the social logic of these motley practices.

Embodied memory, objectified memory

We must start by taking very seriously the endogenous interpretation that consists in people saying that they do not write in their domestic life, that these little means of objectification are not used, because mnemonic abilities are sufficient. In effect, those who are not accustomed to written memos, lists of errands or things to do, notes made in the course of a telephone call or before making a call, jottings in a diary or calendar, etc., frequently appeal to their 'good memory'. Some subjects also speak, for example, of the diary as a 'central memory' (the expression used by a woman with high educational capital) or admit the fallibility of a too uncertain memory. In one way or another, whether people are adept at them or totally reject them, these everyday writings seemed to be, in their very commonplace character, at the heart of the question of memory: objective memory is differentiated here from embodied memory.

'Full-time' housewives, constantly full of all the concerns of the family circle, sometimes have no need to write things down, their embodied memory being permanently mobilized and activated. One woman whose husband was a skilled worker said: 'I've got a good memory. I remember everything I've done. It's me who reminds him [her husband]: "You've got to do this and that," I'm the memory. Yes, I keep everything in my head.' In the same fashion, when you have to keep track of the stock of household provisions on a daily basis, embodied memory is constantly activated and the written shopping list becomes less necessary ('[As I pass along the shelves] that reminds me what I've got and what I haven't.').

Men who very largely 'desert' the territory of domestic writing (Lahire, 1993d, 1995b, 1997b) 'justify' this particularly by appeal to a kind of masculine pride or honour bound up with embodied memory. This kind of memory, oral and alive, seems to be a specifically masculine resource and pride. Women thus note the exceptional memory of their husbands – 'like an elephant's' – who never write anything down, as opposed to themselves who 'haven't the head for it'. It is hard to judge the pertinence of this everyday discourse on 'good masculine memory' and women's difficulty in 'keeping things in'. Not only do women have to think of (family) things from which men are completely disengaged and do not need to keep in mind, but women who maintain that their husbands don't write things down because they 'remember them' may very well write them down instead, so that their menfolk don't forget certain things – thus unconsciously contributing to create the myth of the husband with a 'good memory' (they make lists for their husbands when they do the shopping, or write lists or memos of things for them to do). Sometimes it is even the husbands (or sons) who ask their wives (or mothers) to remind them of certain things or note them down. At all events, resort to writing seems in the eyes of men a proof of 'weakness'. Writing things down to remember them already means taking the risk of not using one's memory. This is particularly noticeable when the husband criticizes his wife for their children getting into the habit of writing things down to remember them instead of stimulating them to use their memory.

I already established from a study of the work-related writing and reading of semi-skilled manual workers (Lahire, 1993b, pp. 57–73) that, tied to their machine and their colleagues at work, caught up in a mimetic mode of embodiment of work, workers were led to read and write only on rare occasions. In fact, if we take the case of assembly plans and certain technical instruction sheets (indicating the number of different pieces that an apparatus contains), then, against what one might rather naively have started by thinking, use of the plan or instruction sheet is not in the eyes of workers a sign of greater skill or competence. Quite the contrary, it is seen as characteristic of a novice, still 'green'. To the extent that the experienced worker immediately recognizes the kind of apparatus to be assembled on the basis of the components supplied, he has no need to consult the plan or read the name of the apparatus. The more skilled you are, the less your need to read a plan or instruction sheet. Writing in this case is clearly associated with beginners, who, deficient in practical bearings, may need written indications reminding or explaining to them what they risk forgetting or what they have not yet completely embodied.

As well as this, a number of statements indicate a sharp criticism of the use of plans: looking at the plan, one worker says, is not working, and not making the effort to remember. Writing is thus considered as apt to destroy or weaken the (valued) capacities of memorizing. In this perspective, the plan and writing are only substitutes, external supports, crutches for the deficient memory of novices who do not have the job inside them, don't have the plan 'inscribed' in their memory – in fact for those who have not embodied the habits of assembly. Through the question of practices of writing, we touched here on the problem of practical sense, since writing seems to intervene when embodied practical sense does not or does no longer suffice.

Writing is thus perceived by a section of my respondents – more commonly those from working-class milieus than those with greater educational endowment, and more often men than women – as a supplementary means of 'reminding yourself'. Once writing is perceived only in its mnemo-technical function, it is viewed as a kind of palliative for a deficient memory. Practices of writing can thus be negatively perceived by those who proudly reply that they 'don't need it at the moment', as if it were a question of a pair of glasses to compensate for a deterioration in vision or a stick to help with walking. Using writing thus marks the existence of a handicap, a difficulty. Quite unintentionally, these studies link up with the critique that Plato gives in *Phaedrus*. Opposing *mnêmê* as living memory to *hypomnesis* as remembrance and consigning to memory, Plato tells us, in the person of Socrates, that writing has not resolved the problem of living memory but, on the contrary, contributes increasingly to destroying this by releasing men from the obligation of making the effort of reminding themselves (certain respondents even say that they 'force' or 'compel' themselves not to write, so as to 'make their memory work').

And yet the idea that writing is for novices is not unique to the world of manual work, but is also met with in a professional milieu as far removed from material production as that of the schoolteacher. In fact, we note a steady reduction – without total disappearance – in the professional written activity of teachers in primary school as their career continues (Delon, 1997). There is less resort over time to a daily notebook and preparation sheets. The reasons for this steady decline are relatively simple.

First of all, writings of this kind are a means of entry into the trade of schoolteacher, of acquiring its identity. A kind of rite of passage, they enable novices to feel a difference in relation to what they were previously, by meticulously and intensely engaging in one of the gestures of embodiment in this new professional world. Application and rigour here are in part a sign of working on identity. But writing what one is going to do in the week or the day is also and above all a way of objectifying in the form of a 'use of time', and keeping in mind what has not yet been completely embodied. This makes it possible to reassure oneself, to 'know where you're going', to 'have a framework', to guide one's action, to 'plan' it for the sake of being 'effective' and not to 'lose your footing'. If teachers say, at a few years' remove, that at the beginning 'I did too much' to be 'secure' or 'serene' in class, they also recognize that this overproduction of writing was an 'indispensable path': 'Beware of improvising, I don't risk this any more.'

When the rhythms, progressions and sense of inscription – in the shorter time of interaction with the pupils and the longer time of organizing the day or week, longer still of programming the year – have been embodied, then internal memory is gradually substituted for objectified-external memory. Teachers, almost like manual workers, call this 'learning the trade', gaining 'experience', 'habit' or 'facility'. Having avoided the risks of adventurous (and dangerous) improvisation, teachers can then leave more place for improvisation based on experience. The early period of abundance of 'written records' is followed by that of steady 'pruning' and a 'reduction to essentials'.

The gradual reduction of this writing, however, is not a linear process, in as much as each change of level challenges the routines formerly acquired, forcing one to 'start practically from scratch'. It forces re-establishing a new capital of pedagogic sequences, exercises and mini-progressions, and consequently reinvesting the time of written preparation. If, as distinct from the case of the manual worker, this writing never completely disappears, it is simply because it is partly destined for others: writing for possible stand-ins, or for the attention of the school inspector. Thus it is also kept up so as to facilitate a change of personnel and to remain within the rules.

Everyday breaks with practical sense

It was analysing an extract from an interview which led me to pose this problem more clearly. A building worker, who left school at the age of fourteen, replied as follows to a question on the use of diaries and calendars:

> I tell you frankly, it's instinct, it's memory. You know that next week you've got something to do; okay then, you don't write it down, you only note . . . Yes, dates that are a bit further ahead, if you like: a dentist gives you an appointment, or an eye test or something like that, they give you an appointment for a couple of months' time. You won't still remember in two months, okay, it's marked down, you know that on that day . . .

It was certainly this worker's appeal to 'instinct', recalling the vocabulary often used to describe practical sense, that put me on the right track. The respondent noted in a diary, or wrote a memo, when it was a matter of appointments some time away that he might forget. But for regular activities, repetitive or close at hand, it was left up to 'memory' or 'instinct'. There is here a kind of implicit theory of everyday practices of writing that intervene when practical sense might fail or not be enough. A large portion of anticipatory, pre-reflexive practical acts are performed without any need to write them down. Someone who wrote down things that were too 'obvious' would immediately be perceived as 'ill' or 'old', or as having lost their memory or their 'head'. Everyday practices are very often carried out before any reflection, in a practical reactivation of non-reflexive habits that have been embodied in the form of subconscious necessity and self-evidence. Who would write down, for example: 'I have to get washed, then take the dog out, then eat, then go and pick up the children from school'? From this absurdity (even if the absurd is still a possible case, as we shall see), we can realize that the obviousness of the world and the majority of practical acts in everyday life assume a kind of non-conscious adjustment of a socialized body to social situations.

A further 'absurd' example that can set us on the path of practical sense is that of the child who systematically writes down lists of things to do or little memos. A mother of three (teacher of German in a grande école) has developed an implicit mini-theory of everyday practices of writing and children's relationship to the world when she explains that her children do not make memos or lists of things to do because they have fewer things to keep in mind and need less preparation in their activities – prepared for them by adults – and they are also more spontaneous than adults: 'They have so many projects going on, things to do, telephone this person . . . When my daughter telephones, it's "I'm going to phone up so and so", and she doesn't wait three days before she decides; it's on the spot.' The projects of adults are opposed to the 'immediate' action of children – planning to simple common sense.

Practices of writing and drawing introduce a distance between the speaking subject (or the acting actor) and their language and give them the means for symbolic mastery of what they had previously mastered practically: language, space and time. The means of objectification of time (diary, calendar, planner . . .), lists of things to say or do (like action plans or future speech), itineraries or routes marked out,[2] personal diaries and the various aesthetic forms of writing (poems, stories, essays, etc.) are all instruments for shaping our temporality, our spatiality and our language, which establish daily exceptions to the pre-reflexive adjustment of practical sense to a social situation. We can note the same distance between the experience of time that simply 'passes' (polyrhythmic) and the homogeneous and linear time organized with the help of means of objectification as between the spontaneous journey of a car driver and the travel itinerary that plans a route, prepares it, divides it into stages, or again as between spontaneous speech in the context of interaction and its elaborated and controlled writing down. Practices of writing thus constitute real acts of rupture in relation to practical sense; they are acts that break with the practical logic of performance of practices in the obviousness of things to be done, with the logic of practical sense as applied in the practical urgency of action (Lahire, 1993c).

We have seen how there exist many different cases of maladjustment or non-coincidence between the stock of embodied schemes and social situations that generate situations of greater or lesser crisis, more or less long-lasting.[3] These moments of maladjustment and crisis (adolescence with its burden of conflicts and sense of misunderstanding, divorce, the transition to retirement, a serious illness affecting a spouse that disorganizes the life regularly lived and breaks the customary ties of sociability, a deep feeling of loneliness or a lack of communication with loved ones who have died or moved away, the break-up of a love affair; Allam, 1996) sometimes give rise, when favourable conditions come together,[4] to an intensive production of personal writing that compensates for an uncertainty or emptiness of identity. On the other hand, the break with practical sense provoked by reflexive, planning, calculating, etc., adjustment is in no way a situation of crisis, but rather connected with ordinary moments of social life. The application of reflexive and planning habits is never something that follows a crisis. It even presupposes practical involvement in activity. These maladjustments and discrepancies sometimes even produce a search for identity on the part of the actors involved (who am I then?), whereas the ruptures that I discuss here do not raise the question of the 'wherefore' or 'ends' of action (why am I doing this or that?), but often remain in the domain of 'how' (how to do this or that?) and 'means'.

It is by gradually reconstituting the different possible cases of recourse to writing in the domestic space that I was able to cast light on the break effected in relation to the logic of practical sense.[5] Rather than enclose oneself in the illusion of the particular case, it is preferable to consider that 'progress is apt to be commensurate with our ability to draw a wide range of pertinent cases into view' (Hughes, 1971, p. 316). The question is thus to practise a systematic variation of cases in order to reach the limiting ones, and even sometimes absurd ones. To understand the reasons why a case is absurd is also a good way of penetrating the logic of normal cases. Besides, each time that a subject says 'I write only when . . .', the sociologist is put on the track of a singular property of the social uses of everyday writing. The sine qua non that is indicated here specifies the use of this writing and defines the limits of its use. 'I never write, except when ...' or 'I always write, except when ...' are apparently banal comments, but they give valuable assistance to the researcher. If the respondents do not talk, the sociologists have themselves to construct these 'conditions' or 'contexts of use' by a comparison and variation of cases.

'Doing it like that'

'Doing it like that' is an expression in everyday language that can be the object of sociological commentary in as much as it seems to denote non-reflexive habits that relate to practical sense – i.e. the pre-reflexively adjusted action of a socialized body (habitus) to a social situation. In the discourse of the respondents, the 'like that' refers first and foremost to a situation in which no cognitive artefact[6] or technical sophistication is used, and in particular no means of writing. The idea that written and objectified memory, means of storing information outside the body, etc., are cognitive artefacts that provide resources in and for action is interesting in so far as several respondents believe that only oral memory is authentic and natural. The written, for its part, is a manner of 'cheating' in relation to the deficiencies or limitations of oral memory. From this point of view, the notion of cognitive artefact at least remains faithful to a portion of the social representations (the written placed on the side of the artificial).

Unskilled workers often describe their entry into a job by saying that they learn it 'like that', 'from the others', 'working it out', 'on the spot', 'seeing others do it', 'imitating' those already there, who in turn had gradually inserted themselves in and through the practice of work (Lahire, 1993e). The respondents often speak in the same way of other learning processes that they had outside of any formal teaching situation.

Here, the respondents often indicate situations in which they recall things or act without recourse to writing, the support of objectified memory, as situations in which they remember and act 'like that': keeping in mind an itinerary 'like that' ('he looked at the map and remembered it like that'), packing a suitcase 'like that' (without a list of things to put in), remembering phone numbers (without an address book), learning lessons without copying them ('I prefer learning it like that, in the head'), doing accounts 'like that' (without a notebook, paper or pencil), doing things 'like that' (without noting in a diary or on a list of things to do), doing shopping 'like that' (without a shopping list), cooking 'like that' (without using a written recipe), and so on.

In the same way, the 'like that' mode may indicate a situation in which the degree of formality of writing is slight. For instance, to say that one writes letters 'like that' means 'without making a draft', or else one makes personal notes, but 'like that' – i.e. without specially using a diary for that purpose ('It wasn't any kind of diary, just jottings like that on a loose piece of paper. It wasn't a diary I used . . .'; a woman bookkeeper). Finally, the expression may define situations in which the order was not chosen with particular care – i.e. where the actor did not particularly have in mind a particular order when they performed their action: making a shopping list 'like that', 'as it comes', 'not in a particular order' ('I write things down like that, okay, not organized'), put away administrative papers 'like that' (not with a particular order of filing in mind), 'sort' or 'put away' post 'like that' (putting it together without classifying it), keep one's recipes 'like that' ('I put them more or less like that, okay. As it comes'), etc.

Memory for the unusual

It is notable that these respondents – whatever their social milieu – make more use of a diary when they have to buy a bottle of gas or dishwasher tablets, as this happens less often, than for their appointment at the hairdresser's, which is a regular ritual for Wednesday afternoon, or the birthday of a loved one, which is unforgettable. Sometimes the only things written on a shopping list are those which are not generally bought ('I do that [write down] so as not to forget things that I don't get all the time, for example the cereal that my daughter likes or things like that, I write them down, but otherwise I know what I have to get. I don't always write it down'; primary school assistant, former bookkeeper), things that are 'special' – for a special meal, for example – 'which aren't systematic' or which 'you don't necessarily think of', as one subject (a doctor) said. You note in the diary 'things out of the usual', but no one would think of writing on a memo pad, a diary or a calendar 'Thursday 2 July: eat lunch'. The opposite of 'dates' so embodied that they are not even thought of as such (e.g. the birthday of a loved one[7] or, better still, the everyday acts of eating lunch or taking a shower) are dates that demand to be noted on a memo, a list of things to do, a calendar or a personal diary (e.g. a hospital appointment); as against regular everyday purchases that require no more than the application of (good) practical sense (flour, oil, sugar, butter, milk, etc.), there are more occasional purchases for a special meal that require a precise shopping list; and as against the usual things that one thinks quite naturally of taking on a journey (e.g. clothes), there are things less frequently used but still necessary (e.g. medicines).

What is written down, therefore, what requires inscription, is the unusual, the extraordinary, the exceptional (as against the usual, ordinary, everyday). In fact, the unusual or exceptional character does not have to be so great that the 'event', 'information' or 'action' would be singled out and memorized more readily in future. Between the ordinary and the routine, which are performed without even a thought, and the exceptional and the singular are many little events that are neither regular and embodied nor sufficiently exceptional and singular, and these are sometimes more particularly the object of inscription.

The ordinary writing of the extraordinary, moreover, is the only example of writing to be found in Xenophon's *Economist*:

> Whatever we use for festivals or entertaining guests or at rare intervals we handed over to the housekeeper; and when we had shown her where they belong, and had counted and made an inventory of each thing, we told her to give every member of the household what he or she required, but to remember what she had given to each of them and when she got it back, to return it to the place from which she takes things of that kind. (Xenophon, 1994, p. 157)

The relationship between shopping list and embodied memory is particularly clear in the case where women reply that they do not make out shopping lists for themselves, but only for their husband or children – i.e. for those without a sufficient practical knowledge of the world of domestic products and the state of supplies to enable them to make purchases 'like that', without a list. Here writing evidently compensates for a deficient embodied programme. Lists can sometimes even be very complex – e.g. when mothers seek to transmit their know-how in such matters. Thus when one mother (salesperson in the family cake-shop) asks her daughter (aged ten) to do the shopping, she draws up lists so that nothing gets forgotten, and even draws a plan of the market so that she can get her bearings: 'I made her a plan of the market and said to her: "This is where to get such and such."' Concerned for the quality of the products, she sends her daughter to shops that she knows and objectifies on the list the choices that she herself makes implicitly (e.g. this product is to be bought from that stall, or, if they don't have it, look for it at this other place, and, finally, if it's not available there, don't buy it anywhere else).

In the same way, travel itineraries are not drawn up when the routes to be followed are embodied, ordinary and routine. These customary routes call only for the mobilization of embodied habits. Reasoning *ad absurdum*, no one would imagine that you would write out an itinerary every morning before leaving for work, to show the different streets, avenues and squares to be crossed to reach there. And it is ultimately for analogous reasons that certain subjects find it quite useless, or even absurd, to write on the back of family photographs or in albums the names of the individuals pictured; they are immediately recognizable in the family circle.

The longer term and preparing the future

Similarly, writing intervenes when it is a question of dealing with relatively longer timeframes and when there is a task of preparing the future, situations that contrast with the immediacy of everyday practices and the immediate relationship to the world. The diary, the calendar and the planner, for example, make possible a division of activities (individual or collective) in objectified time and, at the same time, a planning of (or look back at) what has been done, implying a more reflexive relationship to time (past, present or future). All evidence suggests that domestic use of the diary or calendar is bound up with the extension of timeframes and the increasing complexity of activities to be managed in societies where the bureaucratization and rational organization of activities requires increasing management of meetings, appointment, events, etc., planned in a longer timeframe. This is why it is more distant appointments or events that are written down ('I have a diary, but it's mainly for things that are a long way off', says a home help, with a qualification in bookkeeping) in different ways, from the most basic (memos written on the back of envelopes) to the more elaborate (diary, calendar, or electronic organizer).

Practices of writing for household management thus make it possible to calculate, plan, programme and foresee activity, and to organize it over a longer or less long period. They prepare or delay direct action and to a certain extent suspend practical urgency. Preparing the future may concern the family or personal budget. Subjects sometimes speak of a 'system' in connection with their methods of managing the family budget, the importance of 'knowing where you are', 'knowing what you've spent', and contrast themselves with those who deny the possibility of foreseeing, calculating, planning and methodically managing their life ('living from day to day', 'not being methodical', 'being chaotic', 'taking things as they come', 'taking advantage of life' . . .).[8] The questions that certain subjects ask themselves in doing their accounts, in 'putting aside', in forecasting their expenses – How much should I put aside if I want to buy new furniture this year? If I do buy it, how much will I have left to go away on holiday? If I take a subscription to this magazine, will I still be able to go to the cinema so often? – are well inscribed in the register of the *project*, 'which posits the future as future, i.e. as possible (as being able to happen or not to happen), the possible that is posited as such' (Bourdieu, 1989, p. 19).

As techniques of self-control, practices of writing imply a greater control of one's desires and impulses. The account book or the calculation of the family budget, for example, specifically concern the means of delaying until later purchases that the logic of immediate satisfaction of needs tends to want realized this instant. In this way, a whole capacity to defer (desires, impulses) and plan is constructed, something that is never acquired in advance:

> How dreadful! [she laughs] Oh I make a budget, but no matter how many times I do it, I never manage to keep to it. Yes, at the beginning of the month I set to, I tell myself: 'This month I'll stick to it, I'll note down all my expenses', and then by the fifth or sixth of the month it's finished, the pages are blank. But I don't give up, I do the same every month. Last month I think I stuck to it until the sixth. (Housewife, married to a shopkeeper)

In the same way, memos and planners that make it possible to remind oneself of things that have to be done, and to organize oneself to do them, function as a recall to order addressed to oneself. They amount to genuine techniques of self-constraint, self-discipline: 'And then to make myself see, because it's good, sometimes it's things that I didn't want to do like that, it was to show myself that I had to, and that if I didn't do it no one else would, to force myself a bit.' When the list is addressed to someone else (a servant, for example), its coercive character is readily apparent. Addressed to oneself, the work programme acts as an order to oneself (some people speak of 'policing' themselves). It is understandable, then, what the object is of those people, especially in working-class milieus, who say that they don't want to 'be the slave' of a list of things to do or a planner: they perceive very well the potential power relationship inscribed in these instruction lists and restraining planners.

Managing complex practices

Writing thus sometimes becomes necessary – in the eyes of some people – when one has to deal with the complexity (multiplicity and arrangement of this multiplicity) of practices 'demanding' to be organized, or that can be organized more easily by resort to writing (lists of various kinds, diary, calendar, account book). Certain practices of writing seem bound up with the increasing complexity of family activities; you have to be able to manage and coordinate timetables for work and other activities of both adults and children, as well as the inevitable imponderables of existence: 'There are so many things to think of that I write them down'; 'Sometimes, yes, when I really do have too many things to do, I make lists. On Sunday I do my planning for the week. But the list, I don't mean "buy bread, butter", all that, not at all. I put down "do shopping, go to the bank, visit the doctor, the dentist", that's what I write down, not details, but I do make a plan' (woman, company doctor). When activities multiply ('too many things to do'), when the time for them is 'counted' and yet you have to do everything as best you can, then planning in diaries, calendars or lists of things to do can gradually impose itself as a practice that is necessary to avoid losing 'precious time':

> And then I know that there are so many things to take care of, you always forget – there's something still at the cleaner's after three weeks that I have to pick up, forms to fill in, or go to the bank and I don't know what. Because I'm forced to be organized, otherwise I wouldn't manage. The day before yesterday I had to go out at seven in the evening to buy nappies for my little girl, because they'd run out. That messes up my whole time budget. (Woman, advertising agency sales executive)

Written planners that avoid vagueness and confusion often become ways of acquiring a mastery of sometimes complex situations that is indissociably both psychological (or symbolic) and practical.

It is often when appointments, meetings, movements, etc., proliferate at conflicting times that the diary, for example, is used. This little objectified memory enables some people to free their living memory and manage the complexity of timetables and family activities (the family diary), but especially those of work. And it is clear that the diary is all the more necessary when work and/or lifestyles have a welter of activities, meetings and appointments. Informal sociability, improvised among friends or in the family, in a life whose work rhythms are governed by the routine of a timetable fixed by the employer does not demand the use of this instrument to the same extent.

In the same way, lists (of things to do or say, things to take on a journey, shopping lists ...) are often means of firming up future actions, programmes, plans. Shopping lists, for example, sometimes establish very precise programmes of movement in the big supermarkets (shelf by shelf) and in this way amount to 'plans in which the externalization of the organizing mechanism makes it more determinative, more enduring, more inclusive and more formal' (Goody, 1977, p. 136). 'For example, I classify all the dairy products, all the toiletries, and it's the same in my shopping cart, to save time. So when I'm at the toiletries section, I have my whole list drawn up for the toiletries, the dairy section, if I need milk, butter, yoghurt, I don't mix milk with sponges and then coffee' (woman teacher specializing in deaf mutes). 'I start off with all the cleaning products on one side, I do the rounds of the flat with my list and I take a look at my stocks: bathroom, toilet paper, then I look under the sink. It's a good list, all in order, yes because I know that I get to each section' (housewife, married to a shopkeeper). In this way they make it possible 'to save time', 'not to forget anything' ('Otherwise you run through all the sections'; home help, married to a factory worker).

Not every consumer, female or male, proceeds in this way, but it would be a misinterpretation of a good part of social reality if we viewed them all just as buyers who automatically and naturally browse the different products that catch their eyes in a simple pre-reflexive adjustment to the situation.[9]

The official, the formal and tense situations

Writing is also particularly bound up with official events, appointments and dates, which people are afraid to forget (since this can have serious consequences), or with formal and tense situations that have to be dealt with. In cases of this kind, writing exercises an undeniable function of reassurance in a state of relative tension.

The most official appointments are therefore noted in writing; many people prefer to write a letter to an administrative department, to explain correctly and calmly a delicate or complex situation, rather than make a phone call (where you can 'lose the thread'). If you do telephone, this is after preparing approximately or precisely what you mean to say to the other party, so as not to forget anything and to be precise in your requests. When the phone call is tense, you may resort to writing in order to avoid any shortfall of memory that would lead to having to phone again in order to complete the information.

A housewife, with a vocational qualification, explained about the notes she made before a phone call: 'Yes, that's happened to me. But really, for very important things, for phone calls where you have to hang on for an hour, for example the social security or things like that. But that's quite unusual, I write down everything I have to say so as not to forget, not to tell myself: "Oh, now I've hung up and forgotten to ask the most important thing".' It's when the conversation is tense because of being official that written notes are used to manage discourse. The linguistic habitus, linguistic practical sense, is no longer enough in the face of the tension of the speech situation. Besides, the respondents themselves contrast the spontaneity of informal phone calls between friends or family members with the tensions of discussions with administrative departments, which may require preparation: 'With the administration always, but not with friends, no,' explains a housewife with a skilled qualification; another, with a vocational diploma, says: 'No, not me. Oh yes, sometimes I get everything mixed up, sometimes I'm speaking to my daughter's godmother and we mix up everything, both of us in our own way. You're talking about one thing and then you're talking about something else. And then at the end you remember what you have to say.'

Writing thus makes it possible to manage one's discourse in a more precise and orderly fashion in a composed letter or the everyday act of taking notes before a phone call, when what one wants to say does not suffer improvisation and demands both a precise argument and a certain completeness. Writings of this kind imply a particular relationship to language: concern for form, for verbal and discursive precision, for the order of presentation and for exhaustiveness.[10] Subjects who detest such practices speak the language of 'practical sense': preference for 'improvisation', 'spontaneity', natural speech (as opposed to prepared and artificial speech). Men from working-class milieus are the first to assert their preference for direct contact or confrontation with administrative departments, open and face-to-face, viva voce and thus 'virile', as opposed to prepared oral discourse or the relation at a distance that the writing of letters involves ('I let them know all my states of mind directly') (Lahire, 1997b).[11]

In the same fashion, making notes before a phone call is commonest in the most official and/or tense situations; the use of 'drafts' in composing letters, or re-reading them to look for spelling mistakes, is observed in the most formal situations of writing. Exchange of informal letters between friends or family members is thus often distinguished from letters addressed to administrative departments or unknown individuals. This logic of open versus tense exchange

– 'among ourselves', where norms of legitimacy are not applicable, against spaces of exchange, where these norms assert their presence – imposes itself whatever the social milieu. Tense situations impose formality, preparation, attention, care, concern. Everything happens as if the cultural fault was all the more serious for being public – i.e. under a gaze external to the 'among ourselves'. Thus when mothers spur their children to pay attention to spelling when they write letters, the children particularly resist when it's a question of letters between friends, making the argument of open exchange between children where everyone makes so many mistakes. The difference between social milieus here is that both adults and children from the higher social classes are more often in contact with formal situations, including family ones. Certain children from these milieus internalize early on the use of drafts when writing to a supercilious aunt, grandmother or great-aunt. The 'spontaneous' decision to make a draft seems to constitute an anticipatory practice in relation to the demanding prospective reader. If you know that your linguistic production is under the correcting gaze of another person, then you end up internalizing a corrective gaze on your own production.

In the end, these minuscule practices of writing (notes made before a phone call, successive drafts of a letter), which break with the spontaneity of language produced in a face-to-face situation, are genuine rhetorical techniques. Breaking the logic of direct expression, they liberate those who employ them from the limitation of any spontaneous and direct performance, which can never authorize a backward move. Writing, and written preparation, makes it possible to distance oneself from the immediate situation of utterance and to improve linguistic performance by successive correction, until poor expressions, mistakes in presentation, clumsiness, semantic muddle, etc., are eliminated. Reading, re-reading, replacing one word by another, correcting syntax, shifting arguments or facts around to be more persuasive or pertinent, checking that one has not forgotten anything of what one wanted to say, and so on. Writing makes it possible to select, as with a film, the best takes, with the additional advantage of being able to improve the quality from one take to the next. As a cumulative work in the same space, written discourse is thus distinguished from a high-wire performance without a net, which demands flexibility, adaptation, a sense of the occasion (the *kairos*) and presence of mind. As Charles Bally quite correctly wrote: 'As soon as you take up the pen, you have time on your side; you can reflect, choose, combine, as you see fit' (Bally, 1926, p. 128).

Sometimes the use of notes before making a phone call, or in the course of the call itself, is a matter not just of mastering one's own arguments, but also of a rhetorical technique of resistance to administrative discourse:

> I do it, it depends who I'm phoning. If it's something very important I do it. Because generally people always try to twist your words around, at least that's what I always think. In any case that's how it is for me. And I write things down so as not to get confused. Because they confuse you very quickly. I mean for some things, especially to do with the administration, it's horrific. So I write it down. And if they change the subject, I go back and I've got my note and that's what I do. So that you don't say after you hang up: 'Oh god, I meant to say that and I didn't say it.' (Woman maintenance agent)

Knowing exactly what you want to say, not losing the thread of your request, resisting the tortuous administrative rhetoric, being able to go back and not let yourself be swept away unresisting in the flood of the Other's speech, the administrative speech – that is what writing can also help with. It then becomes a technique of resistance or self-defence. During the whole phone conversation, she 'follows the paper' with her eyes, and doesn't let herself be taken where she doesn't want to go. In the same way, another respondent (woman shopkeeper) said that she writes down during the discussion the information she is given, and if she doesn't understand completely what she's told, these written traces allow her to ask for an explanation immediately after. Writing makes it possible to look back on what was said previously, and helps in not losing the thread of conversation. It makes it possible to check it, to go back to a 'point' that a written trace has isolated with a view to just such a possible return: 'If there are points that don't seem very clear to me, I note them and I let the person speak, and then I ask for clarification, but the important thing is that I write it down.'

The presence of the absent

As against what we are led to believe by those interactionist theories that study only social encounters or meetings that require the joint and immediate presence of individuals who 'are mutually within sight and sound of each other', in relatively restricted physical limits (Goffman), the co-presence of bodies is not always required in social life: phone conversations or written messages on computer networks, answerphones, faxes and, more traditionally, written correspondence. Of course you must have a body in order to act, but the action does not always necessitate the immediate presence of this body in situ.[12]

From this point of view, resort to writing makes it possible to overcome the absence of a 'gift of ubiquity' specific to the human condition: writing continues to mark our presence even when our body is absent. It makes up for the bodily absence in order to continue to perform an action. Here practical sense cannot function, since the body and its embodied habits are not in a situation to act. In the case of a will, for example, the 'desires' of a person continue to act even after they are dead. More generally, institutions – and especially institutions of learning – are like sanctuaries haunted by the absent or dead: texts constrain the action of the living, while those who produced them have long since departed.

Writing makes it possible to act at a distance, or at all events without the immediate presence of the person who wants to act. We can evoke here the *hypomnêmata*, those written instructions mentioned by Plato (*Politics*, 295b-d) which doctors or gymnasiarchs left before setting out on a journey, so that their patients or pupils would remember their prescriptions. We can also think of the written correspondence by which lovers make themselves present to those from whom they are temporarily parted, or the letters by which French emigrants in the nineteenth century were able to continue managing their property, and keep ultimate economic direction of their domain or business.[13] What we should have in mind, though, more broadly, is the written exchange made necessary by the effect of the extension of distance in economic life and social relations.

In the same way, little notes exchanged between members of a family make it possible to mark one's affective presence symbolically ('Have a nice good day. Kisses. Till this evening.'), to remind children or spouse of things to do ('Remember to pick up the things from the cleaner's'; 'Put the chicken in the oven at seven p.m., gas mark 7'). They thus play an undeniable organizational and affective role within the family circle. In fact, when a family is scattered and dispersed by different timetables (school, work, etc.), these little written notes left in a recognized place (on the kitchen table, by the door, near the phone ...) help to maintain family ties despite everything. These words that contribute to maintaining material and symbolic ties between family members are largely bound up with women's work outside the home: to maintain the role that the sexual division of domestic labour confers on them, this is a means that women can use to mark their presence despite their absence, to organize family activities even if they are not – at the moment – physically present. ('Yes, I do that, but only a couple of words. For example, if my husband is out, as I work as a household help, sometimes people phone me about repairs. In principle I stop at four o'clock, but sometimes people say to me: "Can you help me out?" Then I leave a little note: "This evening I'm off at six. Have to take ... to such a place" or "Don't forget to do this or that." Or a phone call: "You have to call back at this time ..."'). As mothers are tacitly or explicitly charged by the family group with maintaining and recomposing forces of fusion (against forces of fission and break-up; Bourdieu, 1994, p. 11), it is they who produce the great majority of these little notes. The exchange is thus very unequal: if mothers give, they don't always get something in return. A housewife (married to a lawyer) speaks of these little notes as a way of 'emphasizing the tie between family members', preserving family ties despite the different activities and rhythms of activity of the various individuals.

When at least one adult is constantly present at home (and when, on top of this, children are not allowed out without permission from their parents), these little notes become useless and hardly find a pertinent context. The physical presence of the adult implies that all information can be transmitted directly and orally. But the use of notes to struggle against physical absence can also be a voluntary use of writing in order intentionally to avoid the co-presence of the sender and the receiver. Thus when a child (ten years old, father an industrial designer, mother an administrative assistant with the SNCF) composes surprise messages that the addressees find only in his absence, he is playing with the possibility offered by writing to mark his presence in the absence of his body. In the same way, when a girl (ten years old, both parents teachers at a grande école) leaves written notes for her father to ask permission to visit friends, this is to avoid a face-to-face with the father who might not give his consent ('In writing it's sometimes easier to say certain things, when you don't have the person in front of you, well she's understood that and that's what she's doing').

Temporary disturbances of practical sense

Borderline cases, but particular interesting ones, are where writing comes to the aid of actors who experience disturbances of practical sense. Practical sense and embodied memory are upset by such things as panic fears (e.g. with the birth of the first child), depression in the wake of serious family worries (e.g. death or illness), or problems of work (e.g. serious interpersonal conflicts) that monopolize the whole of someone's attention, their whole field of consciousness. A mother, for example (doctor, married to a business director), explains: 'The most lists I made I think was when I had one or two bouts of depression after the birth of my kids. I remember then I made lists for the next day, but almost of the kind [she laughs] "Do the vacuuming", "Buy this or that", etc. It wasn't so as not to forget, it was to organize my day, to make the most of it.' In another case, a woman worker explains that, in the grip of family problems and troubles at work, she wrote down in the evening: 'Wash. Go to work', etc. Writing here reinforces the operation of a deficient habitus. What normally functions on the basis of pre-reflexive adaptation of an embodied programme to practical situations may be blocked in certain exceptional situations of disturbance.

In this borderline case, as in all those previously mentioned, writing does indeed stand in a negative relationship to embodied memory. When practical sense (habitus) is no longer enough to 'remind oneself' or act, in view of the unusual nature of things, the extension of timeframe to be mastered and the need to prepare the future, because of the complexity of activities to be managed, the tension due to an official situation, the absence of the body, or temporary mental disturbances and disorganizations, then appeal is made to writing. Objectified memory makes up for the deficiencies of embodied memory. On the one hand, writing is co-substantial with forms of social life that require objectification in writing in order to relieve memory and organize and plan activities. It makes it possible to shape, organize, foresee and plan a practice outside the practice itself, before carrying it out, and at the same time to defy or undo the urgency of practice that weighs on an action. By objectifying the future action, practices of writing effect a distancing of the practice. They enable not only a reflexive look back on action but also its reflexive preparation.[14] If, as Bourdieu writes, 'the social world treats the body as a memo pad', since 'it inscribes there, particularly in the form of social principles of division that ordinary language condenses in its pairs of oppositions, the fundamental categories of a view of the world' (1990c, p. 11), it is when the body comes up against its limits that the memo written outside the body begins to find its relevance. Actors are often caught up in the 'heat of action', but they are also sometimes outside of it (in order to prepare it or rememorize it, evaluate it, rediscuss it, narrate it, comment on it, theorize it . . .).

The use of plans: lists of all kinds

Rather than postulating before any empirical investigation the sovereign power of the plan and planning in action, or on the other hand its total ineffectiveness, rather than making the notions of 'plan' and 'planning' into general concepts of a universal theory of action, researchers in psychology, the cognitive sciences and sociology would benefit by studying the actual plans (particularly written ones) that actors make use of from time to time in order to organize their action.[15]

The shopping list, for example, is a way of fixing and guiding future actions, an action programme, a 'plan'. Some lists of this kind even establish genuine programmes of movement within the supermarket, where the products classified by section follow one another in order as do the different moments of the itinerary followed in the store. A planning micro-mechanism of this kind very concretely allows those who make use of it (generally women) to 'save walking and time', to limit possible forgetting in cases where action has not been prepared. It is only by considering practices of this kind, everyday but observable, that progress can be made in the resolution of theoretical problems.

In order to determine the role or roles of the plan in action, according to the context studied, the first thing is to note that there is 'action' and 'action'. The example of descending the rapids that Lucy Suchman takes to show the practical ineffectiveness of the plan[16] is very different from that of shopping in a supermarket. The specific temporal conditions of the two situations mean that, in the first case, the tempo is such that it is impossible to imagine oneself being able to consult a plan while the action is under way, whereas, in the second case, the list is read in the longer time of the action of making purchases. As against what Suchman believes,[17] it is possible to consult the plan in the course of the action when this is not a short-term action urgently performed. What can be shown by the typical cases presented by these respondents is the fact that planning and routine, reflection and pre-reflexive adjustment, etc., are not incompatible but constantly interwoven, succeeding one another in everyday life.

Let us take the case of a travel itinerary. One respondent (a woman hotelier) explained that making an itinerary brought a saving in time in relation to simply improvising visits to sites: when you know where you are going, you necessarily waste less time. The itinerary remains a flexible plan to the extent that it is adapted to local circumstances, to improvisation as a function of the specific constraints of the situations encountered, rather than constituting an inflexible programme composed of rigid and imperative instructions. The respondent thus explained how her husband and she had to modify their programme at one point because of a miscalculation of distances. All the same, we see in the respondents' assertions that preparing the trip in the form of a plan (each day set aside for a particular visit) does indeed induce the notion of 'keeping to the plan'. When nothing is envisaged and fixed in advance, no one can think that they have accomplished a 'programme', either well or poorly.

Moreover, the most rigid and systematically followed itineraries are those drawn up on the basis of past practical experience. Thus when a couple of shopkeepers (bakers) left for a holiday in Brittany, they followed an itinerary that they had fixed in writing on a card. The plan became all the more rigid in as much as the actors kept to it as closely as possible and proceeded each year to the same operations ('With a place where we always stopped for breakfast, the same place we always stopped for lunch, it was always systematic'). Systematicness and regularity characterized the application of their envisaged plan. As the husband was himself Breton he knew the routes very well, and it was always he who drew up the final itinerary. In this case, the plan thus depended on an earlier experience and a precise acquaintance with possibilities. The husband selected from the possible itineraries the one that practice had led him to view as the most 'convenient'.

Lists of things to do that are drawn up in order to know where to go, to keep things organized, not to forget something, as well as in order to have a sense of moving forward, are also plans susceptible to modification. One respondent (a woman shopkeeper) made herself lists of this kind that combined all the work and household tasks that she had to do. She tried to list things to do in order of importance and degree of urgency. When the tasks on a list could not all be realized, the list was carried forward to the next day. Domestic planning never reaches the rigidity of imperative rules of obligatory instructions, and leaves room for improvisation:[18] 'But I don't mean that I follow this to the letter, because sometimes it may be time to make lunch and I've not done what was on my list – okay, then it has to be done the next day or in the afternoon. But yes, I really do make lists, enormously, to be sure of not forgetting anything.' Embodied non-reflexive habits (practical sense) are thus not incompatible with a planning of action that sets the course, sketches overall strategies, fixes major frameworks or general orientations without ever being in a position to programme the smaller details (e.g. the shopping list enables products to be classified according to their section in the supermarket, to know where you are, to make sure that the task is complete and that nothing has been forgotten, etc.), as in the case of the checklists of airline pilots.[19]

The same respondent gives the example of lists of things to take on a journey, which shows how a practical sense of anticipation is combined with a rationalization of this practical sense. Lists for holidays or weekends away are made in the form of card files and correspond to master lists whose content varies according to whether it is a longer stay or just a weekend, for example, but also according to the season in which the trip is taken: winter or summer. These lists thus permit her to pack her cases quickly without having to reflect on what she needs to take (reflection can be done 'once and for all', subsequent occasions only requiring the product of previous reflections to be re-read, which means both a saving in time and a release of intellectual capacities in relation to reflexive work). Certain theorists of action might think that the plan is of little use in the face of the uncertainties of action and the situations that may be encountered. This respondent, however, already takes into account, in drawing up her lists, singular facts drawn from past experience, such as how dirty her children are in the habit of getting. Lists are already the product of practical anticipations made in the light of what is imagined as likely to happen. Exactly the same kind of situation is also found with another respondent (woman, no occupation, married to a secondary-school teacher), who draws up a list of things to take on a journey in the light of her whole previous knowledge of the situation – i.e. of what she envisages as likely to happen, such as cold days, rainy days, etc. The very writing down of the list thus presupposes the application of a whole practical sense of situations, but this practical sense is triggered more systematically and explicitly than when it is used in 'the heat of action'.

We could show similar situations in the use of account books, calendars and shopping lists. All these analyses bring out an important point: 'planning' is not the opposite of 'improvisation' or 'practical sense', and even rests to a large extent on embodied practical knowledge. 'Good' planning is realistic planning, which already takes into account the specific constraints of real situations. But we cannot rule out the specific rule played by planning by maintaining that, whatever the projected plans, the logic of the situation and the embodied skills applied in the course of action are the sole determinants of action. The plan makes it possible to organize and specify what has been done and what remains to be done, to have a sense of moving forward, to know where one is going and how (in what order) to proceed, etc.

As a consequence, even when lists or plans are not followed to the letter, they introduce a different relationship to everyday activities, and particularly to the future. If 'big projects' that are written down cannot always stay on course in view of the facts of actual situations and their specific uncertainties, the very fact of formulating a project is conducive to organizing action and living it in a quite particular fashion. And so, rather than seeking at all cost to reduce the effects (cognitive, emotional, social . . .) of using plans in action by postulating their uselessness as soon as action is (really) engaged,[20] we should seek to describe the circumstantial effects which vary according to the different types of action under consideration.

The relative pertinence of practical sense

Setting himself against the intellectualist conceptions of his time, Pierre Bourdieu wrote in the fashion of the phenomenologists that 'Time is engendered in the actualization of the act, or the thought, which is by definition presentification and de-presentification, that is, the "passing" of time according to common sense. We have seen how practice need not – except by way of exception – explicitly constitute the future as such, as in a project or a plan posited through a conscious and deliberate act of will' (Bourdieu and Wacquant, 1992, p. 138). But it is this 'exceptionally' that allows us to put these statements about time into perspective. If the plan is an intention for the future in which actors conceive themselves as positing a future and organizing all available means by reference to this future posited as such, as a goal that must be explicitly attained, then the everyday practices of writing that I have studied correspond very well to the case in point. The diary, the list of things to do, the calendar, the shopping list, etc., are indeed instruments for shaping our temporality, the social construction of time, that constitute repeated daily exceptions in relation to the pre-reflexive adjustment of a habitus to a situation. They are everyday practices for constituting the future as such, in a project or a plan, and very often also practices of rationalization[21] (of time, activity, money . . .). Sociological incursion into the practices of writing opens a breach in the unity of the theory of practice or of practical sense.

When Bourdieu – in the wake here of Jack Goody's teaching – emphasizes the importance of written and visual practices as knowledge instruments for escaping the purely practical relationship to practice and the conquest of a theoretical relationship, a logical logic from a more distanced perspective (Bourdieu, 1990a), he forgets a crucial point – but how can one forget this in the case of social formations with formal schooling and a long tradition of literacy? (Furet and Ozouf, 1977). The techniques of objectification that are writings, diagrams, synoptic tables, lists, plans, maps, models, diagrams, calendars, etc., are not instruments reserved for scholars. To be sure, the latter use them more regularly than other actors, and over a far longer time, but it is easy to show that all the techniques of objectification of time, of language and of space to which he refers, and which are deemed to destroy the practical relationship to the world, have on the one hand been inculcated (more or less successfully) by the school institution, while on the other hand they are used daily by actors in their family, personal, work and play activities. How can you speak about the calendar, the list or the plan as used in the scholarly register without immediately thinking of the calendars and plans that are used every day by non-scientific actors? By being most often bound up with educational training, these techniques are unevenly divided socially, but they are present to a certain degree in almost all households as soon as their occupants have acquired the basics of reading and writing.

It is clearly not a question here of projecting scientific reasoning into lay minds, but rather of maintaining that emergence from practical sense is common in everyday life. Besides, what are the social foundations of rational action theories if not the historical invention and deployment of the economic market, mercantile calculation, techniques and strategies of commercialization, methods of accounting,[22] economic or bureaucratic planning, rationalization of the measurement of time, legally attested business contracts, etc.? These theories, like those opposed to them (e.g. a part of phenomenology, the theory of practice, etc.), do not rest on thin air, but systematize different aspects of our forms of social life, different dimensions of our relationship to the social world.[23] Perhaps the effort of theoretical clarification that these theories represent is incompatible with empirical nuance and complexity, but we have to maintain that it frequently leads to excessive generalizations, visible as soon as we observe the social world a little systematically and seriously, instead of remaining caught by the engulfing charm of philosophical theories. An intellectually easy (but socially difficult) polemic against theories of rational, planning and calculating action, which generally are theoretically very weak (but socially very strong), finally ends up no longer being prepared to see what there is of the rational, the planned, the calculated, etc., in the social world. It is impossible to act as if all the inventions mentioned (and many others besides) and their diffusion in many forms on a large scale had left the world in the same state as previously.

Analysis of the everyday practices of writing thus leads to putting in question the universality of the theory of practice. To maintain from the start that all action is the product of the application of a pre-reflexive practical sense, non-intentional, subconscious, etc., that everyday actions imbricate one another in a kind of permanent improvisation (a movement that is unforeseen and completely immanent in the state of things), is to universalize one possible case and remain blind to a large part of social practices. The calendar, the list of things to do, the diary, the shopping list, the account book, the letter, the personal diary and the travel itinerary amount to so many everyday exceptions to the pre-reflexive adjustment of a habitus to a social situation. To make the theory of habitus a theory that 'better account[s] for the actual logic of actual practices' (Bourdieu and Wacquant, 1992, p. 131) is to have a limited view of reality.

For all these reasons, it seems to me that the theory of practice finds its field of relevance or validity[24] in the study of social worlds with a low degree of objectification, societies that are 'without writing' (Lahire, 1993a). Looking back on the origin of the construction of the concept of habitus, Bourdieu was himself led to relativize the scope of its application:

> Some notions that I developed gradually, like the notion of habitus, were born from the desire to recall that as well as the express and explicit norm and the rational calculation there are other principles that generate practices. This is especially the case in societies were very few things are codified; with the result that, in order to account for what people do, we have to assume that they are obeying a kind of 'sense of the game' as one says in sport. (1986b, p. 40)

In these very weakly codified worlds, lacking a number of techniques of objectification of culture, 'the essential things are left to a feel for the game and to improvisation' (Bourdieu, 1990b, p. 80). Practical sense, practical mastery, the practical relationship to practice, improvisation, pre-reflexive adjustment to situations – all these are terms or expressions that perfectly describe the logic of social worlds with a low degree of objectification, and that proved their validity in Bourdieu's studies of Kabyl society.

Even if he maintains that 'analysis of practical sense is valid well beyond societies without writing' (Bourdieu, 1986b, p. 41), the empirical limit of the validity of the theory of practice is now clearly marked, and its author can even invite the reader to 'reflect on the different *modes of existence* of the principles of regulation and regularity of different forms of practice' (1990b, p. 65) within social worlds that are more or less codified, functioning more or less by explicit and formal transmission of skills ('In societies where the work of *codification* is not very advanced, the habitus is the principle of most modes of practices'; ibid., p. 82). It is this kind of reflection that I applied in my own research on practices of writing (domestic, educational or work-related). Asking what are the social conditions for habitus (practical sense, practical mastery) to be the generating principle of practices, raising the question of the forms of social life that allow a symbolic mastery to exist, makes it possible to go beyond the concept thanks to empirical research.

— Scene 3 —

THE PLURAL LOGICS OF ACTION

The ambiguity of a singular practice

Given the multiple uses that are made of it in the social sciences, the word 'practice' is not without a certain ambiguity. It is contrasted, on the one hand, with what pertains to 'discourse'[1] ('practices' and 'discourse') and distinguished, on the other hand, from everything 'theoretical' (practice and theory), sometimes again denoting rather generically the most varied social activities (cultural practices, sporting practices, economic practices, etc.). When Bourdieu speaks of 'the logic of practice' (in the singular – *la pratique*; 2000, p. 50) or 'the universal pre-logical logic of practice' (1990a, p. 19), he thus locates 'practice' in the singular in relation to theory, 'logical logic'. The practical relationship to practice is profoundly different from the theoretical relationship to practice that sociologists apply in their quest to understand specific practices. It is especially in order to mark this essential difference between the scientist and the practitioner, the one in a position to analyse and the other in a position to act, that Bourdieu developed his 'theory of practice': 'One must thus draw up a theory of this non-theoretical, partial, somewhat down-to-earth relationship with the social world that is the relation of ordinary experience' (1990b, p. 20).

But, to be completely acceptable, the epistemological and social break between theory and practice should not be conceived right away as a firm separation between groups of actors (theorist-actors and practitioner-actors). Sociologists who marry, play sport, support a political party, buy furniture or go to the cinema do not generally maintain a theoretical relationship to their own practice. Just like any other practitioner, sociologists are moved by the schemes of action they have embodied in the course of their previous social experiences. They are sometimes theorists and often practitioners. We can therefore distinguish in the scientist two major types of case: that in which they are in the situation of the theorist and that in which they are in the situation of the practitioner.

Things necessarily become a bit more complicated, however, when we consider these same sociologists at work. From a certain point of view, in writing their analyses they are once again in a practical relationship to practice. What they write may well be an atemporal (or de-temporalizing) theoretical vision (*theoria*), at a distance from what others (sometimes sociologists themselves) have in the practical mode, but they are none the less oriented during the time of writing by a practical sense of the sociological trade. What they call upon in their practice of writing are professional habits (conceptual, editorial, stylistic, technical, etc.), and this is not a practice detached from temporal constraints. Difficult here, therefore, to distinguish the theorist from the practitioner, as these are present in the same person and at the same time, the two notions being fundamentally relational: the same person is a practitioner in relation to her act of writing (or already at the stage of research), but a theorist in relation to the practices she is writing about. The break between the theoretical and the practical, the theoretical relationship to the world and the practical relationship to the world, logical logic and practical logic, is thus not simply and solely between two clearly distinguishable realities (two groups of actors – theorists and practitioners) or two types of situation (the theoretical actor – the same actor practising); it also makes a formal distinction that may be applied to the same situation, according to the point of view from which it is regarded.

As I have said about the notion of habit, sociology too often confuses habit as a modality of action (involuntary, unintentional) with the particular kind of habit (whether a habit of reflexivity or not). For example, the footballer has the habit of striking a ball (in different ways), and this gesture does not require of him any reflection or prior planning. But in the same way a grammarian has the habit of casting a grammatical look at sentences (a habit that is triggered without any particular reflexive effort whenever she is in the situation of being a grammarian or philologist). This habit, however, is indeed a habit of reflexivity, of taking a distance from language. Both the grammarian and the footballer are moved by habits that gradually build up in them a 'second nature'. They put these to work without even having to think about it, without being aware or having the impression of committing an unusual act. The grammarian is not absolutely different in this respect from the footballer, who moves easily about the field and strikes the ball into the back of the net. Both have installed in them this 'second nature' of habit, as they have spent years 'doing their scales', repeating thousands of times movements of the body or grammatical operations that are both similar and different. The footballer can also acquire (in his trade or outside of it) habits of reflexivity, while the grammarian has necessarily acquired (in her trade or outside of it) non-reflexive habits; but what separates them is the share of time that they respectively spend on embodying reflexive or non-reflexive habits and, accordingly, the share that reflexive habits (planning, conceptualization, theorization) make up in their respective stock of embodied habits. If this means that the pre-reflexive kind of habit is not the only possible kind, we are forced to maintain that the theory of habitus reduces habit as a modality of action to one particular kind of habit – i.e. the non-reflexive kind.

Pierre Bourdieu, in effect, largely constructed his theory of practice and his concept of habitus against intellectualist theories of practice – i.e. against the idea of a practice oriented rationally, intentionally and voluntarily towards explicit ends, against the idea of reflexivity as a consciousness that was conscious, systematic and calculating. The practical relationship to practice is thus defined as an immediate understanding that is blind to itself (a learned ignorance), a consciousness that is non-conscious, conceptually wanting, pre-reflexive, partial (as against exhaustive and systematic), vague, unintentional, and engaged in the urgency of action. On the other hand, this author has long used a theoretical couple – practical mastery as against symbolic mastery – which initially served to account for differences between dominant and dominated cultural arbitraries. And it is the parasitizing of the general theoretical question about the theory of practice (practical sense, the practical relationship to the world) by the question of cultural differences between groups or classes (practical mastery versus symbolic mastery) that has ended up posing a problem.

If material conditions of existence subject people more or less closely to the 'imperatives of practice' and thus tend to prevent some of them from 'the formation and development of the aptitude for symbolic mastery of practice' (Bourdieu and Passeron, 1977, p. 48), this then means that the members of different social groups are driven by practical sense to a greater or lesser extent, and that some of them have the means, by their material conditions of existence, but also and above all by dint of the instruments of reflexivity that they have acquired, particularly at school, for emerging from the logic of practical sense and mastering the world symbolically, putting a distance between themselves and the world, themselves and their practices.

The concept of habitus seems on the one hand to subsume the opposition between practical and symbolic mastery (Bourdieu and Passeron, 1977, pp. 45–6), while on the other hand falling back on the first term of the opposition (habitus or practical sense is practical mastery).[2] All evidence then suggests that a formidable contradiction is immediately established. In the second figure, the concept of habitus is defined exclusively as 'practical mastery' (or practical sense) – i.e. as knowledge without awareness, pre-reflexive mastery – and for this reason habitus cannot be invoked to account for those social practices – such as educational ones – that function by way of symbolic, conscious, rational mastery. Bourdieu makes it clearly understood that this is indeed how he defines habitus, admitting that this cannot be 'at the origin' of certain practices. He thus proposes, as I have already recalled, that we 'reflect on the different modes of existence of the principles of regulation and regularity of different forms of practice' (Bourdieu, 1990b, p. 65) within more or less codified social worlds, functioning more or less by explicit and formal transmission of skills, and makes clear that, 'in societies where the work of *codification* is not very advanced, the habitus is the principle of most modes of practice' (ibid.). He writes in the same vein that '[it] is, of course, never ruled out that the responses of the *habitus* may be accompanied by a strategic calculation tending to perform in a conscious mode the operation that the *habitus* performs quite differently' (1990a, p. 53). There is thus a conscious mode that is distinct from the practical mode constituted by habitus:

> The immediate fit between habitus and field is only one modality of action, if the most prevalent one ('We are empirical,' said Leibniz, by which he meant practical, 'in three quarters of our actions'). The lines of action suggested by habitus may very well be accompanied by a strategic calculation of costs and benefits, which tends to carry out at a conscious level the operations that habitus carries out in its own way. Times of crises, in which the routine adjustment of subjective and objective structures is brutally disrupted, constitute a class of circumstances when indeed 'rational choice' may take over, at least among those agents who are in a position to be rational. (Bourdieu and Wacquant, 1992, p. 131)

In effect, if habitus is this pre-reflexive, non-theoretical, etc., experience, it is clear that not all practices have habitus as their generating principle.

In the first case, the intention is rather to subsume under the concept of habitus both 'practical habitus' ('functioning more generally by way of practical mastery') and 'reflexive habitus' (functioning more generally by way of symbolic mastery'), and the idea that habitus could not be at the origin of certain kinds of conduct does not strictly have any meaning. The theory of habitus rather assumes major social variations from the standpoint of the relative importance of habits of reflexivity and symbolic mastery in the socialization programmes of different actors in a society. It is this interpretation that I would see as most coherent, removing the multiple contradictions generated by the first option. If, like Bourdieu himself, you opt for the first solution, you are then faced with a pleonasm (practical habitus = practical 'practical sense') and a contradiction (reflexive habitus = pre-reflexive reflexivity). And it is no doubt from trying to tackle different problems at the same time and with the same theoretical tool (response to the epistemological problem about the relationship of social scientists to their objects; response to rational action theories; response to intellectualism; response to those who cannot see the unequal distribution of the instruments of reflexivity) that the tool ends up breaking.

The sporting model of practical sense and its limitations

Merleau-Ponty sometimes used the example of the physical relationship that the footballer has to the playing field to make clear to the reader how the field is not an 'object' to which the player relates, but 'the immanent term of his practical intentions; the player becomes one with it' (1965, p. 168). The theory of practical sense makes generous use of sporting examples to explain the practical relationship to practice, practical mastery, appealing variously to the tennis player, the footballer or the boxer.[3]

The tennis player who takes up the right position to hit the ball, by pre-reflexive anticipation and not in the mode of a reflexive relationship to the future (Bourdieu, 2000, p. 162), is thus brought in to illustrate the practical or everyday relationship to time:

> Everything that I want to say is summed up in the contrast between a project or plan (the plan is an aim for the future in which the subject views himself as positing a future and organizing all means available with reference to this future posited as such, as an end that has to be explicitly attained), and a preoccupation. The preoccupation or anticipation of the player is immediately present in something that is not immediately perceived and immediately available, but that is however

as if it was already there. If you take the example of wrong-footing, the player who sends a ball to the wrong foot acts in the present in relationship to a 'coming' (I say 'coming' here rather than 'future') that is quasi-present, inscribed in the very physiognomy of the present, of the opponent *in the process of* moving to the right. He does not posit this future as in a project: he can move to the right or not to the right ... So I send the ball to the left because he is going to the right, etc. It is determined as a function of a quasi-present inscribed in the present. (Bourdieu, 1989, pp. 21–2)

Or again:

If you want to carry out the experiment, try and do interviews with an excellent player in any sport you like and ask them: 'You did this at such and such time, how did you do it?' You will see how there is an immense gap between this kind of practical mastery, expressed in the immediate relationship to a game by which one is possessed, and which one possesses to the extent that one is possessed by its regularities, its tendencies, and the knowledge of the knowing subject who posits the game as a game, posits the game to himself in a representation of the game, who makes a plan of it ... There is an abyss between the two things. (Ibid., pp. 44–5)

In the conditions of a tennis player in action, you can well understand how this person does not have the possibility – given the urgency of the action – to elaborate decisions, make plans, think of the future as such and envisage rationally and consciously the acts that she might perform, contrary to the conception of a project. The example of the sports player caught up in the heat of the action is a perfect illustration of what practical sense, practical logic, is – i.e. of *practice* (as opposed to theory): 'The conditions of rational calculation are practically never given in practice: time is limited, information is restricted, etc.' (Bourdieu, 1990a, p. 11). Other writers, more inspired by North American ethnomethodology but sharing the same conception of practice, also draw their examples from the world of sports. One of those most commented on is that of descending the rapids in canoe, as developed by Lucy Suchman (1990).

These examples illustrate 'perfectly' the theory of practice held by their authors, but their very 'perfection' immediately renders them suspect. The authors never inquire into the limitations of the sporting comparison and the specificity of the examples given. However, starting from these examples of action and raising the question of their specific social property, one can only be amazed by the reduction of the social world that is ultimately effected by the corresponding theories. Everything happens as if this world were (1) a world of constant urgency; (2) a world of live performance (as on a theatre stage in front of an audience) in which one can never repeat what one has done and has no right to make a mistake; (3) a world of permanent confrontation with situations that impose themselves and require improvisation (the musical metaphor is sometimes added to the sporting one). Taking these 'made-to-order' examples, you end up with one of the most common epistemological errors in the social sciences – that of generalizing from particular cases, or, more precisely, generalizing from a particular variety of case or a particular class of contexts (Lahire, 1996b).

1 In all these cases, the examples describe actors veritably trapped by action, caught in the 'heat of the action', the urgency of things to be done. Urgency is thus a major characteristic of the actions described; it constitutes, we are told, 'one of the essential properties of practice' (Bourdieu, 1990a, p. 82; also 2000, p. 56). There is no time to deliberate carefully when faced with a ball travelling at 100 or 200 kilometres per hour, no rational choice or calculation possible when it is a matter of shooting between two players while being chased by a third, no conceivable plan or project when you find yourself facing your opponent in the ring or descending the rapids. As against the science of practices constructed 'after the battle' (1990a, p. 81) and enjoying far more time, as well as the means – written and graphic – for de-temporalizing action, 'practice' in the singular is necessarily bound up with the obligation to act '"on the spot", "in the twinkling of an eye", "in the heat of the moment", that is, in conditions which exclude distance, perspective, detachment and reflection' (ibid., p. 82). But why should urgency be an essential property of *all* practices? Not all actions correspond to this model. Action is not always reducible to the gesture performed, the word uttered or the decision urgently taken. It may take a few seconds or be extended over several months, even years. You don't do shopping in the same way as you descend the rapids, you don't build a house like you hit a football, you don't prepare an international scientific conference[4] like you box in a ring.

Of course, everything depends on the manner in which the action in question is divided up, but certain actions are organized over a far longer time than those offered in the examples of sporting gestures. Even in different sports, urgency can be greater or lesser. According to whether an action is longer or shorter, it will allow more or less time for reflection, evaluation, calculation, deliberation, soliciting advice, negotiation and discussion. Longer actions, which extend over time, sometimes require the establishing of programmes, planning, calendars, projects, and – *a posteriori* – balance sheets or evaluations. As Anselm L. Strauss remarks, sending the first man to the moon was from this point of view one of the most planned, calculated and carefully prepared actions ever (1993, p. 53). It goes without saying that, whatever its duration, not everything in an action can be intentional, and it would make no sense to assume this. An actor may have the intention of attaining an objective (e.g. travelling to a certain place) without a deliberate programme that precisely mentions all the acts that have to be performed in order to get there. Thus we are always dealing with a subtle mixture of sensory-motor habits and planned or reflexive ones, and it is just as absurd to presuppose that actors are never strategic, intentional, etc., as to postulate that they always all are.

But as in parapraxes, these texts often supply flagrant counterexamples that make the specificity of the sporting examples they give readily apparent: 'You need only think of the impulsive decision made by the tennis player who runs up to the net, to understand that it has nothing in common with the learned construction that the coach, after analysis, draws up in order to explain it and deduce communicable lessons from it' (Bourdieu, 1990b, p. 11). It is impossible then to avoid the question: Why does the trainer's practice not constitute an example of a completely different theory of practice? A theory that asserts the reflexive, deliberate – individually or collectively – and less pressing character of action? Why should one real example be less pertinent than another real example? It is completely possible, in the case of certain actions, to 'overcome the effects of time' (Bourdieu, 1990a, p. 81) by utilizing means that are not reserved just for scientists – plans, maps, diagrams, video recordings, diagrams, etc. Not all actions thus correspond – in all evidence – to the model of urgent action.

2 The model examples all appeal to 'live' actions, in a temporality where time is often scarce and counted, in conditions identical to those experienced by actors on stage in front of an audience. No mistake is permitted, nothing that one has just done can be undone or repeated. Everything happens as if the cineaste-sociologist who films the action privileged those particular scenes: the public football, tennis or boxing match, the real (and not simulated) canoe descent through the rapids, etc. Once again, these examples are perfect to make the reader understand how: 'Caught up in "the matter in hand", totally present in the present and in the practical functions

that it finds there in the form of objective potentialities, practice excludes attention to itself (that is, to the past)' (Bourdieu, 1990a, p. 92). There is no question of a dancer at the Paris Opera recommencing on stage a gesture he has performed badly. He has to pursue his action and catch up with its rhythm. Similarly it is impossible for the player who has wrongly anticipated the ball to say to the umpire, as in a film: 'Cut! We'll replay that.'[5] But the sports player in the course of the match is not the same as the player in training. Why then not also base the theory of practice on the model of the player in training? Here she can replay the same gesture as many times as she wants, stop for breath, reflect on what she's just done, change her grip on the racket or the style of her service, receive advice from her trainer and discuss with him a possible strategy, or envisage with his help different possibilities, and so on. A less compressed timeframe, a performance that is not broadcast live this very day, this minute, when it is important not to go wrong. By focusing our gaze exclusively on the performance, we come to forget the times of preparation and training that are propitious for reflection.[6]

If, at the moment when the player is caught up in the match, she can count only on embodied habitual skills, these may still be the product of a whole work of reflection, correction, calculation, strategy, etc., accumulated through hours of training. The trainer may rationalize the practice of the player, make her conscious of her hits, faults, gaps, 'correct her aim' by orienting her habits in the game. The action performed in a state of urgency, on the day of the match, benefits from all this preparation that is done 'with time', taking one's time, gradually correcting, by repeated rehearsals, the player's gestures, positions and movements (with the aid of video, for instance), her successions of 'strokes' or gestures, in sum by constantly effecting this looking back on oneself and on the past that the theory of practice considers as being by nature impossible in its one and only 'practice':

> This practical sense, which does not burden itself with rules or principles (except in cases of misfiring or failure), still less with calculations or deductions, which are in any case excluded by the urgency of action which 'brooks no delay', is what makes it possible to appreciate the meaning of the situation instantly, at a glance, in the heat of the action, and to produce at once the opportune response. Only this kind of acquired mastery, functioning with the automatic reliability of an instinct, can make it possible to respond instantaneously to all the uncertain and ambiguous situations of practice. (Bourdieu, 1990a, pp. 103–4)

When it is accepted, looking back on past action (but not on oneself)[7] is conceived only in the mode of a crisis of automatisms, habits or routine. It is only when the actor encounters difficulties that put her in crisis that she begins to ask herself questions. But we see very well in the example of the sports player that (corrective) looking back on oneself and one's past action is an everyday and normal condition of advance and improvement in the habits of the game. Besides, sometimes actors also look back on their past action so as to memorize it or rework it in daydreams, to narrate it, laugh at it, 'transmit' it to the next generation, get the impression of mastering it better (e.g. personal diaries), and so on.

The model of 'live' action, however, is not the only existing model. It corresponds to periods of public performance executed in a relatively limited time (exams, certain kinds of match, theatrical and dance performances, musical concerts . . .) but neglects situations in which rehearsal, correction and reflection are possible and even sought after (periods of sports, musical, dance and educational training, simulation of a real situation in the context of a training course, making a film in which scenes are replayed as many times as desired, writing a book with re-reading, correction, deleting, etc., and a multitude of situations of everyday life in which one can repeat what has not been done well). The actor is not always placed in the situation of the tennis player who must take care to succeed with each 'stroke' – which by this fact acquires an absolute and unique value, either leading to victory or steadily condemning her to defeat – with no possibility of error, or of going back and trying again. It is impossible therefore to make this particular moment of the course of action, this type of action, into action *par excellence*. Social life does not unfold at all times in the condition of a public 'live' match.

3 If we are to believe certain examples offered, we might imagine that the social world is made up of permanent confrontations with situations that are not chosen, that impose themselves on actors and in which they have to improvise as best they can. Actors would always be improvising their actions on the spur of the moment, finding their bearings in a course of action that is never foreseen in advance. They would be comparable with the jazz pianist – solo or in a band – who improvises without ever being able to consider, represent and plan his future actions (Sudnow, 1978). Because the time of action is counted, because the actor lives all his actions in a state of urgency, he 'lives in the present, acting continually on immediate circumstances' (Conein and Jacopin, 1993, p. 79; Agre and Chapman, 1987) rather like

the Pengi character in the computer game. A life exclusively in the present, oriented towards action, caught up in the continuous flux of the world's events, the solicitations of the environment that are never mastered but to which one tries constantly to adapt.[8] Practical anticipations are possible, but no project or plan, no objective envisaged.

Donald Norman, in *The Psychology of Everyday Things*, writes as follows against theories of planned action: 'Rather than engage in detailed planning, people embark on their everyday activity when the occasion arises. Thus we do not modify the course of our actions to go into a shop, a library or to chat with a friend. We attend to our activities and if we find ourselves in the vicinity of the shop or the library, or on the point of meeting a friend, we let the opportunity trigger the appropriate activity' (Norman, cited in Conein and Jacopin, 1993, pp. 69–70). This typically aprioristic quotation, by its very naivety, shows very clearly the fact that not all actors are cast on the model of the one described by this author: a bit 'bohemian' and with no particular project, who lets herself be led by the uninterrupted course of things, improvising according to the opportunity of the situation, and who might very well – for better or worse – never reach her place of work, let alone anywhere else . . .

No social life of any kind is simply a constant and uninterrupted flow that carries actors in an endless succession of 'strokes', pragmatically and contextually (in the sense of the immediate context) given or received. Actors do not live in a state of constant improvisation. The same tennis player who has to improvise her gestures on the court as a function of her opponent's style of play, in the practical urgency of the public match, also possesses a planner that foresaw several months in advance the tennis tournament in which she is now executing her performance. Actors often have to juggle between short and long timeframes, immediate tactics and long-term strategies. For example, Anne-Marie Chartier and Florence Janssens show very well how teachers in primary school constantly take into account several timeframes at once in their pedagogic practice ('the strategic timeframe of the school year' with 'mobilizing events'; 'ritualized times' and 'tactical times') and explain why the outside observer does not understand the meaning of the actions, gestures and educational arrangements inscribed in the various different temporal frameworks and perspectives: she observes practices over a given period, but is unaware of the distribution in different temporal frameworks of action that gives them their meaning (Chartier and Janssens, 1996).

According to the framework in which the action is seen, whether the focus is the long shot that shows a sports player planning her season, training for a long period then playing her matches, or rather the close-up on a phase of the game during a match (e.g. wrong-footing or anticipating being wrong-footed), then either planning, foresight, reflection, deliberation, representation, strategy, etc., are highlighted, or else these elements are totally ignored and all that emerges is the pre-reflexive (quasi-instinctive) adjustment to a situation under way.

Intentionality and the levels of context

The question of intentionality in action or the lack of it, consciousness or the absence of consciousness, does not arise in a general or absolute sense, but always depends on the sequence of actions under consideration: a short or a lengthy action, a simple action or a complex one, ordinary or unusual. The dialogue of the deaf between theories of action that reserve a larger or smaller place for intentionality, conscious strategy and aim, etc., is bound up with the fact that very often they are not speaking of the same kinds of action at all. Their champions have in mind such heterogeneous and contrasting examples of action that most commonly their theoretical confrontation is vain and sterile.

Pierre Bourdieu, describing intellectual trajectories, wrote as follows:

> There is therefore an initial reduction that the reduction to utilitarianism enforces: a rational and calculating consciousness, positing ends as being possible as such, is substituted as a relationship to the future for the end as preoccupation, as immediate presence to objectives inscribed in the present. It is by effecting this slippage that one is condemned to cynicism. Cynicism is the act of positing inadmissable ends as such. If my analysis is true, it is possible for example to be adjusted to the necessities of a game, or have a magnificent academic career, without ever needing to calculate to this intention. This would perhaps appear less speculative if we were in a situation of a research seminar, if we were analysing, for example, the biography of an academic or one of the great French linguists of the nineteenth century. A very common theoretical error, committed by many researchers who are carried away (often by a desire for demystification), consists in positing the end-point of a trajectory as if this had already been the end of the agent from the start (Meillet, for example). They transform the trajectory into a project. They act as if, from the moment where Meillet chose a supervisor for his doctoral thesis, a subject, a discipline, he had in mind the ambition of becoming the greatest linguist of his time. They make out that the principle of conduct of agents in a field (two priors struggling

for the staff, or two academics struggling over whether the theory of action should be this or that ...) is always a kind of cynical calculating consciousness. (Bourdieu, 1989, p. 23)

In this case, the sequence of action represents the whole of a personal trajectory. Paradoxically, the different moments in the trajectory could sometimes be interpreted on the basis of examples of short and quasi-instinctive actions. One would then say, for example, that, just as the tennis player does not 'decide' to hit the ball approaching her at high speed, so an actor does not construct conscious strategies to reach a certain position of power (economic, cultural, political). And, indeed, both very short-term and very long-term actions often share this property of making intentionality or conscious strategy unlikely. But the apparent similarity of the two extremes may lead one to believe that the whole spectrum of actions (from the simplest to the most complex, the shortest to the longest, the most to the least probable, etc.) could be viewed in the same fashion. Things are not so simple, however.

Let us take some different examples. Clearly you do not decide to 'go shopping' in the same way as you decide to 'go to the Collège de France'. The former is a simple everyday action, open to anyone able to enter a shop with money to spend; the second is quite extraordinary and certainly not open to all comers. In the same way, to decide on the route I will take to get by car from Lyon to Bordeaux is not the same thing as 'deciding', when I'm in secondary school, to study medicine at university. In the first case, the situation is again rather ordinary and relatively commonplace (car journeys do not present particularly formidable social and political stakes). In the second case, not everything depends on my good intention or good planning: a series of good reports have to be obtained, particularly in mathematics, to get into the top science class, etc., and the social conditions that may enable me to reach my goal may change in the course of time (e.g. I may lose my parents and no longer have either the motivation or the material means to continue my studies, etc.).

If it is hard to imagine, on the scale of social games that Bourdieu takes as the pertinent social context, that actors can set their sights explicitly on goals long in advance (to believe that Meillet got good grades in primary school with a view of being able one day to go to the Collège de France ...), it is very easy to see, on the other hand, that, on different occasions in everyday life, actors can indeed 'posit ends as possible as such' (e.g. to go on holiday to Brittany or Spain, to do shopping or housework first, etc.). These are simply not at all the same kinds of action. And to demonstrate this, it is enough to imagine an actor who shows great foresight in her domestic organization, rationally managing the family organization, accounts and timetables, making shopping lists and lists of things to do, etc. Who would want to qualify her behaviour as 'cynical and calculating utilitarianism'? Just as it is hard to argue that Meillet was already preparing his 'stroke' at primary school, because this involves a very complex series of actions, extending over a very long period of time (almost a whole life), so it is not at all awkward to maintain that someone foresaw, calculated and planned – with all possible cynicism! – to go to the bank at such and such a time, then go to the chemist, etc. If Bourdieu raises the question of cynicism, and if 'calculation' is equivalent to cynicism for him, this is because he places us in the order of positions and practices bound up with high social stakes. Saying that someone getting married does not consciously calculate, as they would in a real marriage market, that taking up this or that prestigious position does not necessarily mean it has been aimed at intentionally, etc. – these are all actions that touch on the social order and its reproduction. But not all actions are quite so 'historic'; they are not all situated at the level of major social stakes, strategies of reproduction of resources, capitals, strategies of subversion or preservation of existing hierarchies. In short, it is because the situations described are considered exclusively at the level of trajectories and fields, with their logic of struggle, balance of forces, reproduction, etc., that the non-intentional aspect of practices can be emphasized – most often quite correctly. One can certainly conduct one's whole life in the mode of rational calculation or intentional aim, but, in a life (or the context of an individual trajectory) that is never entirely controllable, foreseeable, plannable, etc., actors can sometimes develop intentions, plans, projects, strategies, calculations that are more or less rational, in this or that domain, in connection with this or that practice.[9] Critical remarks about intentionality and conscious calculation are thus valid for a particular type of action, at a particular scale of construction of contexts of action, but not universally.

Plurality of times and logics of action

Theories of action and the actor plunge us either into the realm of conscious strategy, calculation, rational decision, reflexivity or conscious intention or else into the world of pre-reflexive, subconscious adjustment to practical situations, the world of practical sense and the logic of improvisation.

As with the tension between plurality and singleness of the actor, it is neither possible nor desirable to settle this question once and for all by theoretical debate;[10] this can only be done by empirical research and inquiring as to the socio-historical conditions that make rational action possible, in which socio-historical conditions actors can apply completely conscious strategies and act in an intentional or calculated fashion. There is nothing in the coherence and internal construction of theories that can decide on the pertinence of one pole or the other in this tension. And it is not unprofitable here to look back to Durkheim. In fact, when Durkheim criticized the recourse that some of his contemporaries had to the notion of 'interest' or 'maximization of profit', he did so not on the basis of a rival conception of human motivation, but rather by criticizing the apriorism involved. Speaking of 'political economy', he wrote that 'this placed at the root of all its deductions an abstraction that it did not have the right to utilize, that is, the notion of a man guided in his actions exclusively by personal interest. Now, this hypothesis cannot be posited immediately at the start of research; only repeated observation and methodical comparison can allow us to evaluate the impulsive force that this motive may exercise on us' (1975, p. 16). Durkheim could have criticized this theory of 'personal interest' from an alternative conception of the social, a different theory of practice, but in actual fact he took a far more distanced (and pertinent) position in not rejecting completely the notion of 'personal interest', but rather the idea that you could stick to this notion as an *a priori* of all research. His target was the *a priori* as such: 'We do not begin', he explained, 'by postulating a certain conception of human nature, and deducing a sociology from this' (ibid., p. 184).

Calculation, reason, rationality, interest or strategy do not lie at the origin of all possible actions. On the other hand, however, it is possible to inquire, for example, what social forms enable certain actors, in certain of their practices, to act by determining 'costs' and 'benefits'. The critique, then, does not depend on an alternative *a priori* conception of the principle of all human action. It is a critique of the mutation of a category of human action that is historically situated into a general concept.[11] But absolutely to insist, conversely, on preserving and defending a 'practico-practical' conception of action (pre-reflexive, subconscious, etc.) is to ignore a large part of what civilizations have built up: calculation, strategy (commercial or military), foresight, programming, planning, borrowing on credit, savings, theoretical speculation, meta-linguistic or meta-discursive reflection, and so on.

A (bad) intellectual habit very often leads to making 'action' and 'reflection' two necessarily distinct realities, whose contact would trigger an explosion. Even to ask whether there is not reflection in action is tacitly to admit, on the one hand, that action (but what kind of action?)[12] is conceivable without any reflection and, on the other hand, that reflection is not in itself an action. 'Reflect or act, you have to choose' would seem to be the generally accepted motto on this question. One thing (reflection) is supposed to prevent the other (action), paralyse it (thinking about what one is doing would block action), so that the two things each live their separate lives. Reflection could intervene before or after action (reflection *on* past or future action) but never during action (reflection *at the same time* as action). One of the reasons for this rather simplistic dualism lies in the fact that reflection is immediately understood (in a logocentric fashion) as theoretical, scholarly, rational reflection. It is implicitly considered that only these scholarly practices merit the name of 'reflection'. Once this equivalence is posited – in the same way, we shall see, as the equivalence between language and theoretical language – it is then easy to show that actors are not little calculating scholars, theorizing each one of their acts, rationally evaluating the pros and cons, the costs and benefits, etc. ('The actor, as [this theory] construes him or her, is nothing other than the imaginary projection of the knowing subject [*sujet connaissant*] into the acting subject [*sujet agissant*], a sort of monster with the head of a thinker thinking his practice in reflexive and logical fashion mounted on the body of a man of action engaged in action'; Bourdieu and Wacquant, 1992, p. 123). It is easy enough to refute such a caricature of an opponent as the rational action theory. But, in passing, the critique shares with the criticized theory the idea that reflection is by nature 'scholarly'. An incompatibility between reflection and action, a logocentric reduction of reflection to scholarly reflection, as summed up in the following quotation: 'Indeed, simply because we pause in thought over our practice, because we turn back to it to consider it, describe it, analyse it, we become in a sense absent from it; we tend to substitute for the active agent the reflecting "subject", for practical knowledge the theoretical knowledge which selects significant features, pertinent indices' (Bourdieu, 2000, p. 51).

Yet if action is not reduced to short-term action, realized in a situation of urgency and with no possibility of rehearsal or replay, it is readily understandable that reflection, including the most rational kind, can intervene in the very course of an action and even constitute the timeframes and stages necessary for it (e.g. organize a cultural event or prepare a long journey, play chess or develop a marketing strategy). But even when an action corresponds to what the theory of practical sense describes, there is always a pragmatically anchored reflection indissociable from the action under way and from the elements of the immediate context, which does not necessarily involve a 'pause' in the action.[13] A theory of action must therefore integrate into its scientific programme the study of different forms of reflection at work in different types of action.

Theories of action have nothing to gain from adopting a strategy of juxtaposing opposites and supposedly overcoming them in theory. In fact, by sparing themselves the theoretical and semantic clarifications required for any construction of a theoretical object (immediately perceived as theoreticist), sociologists sometimes prefer to adopt a rhetorical strategy that is both the most rewarding and the least costly. They believe it possible to 'overcome' the classical philosophical antinomies by contenting themselves with verbally juxtaposing opposing terms, saying both one thing and (what is generally considered) its contrary, rather than seeking ways of saying and describing that avoid the use of these mortal dichotomies. We are thus told that boxing effects the fusion 'of body and mind, instinct and strategy, emotion and rationality' (Wacquant, 1995b, p. 506); that 'corporeal mechanisms' and 'mental dispositions' are so closely intertwined here that they 'obliterate the distinction between the physical and the mental, between what derives from athletic ability and what pertains to the moral faculties and the will' (Wacquant, 1989, p. 36). Indeed, sometimes it is not just the sociologist whose theory overcomes these oppositions, but the actor or his practice itself: 'The boxer is a living mesh of body and mind, defying the border between rationality and habit, bursting the opposition between action and representation, overcoming in practice the opposition between the individual and the collective' (ibid., pp. 36–7). We discover a whole series of pairs of opposites that structure the social sciences as well as a good part of philosophy, and are in this way joined together, aligned and juxtaposed. The culmination of this strategy – in the image of the perverse ingénue – is the use of oxymorons that make it possible to say both one thing and its opposite, putting oneself, if need be, in a position of being able to reply to all theoretical camps at once without having asserted anything more than each one of these taken separately (boxing, for example, is designated as a 'deliberately wild' practice; ibid., p. 47.)[14] The discursive or rhetorical gain is large, but the gain in knowledge of empirical reality is particularly small. If we can agree on a scientific strategy of 'neither . . . nor', which seeks to overcome the classical theoretical oppositions (never mind that this is a philosophical commonplace *par excellence*), this should not lead to the semantic facility of 'both this and that', 'one thing and its opposite', 'A and not-A', which confuses theoretical supersession and semantic collage, if not logical contradiction. At the end of the day, the semantic clarity of Wittgenstein is preferable to the desire of rhetorical juxtaposition of pairs of opposites and the purely rhetorical victory that obscures social realities and sociological interpretation more than it clarifies them.

What is most important, on the other hand, to grasp as accurately as possible is both the reflexive, calculating, planning part of action (moments in which action is prepared, calculated and planned, but also in which it is reflected on, either while under way or after the event) and the part of action that is pre-reflexive, unplanned and not calculated, according to the type of action and the category of actor in question.[15] Rather than postulate *a priori*, and once and for all, the existence of a singular theory of practice (rational actor theory, planned behaviour theory, decision theory, game theory, practical sense theory, situated action theory . . .), it is far better to reconstitute – according to their social world and social milieu, different types of actor and different types of action – the different timeframes and different logics of action: timeframes of consultation, of deliberation (Aune, 1977, esp. ch. 3, 'Deliberation', pp. 112–43; Melden, 1968), of preparation and planning, timeframe of application of embodied schemes of action in a situation of relative urgency – according to the nature of the action – sometimes accompanied by a time of pause, reflection and correction, time to look back on the action, on oneself, etc. It is also useful to investigate those types of action in which actors calculate consciously, those in which they have scrupulously to follow written and explicit rules that are known by all, and again those in which rules (or codes) exist but are less constraining, recalling or marking their presence only in cases of serious fault, those in which there is neither rule nor calculation, etc. To sum up, the point is to develop a sociology of effective logics of action and of the plurality of forms of relationship to action.

Act III

Forms of Embodiment

— Scene 1 —

THE PLACE OF LANGUAGE

The world of silence

With its roots deep in phenomenology, a certain sociological school offers the metaphor of silence and silent bodily negotiation when it has to describe the social processes of embodiment.[1] Running against all those philosophical ideas that see reflexive consciousness and the sign on all sides, these conceptions fall in their turn into the opposite excess and end up in a cascade of elementary confusions: between consciousness and theoretical consciousness, between the verbal and the conscious, between language and reflexivity, language and theory – so much so that any study that discusses language is systematically suspected of connivance with the linguistic turn (Lahire, 1994b). The scientific, serious, anti-intellectualist and anti-structuralist camp then proceeds to a wholesale adoption of the language of the body, of pre-reflexivity and silence. As if man was an animal without language, as if language was necessarily a sign of reflexivity and reflective distance, as if language was always something apart from action, as if it was not itself at times action, as if the 'study of language' systematically meant structuralism or semiology, as if 'thought' necessarily meant theoretical thought, formal, systematic and reflexive – as if L. S. Vygotsky, M. Bakhtin, J. Goody, J. S. Bruner and B. Bernstein had never existed. The logic of 'bending the stick the other way' is sometimes understandable, but by bending it too far you end up breaking it.

To restore to language – its different forms and its different social and mental functions – its proper place in analysing the phenomena of embodiment of habits and schemes of action thus supposes defining it both against approaches that ignore or neglect it and against those that take it into account but abstract from its role and functions in action and the processes of embodiment. Considering language does not automatically mean adhering to the image of society as a great market of semiotic exchange or a communicational space in which information circulates, placing intentionality at the heart of action or adopting a micro-sociological procedure. Nor is it a question of autonomizing language or conferring on it some kind of primacy, still less of proposing a sociological hermeneutics that would make the social world into a text or a book to decipher. Social practices and courses of action are carried out through linguistic practices, but they do not necessarily have the production of these as their goal. Yet nor is it possible to make practices or the embodiment of habits into processes taking place outside of language in an obscure and silent relationship to the world.

Language should therefore be analysed in all its subtle problematic linkages, which delete the traces of language in practices and make it into an equivalent of 'reflexivity' or 'reflexive distance' by reducing it to just one of its social functions. Sociological expressions such as 'the pre-verbal taking-for-granted of the world that flows from practical sense' (Bourdieu, 1990a, p. 68), schemes that go 'from practice to practice without moving through discourse or consciousness' (ibid., p. 74), 'symbolic mastery' as 'consciousness and verbal expression' (ibid.), 'the continuous chain of unconscious apprenticeships that are accomplished body-to-body, by hints, in the relationship between successive generations that is often obscure to itself' (Bourdieu, 1990c, p. 30); 'the social sciences endeavour to theorize the behaviour that occurs, in the greatest degree, outside the field of conscious awareness, that is learnt by a silent and practical communication, from body to body one might say' (Bourdieu, 1990b, p. 166). Philosophical expressions: 'silent relationship with the other' (Merleau-Ponty, 1973, p. 133), 'the feeling one feels, the seeing one sees, is not a thought of seeing or feeling, but vision, feeling, the silent experience of a silent sense' (Merleau-Ponty, 1968, p. 249); 'the silent experienced',[2] and so on. In the struggle against intellectualism, intentionalism, etc., in the end one finally concedes to the opponent his own definitions of 'thought' and 'language', thus casting away the wheat with the chaff (language or thought along with reflexivity, the theoretical, intentionality, etc.), instead of criticizing such reductions themselves. But even Merleau-Ponty, the inspirer of many sociological formulations on this question, accepted the fact that there was nothing to be felt or perceived outside of language, and that the latter was not simply a synonym for reflexive activity. He thus freed the question of language from the intellectualist conceptions that he opposed. In a lecture on Husserl he said that 'language is "interwoven" [*verflochten*] with our horizon upon the world and humanity', that it 'is borne by our relation to the world and to others', but also that 'it supports and creates it' (Merleau-Ponty, 1970, pp. 117–18).

As evidence of the empirical and interpretative blindness to which the model of silent embodiment leads, we can take the example of the sociological commentaries on the embodiment of the boxing trade that rest on this conception which misses and ignores the language of its object of study. Or rather, having dismissed language once and for all (along with intellectualism), the sociologist no longer sees that a good part of the data on which his sociological interpretation is based is constituted of language data produced by respondents either in a situation (when they train, fight in public, discuss among themselves before matches, during breaks or in informal moments in the life of the club, etc.) or outside of a situation (in the context of conversation), and that such 'data' are equally indispensable (which does not mean 'in the same fashion') for the reader seeking to understand pugilistic practice as for the boxer embodying his trade. Without making language the first element of internalization, as Berger and Luckmann do,[3] we can note that the social world of boxing can only be integrated through a series of practices that are indissociably both corporeal and linguistic.[4] It is possible in this way to reconstitute the different types of language to which the author constantly refers, almost without being aware.

The approach criticized here always starts by distinguishing itself from semiological or linguistic analyses, those that dwell on the study of the body as object of discourse, etc., and insisting that the acquisition of a 'specific bodily sensitivity' in pugilistic practice cannot be realized simply by an 'act of will' or a 'conscious transfer of information' (who would imagine that?), but rather by an 'imperceptible embodiment of the mental and physical schemata immanent in pugilistic practice', which does not admit any 'discursive mediation or systematization'.[5] But it is only by an abuse of language that expressions such as 'discursive mediation' and 'systematization' can be presented as semantic equivalents. This is to ignore completely the various types of use of language, from the mere punctuation of practice through to the most complex formalization, via all those forms of discourse that organize, describe, analyse and comment on practice. Elsewhere we read that it is not possible to box 'on paper' (Wacquant, 1989, p. 56). And yet if boxing, a bodily activity *par excellence*, is not learned verbally or in books, this does not mean that it is learned without the mediation of language. Everything indicates that the embodiment of the habits of the boxer's trade is not effected in a kind of silent body-to-body negotiation.

First of all, there is no embodiment of the habits of the 'trade' without learning its words. In the boxing world, as elsewhere, the meaning (and use) of a series of words of action is learned bit by bit, along with the nouns that denote the essential gestures (e.g. 'sparring', 'jab', 'hook', 'shadow boxing', 'upper cut', 'feint', 'guard', 'find your distance', etc.) and the names of objects (e.g. gloves, medicine bag, punchball, wristband, tooth guard), roles ('sparring partner'), times ('round') and places ('gym', 'ring') that are a regular part of practice.

Though the fight is a situation of practical urgency, it is not wanting in language – quite the contrary. This is not polite conversation between the opponents, of course, but the language of the trainers that punctuates the fight, tries to correct the boxer's gestures and positions while the fight is under way, encourages the boxer, reminds him of essential things that he might forget in the heat of the action, comments on punches, demands certain ones, etc. It is also a way of bringing the boxer back to a lucidity that he might have lost in the fight: 'Turn this shoulder, come on, keep the chin in, step in with the jab, chin's too high, gimme a good slot, come on, keep them hands up, keep them hands up' (Wacquant, 1995a, p. 72): '"Hands in the air, Louie, hands in the air", Smithie shouts' (Wacquant, 1991, p. 29). Commentaries that rub things in and advice coming from immediate expertise are delivered in each pause between rounds. These are also the occasion for encouragement and motivation: '"You're too far away, you need to go two steps forward. Block his right and get in closer. Tighten your wrist and don't tense up, you're doing fine ..." "Breathe deep, one more time. Go for it, Louie, we'll win this round"' (ibid., p. 30). And then there are words of commentary when the fight is over, in preparation for future matches: '"Remember to keep your left hand higher, Keith, when you get out of infighting. You're still taking too many hits." After an injury to his hand interrupted a promising career, Butch stood in as a spontaneous technical adviser: "A hitter who charges at you like Torres, you let him come and counter him with dry jabs. Aim at the neck and hit as if you were trying to get past him"' (ibid., p. 18).

During training as well as during the fight, language helps to embody (give meaning to, improve . . .) the experiences one has. Analogy is used to denote the classic linkages of gestures: '"The left hook and the straight right go together like husband and wife", explains Eddie, the second trainer in the hall' (Wacquant, 1991, p. 17); positions, gestures, rhythms are all roughly corrected ([the boxer working on the medicine ball] "Hit it to me! And give me a right behind" ... "Move your head, for chrissake! It's not a bag you've got there, Louie, it's a man!" growls DeeDee. "How many times have I got to tell you you've gotta think. *Think! It's your head you box with!*"' (ibid.)). More generally, only discourse can order experiences, place them in a hierarchy, ascribe them their respective values: 'Forget the ring; it's in the anonymous and everyday penumbra of the training hall, both refuge and workshops, that the fighter is forged ... "You win your fight in the gym," the veterans keep repeating' (ibid., p. 16). And it is impossible to deduce, from a reminder of the kind: 'You're not in a social club, here, you're at work' (ibid., p. 18) the idea that the boxer's trade functions without discursive mediation.

If the infighting during the match is not itself lacking in linguistic mediations, it is preceded and followed by times that are less 'pressing', when commentaries circulate, typical stories and anecdotes that recall the values of the trade, its rules, the discipline it imposes, etc. Words then also frame the experience of the boxer that continues outside the 'gym': '"Being a boxer is a trade that keeps you at it twenty-four hours of the day. You have to have it always in your head. You can't do anything else if you want to do it well"' (Wacquant, 1991, p. 15), recalling the diet the boxer has to keep to, relate the difficulty experienced in relation to the sexual abstinence required for three weeks before the match, and repeat this demand or advise respect for hours of sleep: 'But the sacrifice does not begin or end at the doors of the hall. "Work at the gym is only half the story. The other half is discipline: eat properly, go to bed early, get up the morning for your job, leave women alone, and all the rest – take care of your body, ok." Food, sleep, sex: the holy trinity of the pugilistic order' (ibid., p. 21). '[The club trainer] storms: "Being hungry is nothing! It's in your head, it doesn't exist – once and for all." ... Shanti reminds me: "Leave your woman alone now, Louie, you're only three weeks from the match"' (ibid.). Discourse also comments on the – unfortunate – cases when certain boxers break the rules: '"That sex, it's a monster, man. It kills you, I tell you because I've tried." ... "It's a crying shame. Fred, he was a bloody good boxer. He's tough, he punches, and he knows how to take it. But he's too fond of girls"' (ibid.). Mythical discourses abound about sexual abstinence and the connection between sexual relations and loss of strength and energy: '"When you come, you lose blood from the vertebral column"' (ibid.). It's also in informal conversation in the gym that more general knowledge is embodied about the morphology of boxers (type of musculature, height, weight, etc.):

'The fit between bodily capital and style is suggested in this excerpt from a gym conversation in which a noted manager talks about a tall and filiform fighter known for his quickness and reach but lacking in bodily strength' (Wacquant, 1995a, p. 69).

Words give meaning to the corporeal experiences and sufferings experienced or expected: 'Becoming a boxer, preparing for a fight, is like going into a monastery. *Sacrifice!* The word constantly recurs in the mouth of the old coach DeeDee, who is well acquainted with the subject' (Wacquant, 1991, p. 14). The same goes for the first fight, which is surrounded by discourse aiming to prepare and give meaning to the event: '"Your first fight, you've got two opponents, the guy opposite and then the crowd. Sometimes you're so impressed that you don't know any more what to do. That's how I lost my first two amateur matches. I was so depressed afterwards that I wanted to give it up"' (ibid., p. 23).

Like the embodying of habits bound up with the practice of boxing, studies of other corporeal practices establish the polymorphic and multifunctional presence of language. On close examination, therefore, language (the great variety of language games) is just as omnipresent in the apprenticeship of dance (Faure, 1994): the naming of steps, positions and gestures, the use of metaphors and analogies, pedagogic and/or scholarly explanations (anatomical and physiological, in particular), various kinds of verbal remonstration, congratulation and correction, video recordings with commentary, counting to make sure of rhythm, etc. The body of the dancer is itself constantly objectified in the work of embodying sensory-motor habits. Use of video or the mirror to objectify one's body in movement and note 'faults' or clumsy gestures, looking at others as doubles of oneself in order to correct oneself, explicit verbal or corporeal correction on the part of teachers, the use of dance manuals in which 'good' and 'bad' bodily positions are shown, or again the regular objectification of the body and control of its movement by frequent weighings – this all contributes to taking the body as the specific object of attention and concern, and to objectify it in the very process of embodiment.

We can then note that researchers often crudely confuse 'discursive mediation' or 'language' with 'verbal', 'formal' or 'rational' explanation, 'commentary on practice', 'theory or reflection on practice', etc., broadly sharing here the common sense of the actors themselves, who often see 'talking' or 'conversing' as 'doing nothing'. Speech or language, when referred to by certain actors, are immediately conceived as autonomous periods of time opposed to practice ('When you talk, you're doing nothing', said a skilled worker that we interviewed:

'Enough chatting! Down to work!', you can hear in a workshop where two workers are having a discussion by the coffee machine), and never as elements totally embodied in the action, work, activity itself (Sharrock and Watson, 1990).

Researchers who do not question this conception of common sense reformulate in more scholarly language, but without questioning them, the same erroneous conceptions ('without discursive mediation'). The same goes for the salt-cutters studied by Geneviève Delbos and Paul Jorion, who claim that their fathers 'never spoke' to them: 'I sometimes asked him: "Why do you cut here rather than there? And why now?" Things like that. My father never spoke . . ." But he certainly did, no doubt to explain, but certainly to reproach and forbid' (1984, p. 126). There is again here a confusion between 'speech' and 'explanation', while the latter can include orders, prohibition, reproach or commentary outside the practice of the trade: 'The trade is not learned only in the practical conditions of its exercise, it is also learned from everything that happens in daily life, a chance conversation discussing it or something quite different, for example' (ibid., p. 140). There is also a question of focusing or dividing up. One can always focus on a silent moment of activity, a wordless scene, with no verbal intervention of any kind. But it is necessary to widen the frame slightly, or relocate the scene in a longer timeframe, to establish that, if people don't speak in the throes of action (which is not always the case), they often speak before or after.

The punctuation of action and its theorization

Far from being the first form of linguistic exchange, conversation as an autonomous and specific activity, detached from other social activities, is only a very particular mode of use of language. Language is very often inserted and embedded in the course of action, helping to advance it, modify it, etc., but not extricated (or extricable) from gestures, motions, movements, and the like. It can be 'an auxiliary and a marker of action' – in other words, 'a means of attracting attention to the relevant features of what is happening' (Bruner, 1991, p. 72). And the question is never raised as to what the most practical actions (those of the boxer, the factory worker, the salt-cutter) would be without this linguistic punctuation. In this sense, language is very often a constitutive element of practices, or of an action that would not exist without it. It is not opposed to action, but is in fact one of its motors. To take an example from Basil Bernstein, 'the speech used by members of an army combat unit on manoeuvres', characterized by 'syntactic and lexical options' (1974, p. 124), is indissociable from the manoeuvre itself, which cannot take place and be organized except by this kind of language. The social practice known as a 'manoeuvre' is woven out of specific language practices made up of gestures, shouts, syntactic utterances and a particular vocabulary (you can't carry out a manoeuvre using the specific forms of poetic language). By reducing language to its function as 'commentary' on action, or an 'account' of action, you end up no longer seeing that language is as much 'inside' as 'outside'.

The work of Erving Goffman displays two contradictory tendencies. One of these presses him to absolutize one mode of utilization of language ('In sum, talking is likely to involve the reporting of an event – past, current, future or conditional'; 'All in all . . . I am suggesting that often what talkers undertake to do is not to provide information to a recipient but to present dramas to an audience'; Goffman, 1974, pp. 506, 508). The other leads him to recall that the contexts of activity in which language is inserted are not always conversational:

> Observe, too, that something more than thrusts from the physical world into the spoken one are possible. For quite routinely the very structure of a social contact can involve physical, as opposed to verbal (or gestural) moves. Here such words as do get spoken are fitted into a sequence that follows a non-talk design. A good example is perfunctory service contacts. A customer who comes before a checkout clerk and places goods on the counter has made what can be glossed as a first checkout move, for this positioning itself elicits a second phase of action, the server's obligation to weigh, ring up, and bag. (Goffman, 1981, p. 38)

As against the conversational model that envisages only linguistic exchange, verbal intervention may follow a gesture or an action; it may also trigger non-verbal responses.

Psychologists studying the entry into language have shown well the major role of language as a direct handle on action in the development of the child, including the embodying of sensory-motor skills. Mothers, for example, in the course of their play activities with the child, use language to 'restore joint attention' (Bruner, 1991, p. 179). The same mothers symbolically mark the different stages of action under way and in this manner contribute to shaping the action materially and symbolically. If an action is named by the adult, or the 'end' of an action (the child pulling, pushing, catching . . .) is punctuated by an onomatopoeia indicating to the child the end (and success) of the action ('And then!' 'Ye-es!' 'That's it!' 'Well done!'), it is divided up by the adult, creating discontinuity in the continuous chain of gestures and movements. And it is clear that, in a case such as this, language is not necessarily directly present in the situation, but marks its presence in the implicit categorizations that the adult, providing a framework, indicates to the child by defining the action's beginnings and ends (start to pull/finish pulling; start to push/finish pushing; start to climb/finish climbing, etc.). In a general sense, even before being able to speak, the child is placed in schemes of interaction with the adult, guided by her, and these are indissociable from classical verbal interactions (question/answer; proposition/counter-proposition: proposition/confirmation . . .). There is thus an analogy between types of interaction that are non-verbal ('formats' of exchange, as they are sometimes called in psychology; Garvey, 1974), but structured by adult mediators who are already speaking subjects and who perceive the world – objects, actions, etc. – through the categories of their language, and types of verbal interaction that the child will gradually integrate with the help of these adults. These tutors punctuate the actions of and with the child by linguistic interventions, and in this way give it the means to grasp these (Bruner, 1991).

Moreover, it seems indeed that, by naming actions, series of gestures or 'formats' of activity, and having the child who is able to talk name them ('this is the game of . . .'), their memorizing and future repetition is facilitated (I can do 'this' and 'that', I recognize and know how to reproduce a 'loop', a 'round', a 'square', etc.). The capacities of designation thus make it possible, in certain cases, to contribute to the fixing of habits. In fact, by providing children with a language adapted to activity, adults provide practical means (stenographic and portable, embodiable) that help in organizing and structuring such activity in the future.[6]

But language can also intervene in the mode of recapitulation, commentary or recording/authentification,[7] in the wake of an event or an action, or in the mode of deliberation or planning with the view of an action to accomplish. We have seen this in relation to school, and it can sometimes go as far as formalizing or theorizing practices. How can we imagine that rational thinking could take shape, and establish itself, without the instruments of language (oral, written or graphic)? Without writing, without listing and tabulation, without graphic procedures of counting, algebraic symbols, diagrams, maps or plans of all kinds, rational thinking – whether philosophical, grammatical, logical or scientific – would not exist (Goody, 1977, 1987; Lahire, 1993a).

Language and the forms of social life

> Musical language is not some instrument invented after the fact to fix and communicate to musicians what certain among them have spontaneously imagined. On the contrary, it is this language that has created music. Without it there would be no society of musicians, not even musicians, just as without laws there would be no city and no citizens.
> (Maurice Halbwachs, *The Collective Memory*)

> Men already living in a certain social interdependence (as a result of language, an indispensable precondition).
> (Karl Marx, *Capital*, Vol. 2)

Since language is present at the heart of every practice, every form of social life (in economic practices, as much as in educational, religious or sporting ones), it makes no sense in the end to take it as the *particular* object of sociological investigation (Lahire, 1990). Those who try to do so fall either into a theoretical trap or into a reduction of the question. The trap consists in autonomizing language (or discourse), seeing it as no more than signs, signifying exchanges – languages of fashion, space, architecture, consumption, etc. – in the context of a generalized semiology.[8] The reduction is that made by those who challenge semiology and structuralism – for their failure to take into account the social conditions of use of language – while tacitly accepting the opposition between language and society, the discursive and the social. This is the sociolinguistic or variationist approach, which studies language as a relatively autonomous (sub-)system (from a phonetic, lexical, syntactic, stylistic, etc.) point of view, in which social differences and social interests, etc., are retranslated. It is this position that was formulated very precisely by Pierre Bourdieu and theorized into sociology: 'a structural sociology of language, inspired by Saussure but constructed in opposition to the abstraction he imposes, must take as its object *the relationship between the structured systems of sociologically pertinent linguistic systems and the equally structured systems of social differences*' (1991, p. 54).[9] Whether conceived as orders to be studied separately (the Saussurian conception of language) or as separate orders whose relationship can be studied (the sociolinguistic conception), the social order and the linguistic order are viewed as two distinct and relatively autonomous realities.

Practices of language are not surpluses, add-ons, reflections, superstructures, marginal illustrations, secondary practices in relation to the 'really objective' realities. They do not just complete the materiality of an infrastructure or cement the foundations, the in-itself, of the

Objective, the material, the real that is already there, and we should seek to avoid any metaphor that uses this conception of a 'volatile' symbolism added on to the 'solid'. Language is not merely a veil placed over the 'real' world and determined by it.

Rather, therefore, than making a firm partition between the discursive and the non-discursive, the linguistic and the social, and so on, it is preferable to maintain that no practice, no action, no form of social life exists outside of linguistic practices (discursive practices, if you prefer), which take varying forms (from the interjection to the scientific treatise, by way of more or less informal conversation, news reports, contracts, legal texts, certificates, account books, literary genres, mathematical formulae, lectures, dissertations, trade-union leaflets, exchanges of letters, school exercises) and whose social functions are many. We could say the other way round – i.e. addressing linguists rather than sociologists – that no linguistic or discursive practice is detachable from the forms of social life from which it stems.

Certain formulas of Foucault have helped to obscure this question. By speaking of 'a field of non-discursive practices' (Foucault, 1972, p. 75) to designate variously institutions, economic and pedagogic practices and processes, educational practices or political events (ibid., p. 179), he suggested that these 'realities' were outside of any kind of language. It seems evident, however, that neither economic processes, nor pedagogic practices, nor political events happen outside of linguistic practices (in the first case, practices of accounting, contracts, negotiations, commercial exchanges, bank records, etc.; in the second, exercises, lessons, school textbooks, etc.; in the third, oral or written political speeches, discussions among activists, public debates, posters, etc.). Foucault spoke of particular linguistic practices: discursive practices (major scientific, philosophical, moral, political, discourses) that were based and articulated on fields of practices that were themselves already woven out of linguistic practices, discourses about practices that were not themselves outside of linguistic practices (a sort of meta-discourse).

The mysterious inside

Certainly, language is not simply a means or an instrument analogous to a hammer or a file. Its use is not simply to help communication between minds which to begin with were separately constituted. It is itself constituent.
(Henri Lefebvre, *Critique of Everyday Life*, Vol. 2: *Foundations of a Sociology of the Everyday*)

I would like to suggest that language is not an ordinary tool, but a tool that enters into the very constitution of thinking and social relations. We can see how this point of view is opposed to the Piagetian image of language as an 'idle' system that only relates thought and is just a kind of 'symptomatology'.

(Jérôme S. Bruner, *Le Développement de l'enfant*)

Except at the cost of abandoning any intention to explain human practices scientifically, it is essential to abandon the idea that 'thought', 'psyche', 'mental activity' or 'consciousness' possess some kind of existence anterior to their 'expressions' or 'manifestations'. To say that linguistic activity (in all its forms) is simply the 'expression' of something already formed in consciousness outside of any linguistic instrument, an 'expression' 'making public' in some way an 'internal', 'private' or 'intimate' activity, would be equivalent to maintaining that the tail wags the dog. In fact, internal consciousness only takes shape because it is the consciousness of one individual in relation to others and, as a result, one with the experience of multiple linguistic activities. The linguistic and social character of thought does not appear at a subsequent time:

> The 'Cartesian' (in the Chomskyan sense of the term) conception readily gives the impression that we think in a certain manner *outside of* language, and that we use language as a kind of more or less arbitrary code to externalize what we think. This is to forget that the language in which we communicate is also the language *within* which we think, that we think to a certain extent in words, and often in the same words that we use to communicate our thoughts. (Bouveresse, 1987, p. 68)

The embodying of habits (or schemes of action) that enable us to act in various social contexts is not effected without a 'psychological instrument' (Vygotsky). Spoken or gestural language, writing, mathematical symbols, various graphic procedures (lists, tables, diagrams, maps, plans) – it is by way of these tools, that are appropriated, utilized, manipulated, that we construct our 'intellectual faculties'. The link that Émile Benveniste established between 'linguistic form' and 'thought' (the former being 'not only the condition for transmissibility, but first of all the condition for the realization' of the second; 1971, p. 56) must be conceived more generally as existing between all linguistic processes (oral, gestural, written, graphic, iconic) and the activity of thought. We can thus posit in a radical fashion, following Mikhail Bakhtin, that outside of its construction in a linguistic material (whether this is shout, gesture, speech, writing, graphic representation, etc.), 'consciousness is a fiction' (Bakhtin, 1973, p. 90).

— Scene 2 —

WHAT EXACTLY IS EMBODIED?

Processes of embodiment–internalization

A theory of action would remain incomplete if it were not accompanied by an analysis of the formation and constitution of schemes of action. Yet researchers who speak the language of 'internalization of externality' (or 'the embodying of objective structures') and the 'externalization of internality'[1] have not really given flesh to this dialectic (by ethnographic description and theoretical analysis), so that today it plays more of a rhetorical role in the conceptual economy of theories of the social and a strategic role in opposition to other theories, rather than a genuinely theoretical role aiming at the construction of scientific objects.[2] If sociologists should prove incapable of grasping particularly how the various types of 'disposition', 'scheme', etc. (types of 'habitus'), are constructed by social experience, these terms would lose any heuristic interest and constitute simply one more *asylum ignorantiae* in the history of sociological concepts.

The sociology of education and culture – at least that which is not enclosed in the limits of the school institution or of so-called cultural projects – interested as it is in the different modes of socialization and the different modes of transmission or construction of culture, should be able to contribute to illuminating these processes of social construction of the structures of behaviour and thought. And yet it has for a long time been content to see education (family and school) as simply a means of social reproduction, without describing its specific order and processes. We know that, through socialization in the family, school, etc., the (unequal) order of things is reproduced, but there are few descriptions of the socializing practices themselves, the effective modalities of the various forms of socialization.[3] As Bernstein writes:

> From a certain point of view, 'habitus' is more of a concept that requires a language for its own description and construction, rather than a structural model. It is defined more by its operation and functions than by the specificities that make this or that habitus possible; we are given no rule as to its formation in particular cases, but left with a mere retracing of the realizations of class habitus – which are historically contingent. Everything relating to the processes underlying the different modalities of transmission of habitus is in some sense passed over in silence. Habitus is thus a theory of the specialized subject that lacks a theory able to specify its own construction. (Bernstein, 1992, p. 23)

Bernstein concludes that, if theories of reproduction and resistance do not supply descriptions of the processes by which habitus is constituted, 'this is quite simply because these theories and approaches are not really interested in this kind of description. They simply propose to understand how external relations of power are conveyed by the system; they are not interested in describing the support, but simply in diagnosing its pathology' (ibid.).

Before embarking on the necessary task of describing the modalities of socialization in its very varied forms, however, we can begin by asking how a 'social structure' can be internalized or embodied in the form of 'mental structures'. Saying that 'social structures are embodied' is a metaphor that can rapidly prove an encumbrance when we study the construction processes of schemes of action (sensory-motor, perception, evaluation, appreciation, etc.) (Lahire, 1995a, pp. 285–9). What the child, adolescent and eventual adult embody are not, properly speaking, 'social structures', but rather corporeal, cognitive, evaluative, appreciative, etc., *habits* – i.e. schemes of action, ways of doing, thinking, feeling and saying that are adapted (and sometimes limited) to specific social contexts. They internalize modes of action, interaction, reaction, appreciation, orientation, perception, categorization, etc., by entering step by step into social relations of interdependence with other actors, or by maintaining, through the mediation of other actors, relationships with multiple objects whose mode or modes of use and appreciation they learn.

James Wertsch (1979), for example, shows how children between two and five learn, in their interaction with their mother, to form, control and consolidate their habits in the example of constructing a jigsaw puzzle. First of all the child has to understand that the information provided by his mother relates to the images represented on the pieces of the puzzle and not to the external environment (for example, at the start the child believes that his mother is referring to the window of the room in which they are sitting, whereas she is speaking of the one represented in the puzzle). The child must in some way recognize the right 'language game' (in Wittgenstein's sense) or the right context of activity: 'doing a puzzle'. He then shows himself capable of realizing the action demands explicitly formulated by his mother, but not yet those that are implicit, which would assume he is able to interpret beyond the words, by mastering the overall strategy of completing the puzzle. Finally, the child gradually takes in hand 'the strategic responsibility for the task' and moves on to an egocentric language (addressing to himself the questions that his mother had asked him to help her with in doing the puzzle), while the mother now only has to intervene verbally to confirm the relevance of the choice, support the effort undertaken, etc., and thus definitively consolidate the habits now incorporated.

Here, then, we have an example of internalization or embodiment that makes clear the transition from the inter-psychic to the intra-psychic, as the child's internalization of a definition of the context of action ('doing a jigsaw puzzle'), of ways of proceeding in order to reach the desired result, of the (right) questions to ask himself in order to succeed with the task, etc. Helped by the adult, the child internalizes the questions, gestures and strategic procedures that he uses so as eventually to manage to do by himself (autonomously) what he had previously done under tutelage. The adult frames and channels the task, indicates and attracts the child's attention, then asks questions, reduces his field of freedom, explains or defines the task step by step, point after point, supports and comforts him when he fails, guides him when he takes a wrong turning, encourages and rewards him when he succeeds (see also Bruner, 1991). The child, for his part, sustains his effort with the perspective of gratifications – positive sanctions – that he may obtain from those around him. The desire soon to be able to do it himself, 'like a grown-up', which remains for the time being inaccessible, and the identification with a (positive) future image of himself (to 'see himself there') are also far from negligible as motives in the work of constructing habits (Delbos and Jorion, 1984, p. 129). What is embodied or internalized does not exist as such in the 'external' social world, but is reconstructed bit by bit, for each individual, in the repeated interactions that he has with other actors, by way of particular objects or in particular social situations. The child internalizes not the 'social world' or the 'objective structures of the social world', but rather schemes of action (schemes of perception or categorization, sensory-motor skills, strategic schemes . . .) which enable him to 'use' a jigsaw puzzle or resolve a problem (such as how to put it together).

The same holds for the child's construction of tastes in reading. What the child likes to do alone, what she is able to do alone, is simply the internalization of activities that were previously guided or done by others. For example, since Marion, aged eight, was very young, her parents (computer programmer and social security employee) had read her stories not just in the evenings but also at breakfast, which is rather uncommon. In fact, as Marion was reluctant to eat in the morning, the habit caught on of reading her stories to encourage her. After internalizing these moments of reading done by her parents, Marion now reads every evening by herself (20 to 25 minutes) and in the mornings over breakfast (Lahire, 1995d, pp. 72–89).

Besides, the idea of an 'inscription of social structures in the brain' masks the processes by which not 'social structures' but relations to the social world and to others, ways of acting in particular situations, with others and with objects, are gradually embodied. This impression is strengthened by the metaphors of cultural 'transmission' (the 'transmission of cultural capital') or cultural 'inheritance' (the 'inheritance of cultural capital'), which are in themselves powerful obstacles in the way of apprehending these phenomena of embodiment. To be aware of this, one need only compare systematically 'material transmission' (material inheritance) with 'cultural transmission' (non-material inheritance).

1 To 'transmit' a material inheritance to someone is to give them a thing that the giver possessed until then and that passes in this way from one owner to another. What magical quality does 'transmission' then have when it is cultural, so that, when the 'transmission' is accomplished, the initial owner remains in possession of what was 'transmitted'? As against all forms of material inheritance, where finite stocks of material units are divided between different owners and can never belong to everyone at once, cultural inheritance in its embodied form has the original feature that it can be 'transmitted' from one owner to another without the former being obliged to diminish their share of the stock of embodied schemes. To give to someone else in this case means enriching them without impoverishing oneself. If there are culturally 'rich' and 'poor' (not everyone 'knows' everything or how to do everything), the economy of 'cultural transmission' is unfamiliar with either impoverishment, loss or dilapidation.

WHAT EXACTLY IS EMBODIED?

2 In the transmission of a material inheritance, the latter remains unchanged during the process of transmission, as well as when the transmission has been completed (e.g. a painting by Degas or a piece of furniture remains, apart from the material wear and tear that may be occasioned, identical to itself at whatever the moment in the process it is considered). Once again, a strangeness of 'cultural transmission' is that culture is never 'transmitted' identically, but rather distorted as a function of the conditions of its transmission and the social relationship established between the person who already 'knows' and the one who does not. The embodied culture is not 'poured out' but rather appropriated and transformed (cf. in particular Singly, 1996). The person who embodies social dispositions, habits, ways of seeing, feeling and acting, appropriates gestures, practical or theoretical reasonings, ways of saying or feeling, etc., according to what they are already – i.e. according to their existing stock of habits embodied in the course of their previous social experiences. The metaphor of 'cultural inheritance' (or 'cultural transmission') elides the inescapable distortions, adaptations and reinterpretations that the 'cultural capital' experiences in the course of its reconstruction from one generation to the next, from one adult to another, etc., under the effect, on the one hand, of the gaps between the supposed 'transmitters' and 'receivers' and, on the other hand, of the (contextual) conditions of this reconstruction.

Sometimes, indeed, the processes of 'transmission' may get muddled for various reasons, and its success prevented. The bearers of the embodied culture may not be in a position to assist others to construct certain elements of this culture in their turn. They do not have the dispositions available. This is the case, for example, with a number of embodied cultural dispositions which cannot always find conditions for their actualization in the family world, given its absorption (in terms of time and mental investment) by the world of work. It is also the case with family situations which render the child unavailable or indisposed to enter into the process of construction (e.g. difficulty with the exercise of parental authority, 'psychological' blockage bound up with repeated traumatizing experience or with the internalization of an unhappy relationship to this or that kind of situation, practice or knowledge).

3 A material inheritance can be 'transmitted' in a relatively short space of time (the time of transfer from the giver to the beneficiary, which is sometimes even immaterial). Cultural 'transmission', for its part, is most often a matter of time, repetition and exercise, as

it involves the gradual establishment of habits in the body, whether these are mental or gestural, sensory or intellectual. According to the habits in question, this time may be longer or shorter: short – but not without the need for repetition on the part of the child – in the case of the simple gestures of everyday life (pull, push, swing, take, grasp . . .), but sometimes very long for complex habits of reasoning (mathematical or philosophical), the specialized habits of trades (such as those of watchmakers or carpenters) or moral habits (modesty, asceticism or loyalty are not improvised from one day to the next).

4 A notable difference bound up with the former one is that the transmission of a material inheritance may be effected independently of the feeling that the beneficiary has towards it, whereas cultural transmission has to rely on the desire to construct habits, a desire that is particularly required to support and encourage effort when the transmission is a matter of several months or years. As a stockman cited by Denis Chevallier and Isaac Chiva says about learning the trade of shepherd: 'The desire for the mountains comes if the child has been nourished with it at home; they have to hear them spoken about, they have to see how it is done; then they look forward to having fine cows and sheep. And you say to them: "Up in the mountains they grow well, and it's you who will look after them." That is how you make shepherds' (Chevallier and Chiva, 1991, p. 1).

But we could also mention here the musical-affective programme that Leopold Mozart, joint head of the Salzburg orchestra, set up for his son Wolfgang. From his third year of age, the child was subjected to a rigorous work regime, an implacable discipline based on the regular exercises composed by his father. Very soon, his life was essentially reduced just to music. But if Wolfgang continued to keep to the severe programme imposed on him, it was because his father was also able to weave ties of affection with him which constantly passed through music. As Norbert Elias writes, Wolfgang 'was rewarded for each musical achievement with a big prize in terms of affection. This undoubtedly favoured the child's development in the direction desired by his father' (Elias, 1993, p. 57). If 'each sign of musical talent in his son delighted the father' (ibid., p. 75), we can understand how, for Mozart at an early age, attracting the admiration, love and joy of his father presupposed playing music and progressing musically.

5 The transmission of a material inheritance is always conscious, and the person transmitting or bequeathing it knows what the content of the legacy or inheritance transmitted is. A large part of culture,

on the other hand, is 'transmitted' unknowingly both to the 'transmitters' ('donors') and to the 'receivers' ('heirs'). Although formal situations of teaching themselves involve an 'underground transmission', they privilege the explicit pedagogic transmission of objectified knowledge contents. But not all situations of 'cultural transmission' follow this model of formal and explicit transmission, of knowledge that is itself explicit. In certain cases, the child (or adult) is led to construct habits, dispositions, knowledge and know-how in socially organized contexts, without there being a really 'express' (voluntary, intentional) 'transmission'.

Thus in many informal situations of learning a trade, what is 'transmitted' is not 'knowledge' but rather 'work' or 'experience', as Geneviève Delbos and Paul Jorion showed in the case of the salt-cutters: 'But what does the child see? His father and mother at work in the marsh. He sees people working, he does not see any "knowledge" or "skills"; these are either communicated or abstract, in the latter case by a specific work' (Delbos and Jorion, 1984, p. 128). There is the same invisibility of 'knowledge' in the appropriation of jobs by semi-skilled workers in a firm manufacturing and assembling refrigerators (Lahire, 1993e; 1993b, pp. 33–56). To listen to these workers talk of the way that they 'suddenly' entered their job, without any preparation whatsoever, one might believe that no technical competence was required, that it was chiefly a question of having (or not having) a pragmatic disposition ('being able to work things out' or 'muddling through'). When knowledge and know-how are not objectified, but on the contrary indissociable from the people (the bodies) who apply them, learning can only be conducted in a mimetic fashion (watching and copying) and in an interpersonal relationship. The important thing is concentrating on what you are doing and not 'having your head somewhere else'. Knowledge is not apparent as such, and the workers themselves consider their work as 'not complicated'.

Analysis of these work situations can be repeated in connection with a large number of situations of socialization (families in particular), where what children encounter is not contents of knowledge to be appropriated but rather forms of activity, gestural or linguistic habits, etc. Of course, the child constructs her 'cognitive structures' by way of her insertion in these multiple forms of social life (and language games), but she does not engage in these practices in order to 'learn', 'build up knowledge' or 'construct knowledge and know-how'.

Children, moreover, can always constitute 'undesirable' dispositions (moral or cultural), given the place that they occupy in the configuration of family relations of interdependence, without anyone having wanted or desired this. Anxieties, complexes, discouragement or inhibition in the face of certain situations, low self-esteem, mental and sensory-motor blockages, anxious relations towards certain tasks, etc. – all this can also be 'transmitted' and disturb or make difficult other mental and physical constructions.

The metaphor of 'internalization–incorporation of social structures'[4] is as little relevant as that of saying that the child learns her 'native tongue': except when she is well disposed towards language in a school situation, as we have seen, with lexical, orthographic, grammatical, stylistic, etc., rules, the child who learns to speak embodies not a 'language', a 'code' or a 'linguistic structure', but schemes of verbal interaction, types of verbal exchange and modes of use of language.[5] To use Wittgenstein's terminology, we could say that this is a typical situation of linguistic pathology.

If what are called 'objective structures' or 'social structures' are in this case rather scientific constructions of reality based in most cases on statistical data ('scientifically apprehended as possibilities' [Bourdieu, 1990b, p. 90] and constructed by the social sciences 'through statistical regularities such as the probabilities objectively attached to a group or class' [Bourdieu, 1990a, p. 54]), it is hard to see how actors could embody these 'objective structures' and how they could then be reproduced, converted and transfigured into 'mental' or 'cognitive' structures (reconstructed on the basis of direct or indirect observation of practices). 'Objective structures' and 'mental structures' are not two different realities, one (mental structures) being the product of the internalization of the other (objective structures), but rather two apprehensions of one and the same social reality. Descartes already warned against the error of taking a formal distinction between two attributes of the same substance, or between a substance and its attributes, as a real distinction between two substances, and Nietzsche recalled that, while lightning is simply a manifestation of thunder, we customarily think that thunder and lightning are two different phenomena and that the first is the cause of the second.[6] A tendency is thus often observable in sociology 'not to make two things into one, but rather one thing into two' (Rosset, 1995, pp. 37–8).

WHAT EXACTLY IS EMBODIED?

The polymorphic embodiment of written culture in the world of the family

I began my life as I shall no doubt end it: among books. In my grandfather's study, they were everywhere; it was forbidden to dust them except once a year, before the October term. Even before I could read, I already revered these raised stones; upright or leaning, wedged together like bricks on library shelves or nobly spaced like avenues of dolmens, I felt that our family prosperity depended on them.

(Jean-Paul Sartre, *Words*)

No, I had no headache, but until the age of six, I was no longer allowed to enter a classroom or open a book, for fear of a cerebral explosion.

(Marcel Pagnol, *My Father's Glory*)

Study was a penance forced on me to obtain a good position and not marry a worker. But the fact that I liked to rack my brains struck him as suspicious. A lack of life at this tender age. He sometimes seemed to believe I was unhappy. . . . He said that I learned well, never that I worked well. Working could only mean working with your hands.

(Annie Ernaux, *La Place*)

Certain particular features of 'cultural transmission' can be observed in the case of the various forms of appropriation by the child, within the world of the family, of a multiform culture of writing (read or produced). In connection with two studies of primary-school children from socially differentiated families (differentiated economically and culturally), one of fifteen children aged from eight to ten (Lahire, 1995d) and the other of fifteen children of ten and eleven (Lahire, 1995e), I sought to grasp the modalities of intergenerational relationship that the written text (writing and reading) solicited.

The object was to reconstitute the contexts of usage, the functions and representations of writing, within a range of socially different families. The children's mental and bodily constructions relative to writing within the family world involved both tastes and distastes, social roles, social functions linked with the various practices of writing and reading (e.g. aesthetic, documentary, practical, etc., functions of the activity of reading, or mnemonic, calculatory, planning, checking, identity, play, etc., functions of practices of writing), as well as diverse contextual norms (e.g. learning to first make a draft or to correct spelling mistakes, in letters destined for a linguistic market that was particularly fraught . . .).

Concerning the social functions and representations bound up with the various practices of writing, it emerged that children can internalize very early on – before and even outside of any act of writing or reading – the 'reasons' for or 'context' of resort to the written word. To take one example, Audrey (eleven years old, father a fork-lift truck operator, mother a teaching assistant) shows by what she says that she has understood well the checking function of the list of things to take away on holiday. In a similar vein, Salima (eleven years old, father a building worker, mother a housewife) is particularly able to explain the different reasons for resort to domestic writing: she remarks that written memos are useful when you leave the area of regular things and remembering is no longer automatic; she contrasts dates that are remembered without special effort, thanks to regular, embodied memory, with those that demand recourse to an objectified support; she also explains very clearly how the list of things to do for school enables her to know where she's got to, to organize her time, to check things have been done, to have the sense of going forward (by noting what has been done), and possibly postponing what she has to do. Pierre-Étienne (eight years old, father an anaesthetist and mother an ophthalmologist) kept a diary for two weeks in order to note in a very detailed manner everything he had done each day; Akim (ten years old, father a truck-driver and mother a housewife) learned to note the dates of his football matches in a diary. In terms of reading, Marion (eight years old, father a computer programmer and mother employed by the Social Security) or Clémentine (eight years old, father an engineer and mother a teacher of classics), among others, hear their parents talk about their books and discover in this way the particular modality of relationship to books that is commented reading, hermeneutic reading that leads to discussion and invites the sharing of opinions.

It emerges from the two studies that children in the family enter the world of writing in different ways, which produce their socializing effect only in their particular combination. There may be first of all explicit and quasi-pedagogic parental incentives and solicitations: an almost school-like teaching of reading and writing (sometimes with the help of school textbooks), explicit learning of intellectual techniques and strategies (e.g. making a draft when you have to write a letter, re-reading it to correct spelling mistakes, copying a lesson in order to learn it, using the dictionary . . .), invitations to write texts during the school holidays to get into the habit of relating one's own experience, express requests for the child to take down written messages when she picks up the phone, verbal explanations to make the child understand the advantage of resort to memos or the calendar to prepare her activities and not to forget important things to be done, or constant solicitations to reading (giving books as presents, a subscription to a magazine, taking the child regularly to the library, reading her stories, asking questions on what she is reading, asking her to read aloud, etc.).

Entry into the written word is also carried out by various kinds of direct collaboration and participation in practices of writing and reading to which children are invited (and sometimes forced). Children may contribute to drawing up shopping lists or lists of things to take on holiday, by noting things down themselves, by asking adults to do this for them, or by writing under the parents' dictation; they may be able to take charge of the list in the supermarket, to check what still has to be bought (sometimes crossing off items that are already in the cart), gradually enter a culture of exchange of letters (from the minimum mark of entry into this culture constituted by their signature, to a few words added at the end of their parents' letters), take part in drawing up a holiday itinerary, help their parents to organize and comment on family photographs, make their contribution in labelling video cassettes, and so on. As far as practices of reading are concerned, children can help their mother in cooking by reading the instructions from a written recipe, read comic strips or stories with their parents, hunt out with them elements for a school project to be done, consult magazines with them on a subject bound up with holidays of cultural outings, etc. In many cases, they participate in this way in their parents' activities of writing and reading, joining these in the mode of 'help' or 'equal' participation, but undoubtedly learning about the activity, its functions and its context in general, as well as the role that is given to them. Before being able to do these things 'by themselves', children thus learn about activities and contexts that imply the use of the written word; they close in on these. Thanks to these various kinds of collaboration, they are able to master their functions and contexts of use long before taking charge of them personally.[7]

Children may also try to 'see themselves doing it' – i.e. see themselves already 'grown-up' – by imitating roles, attitudes and practices that are characteristic of their parents. And as family practices of reading and writing are very clearly articulated to the sexual division of tastes, habits, roles and tasks, associating women particularly strongly with the written word (Lahire, 1993b, 1993d, 1995b, 1997b), these imitations of regular parental behaviour are indissociable from the identification with gendered adult roles (to do what mummy or daddy do – which can also mean not doing certain things). Parents thus describe the various regular situations of imitation of their own gestures, mannerisms or manias as readers or writers. Children may also amuse themselves with role games that imply writing: playing 'schoolteacher' (a woman, rarely a man), 'shopkeeper' (likewise, generally a woman), 'doctor' (a man, not a woman) or 'librarian' (again, a woman).

Finally, children embody functions, representations, and certain specific cognitive and organizational effects of the written word by indirect and diffuse impregnation – i.e. by a whole family atmosphere rather than by specific acts of writing or reading (solicited or explained, undertaken as collaborator, observed and imitated). Whether it is explicit styles of speech that are lexically and syntactically articulated to habits of written discourse, semantic discussion (about the meaning of words), grammatical (or syntactic) correction, literary or philosophical (which gives those hearing them evidence of the hermeneutic modes of reading), logical or mathematical styles of reasoning (everyday mention of notions of proportion, contradiction, etc.) or styles of domestic organization, relations to time or to order (bound up with the use of writing for organizing and planning . . .), the written word quite indirectly imposes its subliminal presence through various attitudes and practices on the part of adults.

When the world of the family offers a pedagogic stimulus, letting the child participate in activities that require reading and writing, providing convenient practical models of identification to give the child the desire to imitate, to 'do like', and generally 'diffusing' cognitive or organizational effects bound up with the parents' own embodiment of a culture of the written word, then children are in ideal conditions for building up skills, representations and tastes for writing and reading. The combination of these different ingredients is encountered only in families with a particularly well-established access to school and writing. In fact, children whose grandparents and/or parents are more or less illiterate or have difficulties with the written word stand in great contrast with those whose parents, grandparents and, sometimes, several earlier generations not only are or were literate, but underwent an extensive educational trajectory.

Children who discover the world of school as a relatively new and foreign world depend most completely on the school to appropriate the elements of a written culture. When they manage to do so, they often succeed by dint of the written culture of the school rather than a written culture of the family, which may be completely non-existent. In all these cases, mothers who take responsibility for integrating the written culture of the school into the family world are like missionaries or combatants of the school culture of the written word. When the family world is not 'naturally lettered' – i.e. has not already been 'lettered' for a long time – children always resist parental injunctions to a greater or lesser degree.[8] It is sometimes hard for children deprived of a 'lettered' family environment to conceive reading as an extra-curricular activity, something not associated with work. When her contact with the written word (writing or reading) is almost exclusively in the context of school (to be specific, when the only books in the home are school books), it is really difficult for the child to envisage reading or writing other than in the form of school *work*. Despite all the efforts that her parents may make to 'make her like it', to 'push her to like' what they do not like themselves,[9] love of reading always remains a rather forced love, a marriage of reason rather than a marriage of the heart (the child prefers, for example, to receive something other than books as presents).

When the parents do not offer practices of reading and writing that could play the role of examples for the child, the only solution for them thus lies in focusing their attention and educational energy on school activities. Unable to rely on the force of family habit in terms of written culture (sometimes almost non-existent) or on transfers that would lead from family practices towards the world of school, they therefore directly follow the practices of the school world in a kind of primitive accumulation of educational capital. When the educational energy of the family focuses on school practices, educational behaviour is never the behaviour of capitalists confident in themselves, but rather that of adventurers building up what they do not yet have. Sometimes, when those in this process of constituting an educational capital obtain good results, there is no longer even any sense of limits to the work of accumulation, the point at which it comes to an end. One never knows whether calling a halt, relaxing tension and attention, might not be fatal for the educational trajectory. Children from this kind of family configuration who succeed at school are with equal fatality pure products of the educational system, since they depend on it more completely in order to succeed than does any child whose family culture of the written word, on account of its long-established character, is wider than the written culture of school.

If this school culture has precociously penetrated the world of the family, educational success even becomes a major precondition for the emotional economy of both individual and family. One can thus sense with the mothers of Julien (eight years old, father a skilled worker and mother a nurse) or Nadège (eight years old, father a delivery man and mother a hospital orderly) a kind of identification with the school that leads them, on the one hand, to bring the school home (taste for reading books, help with homework, additional school exercises, holiday tasks, correctional habits in matters of language, etc.) and, on the other hand, to besiege the school itself (treating the teacher as a member of the family, often going to talk with her at the end of the school day, offering to help with school projects and events . . .).

At the opposite extreme from those families focused on educational practices, who can conceive their children's practices of reading and writing only in a school context, we have those families where several generations have completed secondary school or university, who have totally embodied the school culture, appropriated it in their own fashion, and can thus allow themselves to live a more relaxed relationship with the world of primary school: families in which parental reading is diverse and varied (from newspapers to books, via magazines and comics),[10] where more legitimate readings have been selected and others rejected, where the parents talk about their books and sometimes even take part in book-related social activities (reading groups, library exchanges) and where, finally, reading goes beyond the context of school and is integrated into the most everyday moments of family life to become a fundamental family value, a central cultural option. These same families offer their children frequent practices of writing, from the most pragmatic to the most formal, the most utilitarian to the most aesthetic. A mother (a housewife whose husband, a lawyer, heads a law firm of ten persons) even says that she feels more at ease with writing than speech to express her thoughts, thus reversing the customary order of facilities.[11] For children living in family environments such as this, writing and reading are family realities before being experienced as school ones. They may have internalized the desire to correspond in writing, taking the initiative in writing their first letter where other children do this only at school, writing stories and poems, keeping notebooks during the summer holidays, etc. Sometimes they have internalized the pleasure of receiving books as presents or consulting dictionaries and encyclopedias.

Fathers and mothers thus act both as intermediaries and as models of identification in the matter of written culture. Everything that underlies the world of school is already broadly embodied in the world of the family in the form of habits of life, taste, style of conversation, relationship to language (orthographic control and vigilance are integrated into the practices of correspondence, meta-linguistic reflexivity on vocabulary is exercised not only in moments of reading but also in the course of everyday conversation, etc.), cultural options, asceticism and rigour.

But the world of the family may be wanting in all such features favourable to the child's construction of a culture of the written word. This is the case with Damien's family (see note 11, p. 249), where the almost total absence of parental examples (in terms of reading and writing), combined with poor educational capital and a weak belief in the value of educational practices, leads to incentives that are objectively negative (not deliberately or intentional). Thus we observe in this family the effect of negative parental attitudes and dispositions towards reading and writing. Damien's parents have neither the disposition (formed more in the perspective of increasing economic capital: they refer to themselves as 'manual' rather than 'intellectual' and implicitly criticize the ephemeral character and futility of cultural production as against economic advantage) nor the time needed for this kind of missionary educational energy.

Negative identifications and the force of implicit injunctions

Far from simply being the product of very explicit parental inventive and solicitation, and more generally of the educational intentions of adults, children often construct themselves between formulated injunctions and the wider contexts in which these injunctions are uttered. Such contexts themselves constitute a kind of implicit injunction, unspoken but readily apparent. When the explicit injunction is (too greatly and/or too often) contradicted by the implicit injunctions of everyday practice and counter-example, it has very often lost its traction. In such conditions, explicit parental injunction has to be particularly strong in order for children to be able to respond to it positively.

I noted the opposition that parents in a working-class situation encounter when they press their children to read without themselves having the taste for or practice of reading. This opposition and resistance is recorded by statistical investigations: 'By comparing young people whose parents read only a little or not at all, but who have encouraged them to read, with young people whose parents read a lot while abstaining from asking them to do the same, it is clear that it is parental example that carries the day' (Singly, 1993c, p. 57). There are little gestures that say more about this – and more effectively – than do words.

There is no need here to mention unconscious forces supposed to circulate mysteriously between parents and children. There is the said and the unsaid, what is said and what is done ('Do as I say, not as I do'), the conscious and the unconscious: parents who incite – sometimes even with heavy sanctions – without being in a position to give an example, who make demands without always being able to check that these are satisfied, who occasionally assert principles without deploying the whole series of little everyday tactics that would force or lead children to apply them spontaneously, or who wage a daily battle to try and impose on children habits that are constantly put in question by the weight of things, by the counter-examples of the material and social context (e.g. keep the environment clean and don't damage the urban space, when this is constantly dirty and in bad condition).[12]

The male relationship to the written word, which I have steadily brought to light in the course of a series of studies, is equally revealing about these gaps between explicit and implicit injunctions. As I have already recalled, practices of writing are very strongly feminized within the domestic space. Incentives to read and write thus come most frequently from mothers. But this situation proves problematic for boys, who do indeed have to respond (as children) to repeated maternal incentive (take the time to read, practise your writing, get used to writing letters . . .) but also have to construct their masculine identity, even when their fathers may be absent – totally or in part, according to the social milieu in question – from the terrain of domestic, personal or family writing. Everything happens as if the boy listens to his mother or looks at what she is doing with the subtle distance appropriate to someone learning, as Berger and Luckmann put it, to recognize the 'feminine version' of reality without identifying with it. He then enters into a process of (more or less) negative identification: if (domestic) writing is feminine, since borne essentially by the mother (and when the boy has a sister, the energy that she puts into writing secretly in a personal diary, or writing letters, only reinforces his implicit convictions) and not very popular with the father, then too deep a commitment, too enthusiastic an investment in such practices, will have something suspicious about it. Boys then resist, shirk, sulk, practise a policy of last-minute concession (after repeated reminders or endless insistence from the mother, she succeeds in extracting a signature or a nice word at the bottom of a letter), and at all events only very rarely launch themselves spontaneously into such ambiguous activities (activities of adults, but women's activities). Where a girl can identify fully and gradually make her own, with pleasure, practices that have initially to be solicited – evidence of a complete and successful internalization of habit or disposition – boys may, in the wake of a kind of practical deduction, express their disinterest or insensitivity towards the writing (whether intimate, domestic or familial). They construct their own gendered identity by way of a more or less firm resistance (particularly depending on the degree of domestic desertion by the father) to these types of written word. This means that, as against what is generally believed, disinterest or indifference precedes (and ends up generating) inability or effective incompetence. The case of the relationship of boys to writing has the virtue of recalling how, to take up the words of Max Weber, the child only embodies habits, knowledge, know-how, etc., when its 'interest' in learning is greater than its 'interest' in not learning. This interest (or desire) is constructed in the always complex, and sometimes contradictory, space between explicit and implicit injunctions.

Act IV

Workshops and Debates

Scene 1

PSYCHOLOGICAL SOCIOLOGY

> All sociology is a psychology, but a psychology *sui generis*. I would add that in my belief this psychology is destined to give new life to many of the problems posed at the present time by purely individual psychology and even have repercussions on the theory of knowledge.
> (Émile Durkheim, *Rules of Sociological Method*)

Gradually, without even recognizing it or being in a position to assess its consequences, sociology has come to interest itself in socialized individuals as such, as well as in social groups, structures, contexts and interactions. When the notions (and the realities to which they refer) of 'cognitive' or 'mental' structures, 'schemes', 'dispositions' (or 'habitus'), 'embodiment' and 'internalization' were not themselves the focus of study, but served only, in the accounts of investigations, as transition points needed to account for practices by introducing embodied past socialization, these theoretical models could appear satisfactory. Terms borrowed from psychology (that of Piaget, in particular) made it possible to denote a void or an absence between the objective structures of the social world (grasped statistically) and the (observed) practices of actors.[1] Habitus could then be a feature of a group or a class, as much as of an individual. That did not pose any particular problem, since no specific attention was devoted to it, and the theory did not really propose to study these realities (cognitive, mental, etc.) empirically. This was broadly sufficient for the craft of the sociologist, and no doubt still is so for a large number of researchers. In fact, many sociologists continue to practise sociology without even having any need to give a name to these matrices (cognitive, emotional, corporeal, ideological, cultural, mental, rational, etc.) of behaviours, actions and reactions.

But it was not possible to speak with impunity – without drawing conclusions, and especially without attracting critical attention and questioning from more recent researchers – about 'mental structures', 'cognition', etc. Everything that was accepted at face value and went without saying is now open to reconsideration and questioning: Transposability? Transferability? Dispositional explanation? Cultural inheritance? Transmission of cultural capital? Schemes? A system of dispositions? A generating formula of practices or a unifying principle? Internalization of objective structures? Embodiment of social structures? Rather than presupposing the existence of such socio-cognitive processes (the construction of schemes, systematic analogical transfers and transpositions, the general character of dispositions, their systematic and universal application, the internalization of externality, etc.), rashly short-circuiting the long and laborious series of research activities that it would be useful to undertake, we have to start out again on the paths of contextualized questioning with our sole companions a Cartesian doubt and some results of empirical studies. By universalizing the findings of a certain state of contemporary (Piagetian) psychology (not completely outdated, that goes without saying), we have imported into sociology, in a petrified form and unchanged for two decades, psychological concepts that – like all scientific concepts – were no more than a kind of résumé of the state of some of the most advanced psychological work on the question of childhood development at that time.

The field of a psychological sociology (rather than a social psychology) is thus opened up, something that no one intended but which everyone has gradually contributed to create. To study the individual who crosses different scenes, contexts, fields of force and struggle, etc., is to study social reality in its individualized, embodied, internalized form. How is external diversity made flesh? How can it inhabit a single body? When sociology was content to introduce the individual, actor or agent simply in relation to a singular activity or field of practice (a worker, a father, a spouse, a friend, a reader, a user of this or that cultural institution, a speaking subject, etc.), it could spare itself the study of these individualized social logics. But once the focus is on the individual (not as the atom or basis of all sociological analysis, but as the complex product of multiple socialization processes), it is no longer possible to rest content with the cognitive models used up until now.

The slippage has been gradual and imperceptible: an insensible shift of focus, of scale of contextualization, and everything becomes different (Lahire, 1996a). The entire landscape has altered. Matters would no doubt have been more clear if those who did not privilege the study of 'dispositions' and 'schemes' (mental, cognitive, appreciative, emotional, etc.), their construction and their activation, had not claimed a relevance for their assertions whatever the scale of contextualization (from the largest social group to the most singular individual). We would then have perceived the specific contributions of various people, the relative relevance of different analyses. But the desire for a powerful theory can lead researchers both to reinforce their theories (like besieged fortresses) and to inflect and nuance them with a view to 'keeping control', ready sometimes to say the opposite of what they had previously maintained loud and clear. That is the way of science, its models and its researchers.

An exit from sociology?

Contemporary sociological work often uses expressions such as 'dispositions', 'cognitive' or 'mental' structures, 'interpretative procedures', 'categories of perception' or 'representation', 'ethnomethods', 'stock of knowledge', 'reserve of previous experiences', 'relations to the world' or 'views of the world'. But the authors in question are most often satisfied with presupposing the existence of these 'dispositions' or 'structures' within the actor, rather than actually taking up as a research programme the study of their construction and their possible (but not necessarily systematic) reinvestment in new social contexts. It is not possible without impunity, however, to employ a vocabulary close to that of psychology without at some point triggering the desire, a genuinely sociological one, to subject this to a critical questioning and empirical evaluation – in brief, to examine it more closely. If we bear in mind that sociology, and not just psychology, is concerned to analyse the functioning of these 'little machines' producing behaviours, actions, evaluations, appreciations, choices, etc., that are actors, it is important to equip oneself with adequate conceptual tools for making headway in this domain. One aspect of future sociology, it seems to me, will have to be a concern with the ability to rise to this theoretical and methodological challenge in empirical work.

One might nevertheless believe that 'individual mentality' is not a sociological object but a strictly psychological one (in the broad sense of the term), so that sociologists could draw on the work of psychologists without having to study this question for themselves. This conviction – supported by the common image of sociology as a 'generalist' science of the collective, of social groups or, in the worst case of 'averages', 'average behaviours', etc., and by the same token as a science incapable of seeking to account for individual singularities[2] – sometimes has its roots deep in the Durkheimian conception of a strict division between collective consciousness and individual consciousness:

> In each of us, it may be said, there exist two beings which, while inseparable except by abstraction, remain distinct. One is made up of all the mental states that apply only to ourselves and to the event of our personal lives: this is what might be called the individual being. The other is a system of ideas, sentiments and practices which express in us, not our personality, but the group or different group of which we are part; these are religious beliefs, moral beliefs and practices, national or professional traditions, collective opinions of all kinds. (Durkheim, 1956, pp. 71–2)

This division between two 'individuals' or two 'groups of states of consciousness' (Durkheim, 1987, p. 330) was undoubtedly made originally with the strategic intent of demarcating sociology from psychology (as 'science of the individual mind' [Durkheim, 1982, p. 40]), and to block any attempt to reduce sociology to psychology, to the individual (the social should be explained by the social). There thus remained, according to Durkheim, a psychological or mental 'residue' after the interpretative procedure of the sociologist, a 'residue' that provided the legitimate object of psychology.[3]

Contemporary sociologists, however, so chary sometimes towards the idea of upsetting disciplinary conventions in the way that objects and fields of research are divided up (sometimes based on nothing more than realities of an institutional order), forget the moments at which Durkheim wrote, with greater sociological boldness and less concern not to tread on the discipline of psychology, that 'psychology is also destined to partly renew itself' under the influence of sociological research, 'since if social phenomena penetrate the individual from outside, there is a whole domain of individual consciousness that depends in part on social causes which psychology cannot abstract from without becoming unintelligible' (Durkheim, 1975, p. 35, n. 5), or again that 'the whole of sociology is a psychology, but a psychology *sui generis*. I would add that this psychology is destined, I believe, to refresh many problems that a purely individual psychology, and indirectly even the theory of knowledge, currently presents' (ibid., p. 61). Sociology, in the end, 'leads of itself to a psychology', but a psychology that Durkheim deemed 'more concrete and complex than that practised by the pure psychologists' (ibid., p. 185) of his time.

If I could claim just one theoretical legacy, therefore, it would be that of Durkheim – at all events, the Durkheim who did not concede any particular ground to the other human sciences, and who indicated the way in which sociology could tackle – from its particular perspective – all domains imaginable. By not ruling out any object *a priori*, sociology could take a further step on the path towards scientific autonomy. As with the most 'pure' literature, which, to show its break with external demands, maintains the primacy of form over function, the mode of representation over the object represented, sociology had to show that there is no empirical limitation to what it is able to study (no objects are more sociological than others), but that the essential thing lies in the sociological mode of treatment of the 'subject'.

Everything, therefore, contrasts my own sociological approach with those that variously consist in adding on insights from other disciplines (pluridisciplinarity), assembling in a theoretical bric-a-brac concepts hailing from different disciplinary traditions, these often themselves being attached to different theories of knowledge (interdisciplinarity),[4] or illicitly introducing into a discipline different principles arising in another discipline (e.g. what is today presented as a 'naturalistic programme in the social sciences' and calls for the development of a 'natural science of society'). These various impasses have in common that they all involve an abdication of sociological interpretation, bound up with three illusions: the illusion that such a dual (triple, quadruple) perspective can delivery a better vision; the illusion that this mixture of theoretical and heteroclite principles and orientations can give rise to an enrichment (rather than an explosion or implosion); and finally the illusion that a science with high legitimacy ('hard' science) can provide the foundation for another ('human') science.

Dan Sperber's book *Explaining Culture : A Naturalistic Approach* (1996) offers a fine example of the third kind of illusion just mentioned. The author puts forward here a series of theses, among which:

1 'Socio-cultural phenomena are ... ecological patterns of psychological phenomena. Sociological facts are defined in terms of psychological facts, but do not reduce to them' (1996, p. 31);
2 cognitive psychology consequently offers one of the principal sources for the explanation of cultural phenomena;
3 in order to naturalize the social domain, passageways must be established with the cognitive sciences;
4 the human mind is a combination of several mechanisms that are in part genetically programmed;

5 humans have an innate disposition to develop concepts according to certain schemes; the individual formation of concepts, just as their cultural variability, is governed by innate schemes and mechanisms (such concepts as norm, cause, substance, kind, function, number and truth are 'preformed in an innate manner'); and
6 if all representations do not have an equal chance of multiplying in the human population, this is partly because they are 'filtered' by universal human cognitive capacities.

The scientific programme sketched out above is manifestly anti-Durkheimian (there is no autonomy of the social, the social is not to be explained by the social but rather by psychology or neuropsychology) and close at times to certain developments of methodological individualism (to explain macro-phenomena by the cumulative effect of micro-phenomena) or other scientific programmes, such as that of Gabriel Tarde on phenomena of imitation.[5] Moreover, defining the cultural (or social) aspect of representations by their extent and durability, the author totally overlooks recent developments in the social sciences that tend to study the social tissue in its most singular folds.

By introducing certain borrowings from the cognitive sciences into the explanation of social (or cultural) facts, Sperber in fact prematurely abandons a specifically sociological interpretation (in the broad sense of the term). If we accept that the poor success (the low degree of contagion) of certain mental and public representations is explicable in terms of 'the organization of human cognitive and communicational capacities' (1996, p. 66), what interpretative work then remains for the social sciences? If 'humans have a disposition to develop such concepts as that of bird' (ibid., p. 69), and the category 'black ... is innately pre-wired, so that, when you learned the word "black", you merely acquired a way to express verbally a concept you already possessed' (ibid., p. 94), is it really useful to describe and analyse socio-historical facts sociologically? Too often, what is simply the product of the social relations that human individuals maintain with others, and with the products of their social activity, is placed in the individual herself – as if encapsulated in the brain. And if it is true that cognition 'needs' a brain, it is not the brain that controls those variations in the matter of mental operations that are so manifest both historically and sociologically.

We can find, on the other hand, solid support on the side of cultural psychology and/or North American psychology (sometimes of Vygotskyan inspiration), which fundamentally follows the trajectory we are proposing in a different direction.[6] In fact, this seeks to integrate culture or the social into its traditional objects (study of individual cognition, perception, memorization, etc.),[7] whereas we call for the opening of the mysterious sealed boxes that sociologists have most often been satisfied to refer to in terms of 'scheme', 'disposition', 'cognitive transfer', 'mental or cognitive structures', etc. What is involved here is not an interdisciplinary or pluridisciplinary encounter, but rather an unprecedented historical convergence between procedures that share not only the same epistemological orientations (e.g. they seek to grasp social, historical, geographical, cultural, etc., variations, rather than emphasize the universal character of human behaviours, competences, characteristics, as do biology, neuropsychology, etc.) but also related or congruent theoretical views (cultural psychology would be hard pressed to find solid support from the most objectivist and statistical sociologists, who can think only in terms of groups).

The objectivity of the 'subjective'

The character is no longer a psychological abstraction, as all the world can see.... Our aim is the exact study of the environment, establishing states of the external world that correspond to the internal states of the character.

(Émile Zola, *The Experimental Novel*)

Norbert Elias devoted himself to exploring the transformations of mental economy and personality structures in the course of the constitution and consolidation of the modern state, which by the monopolization of legitimate physical violence brought about a pacification of social life and a civilizing of manners. He studied the psychology of restraint, maintenance and self-control of impulses, and the mastery of emotions (Elias, 1994). But since these are mental, immaterial, realities that are inaccessible as such, it was by an analysis of manners, ways of eating, talking, etc., that he sought to objectify them.

Analysis of ways of doing and saying is thus a means of access to the mental economy of individuals. But is there also a different way of proceeding? Psychology – both contemporary and historical – can only be objectivist and materialist, in the sense that it starts from the observation of the visible and outward behaviour (often discursive, sometimes non-discursive) of actors, and seeks from this to deduce and understand subjectivity, mentality, cognitive style, ideology, representations, values, views of the world ... In this sense, such notions as those of 'mental structures' or 'psychic structures' should be used with precaution, if one is not to set real theoretical traps for oneself, and it is often preferable to speak of the objective structures of thought, perception, evaluation, appreciation, belief, etc., as these are expressed in actions and practices (linguistic and otherwise).

It is beneficial today, in this respect, to re-read the French psychologist Pierre Janet, for whom the object of psychology was not consciousness but rather action, and who believed that the only way to reach a knowledge of consciousness was to study in detail its contextualized manifestations (Janet, 1988). Likewise, if behaviourism today has a bad reputation, it at least had the merit of recalling the objectivity of the subjective within a psychological (and also sociological) culture marked by mentalism and introspectionism, by defining the domain of psychology as made up of 'the objectively observable behaviour of human beings' (Naville, 1942, p. 13). It appeared quite evident to Watson's eyes that behaviour meant 'what the organism does and says', and that 'speech is an action like any other'; 'Saying is doing, i.e. behaving. Speaking aloud or to oneself (thinking) is a type of behaviour just as objective as playing baseball' (ibid., p. 16).

Sociologists very often distinguish two realities that are not actually different. They oppose the 'objective' to the 'subjective', referring on the one hand to everything that can be grasped outside of the actors' subjectivity (but not the sociologists') and on the other hand to the 'meaning that actors give to their practices', their 'point of view on the world', their 'representations of the world', etc. Yet we are not dealing here with radical differences, simply with differences of degree in the objectification of realities. The domain of reality denoted by the term 'mental structures' is just as objective as that denoted by that of 'material structures'. These 'mental structures' are constantly objectified in the words of the actors' language and their modes of behaviour. There are thus no objective realities distinct from subjective realities, but rather realities objectified in objects, spaces, machines, words, ways of acting and saying, and so on.

Those realities marked by a high level of social objectification are often described as 'objective': economic capital, a house, a car, a plot of land, etc., whereas an opinion, an idea, a point of view or a representation are called 'subjective', even though in concrete terms these subjective realities are every bit as objective: they are materialized in the sounds of an oral discourse, in the traces of a written or printed manuscript, in the strokes of brushes or chisels that create paintings and sculptures, etc. The 'psychology' of an author or the 'mentality' of an age are equally visible in the objects, spaces, tools and machines they produce: we know just as well the 'mentality' of the Athenians of the fifth century BC, in particular the dissociation they made between what pertained to economics and what to religion or morality, from considering the appearance and spread of coinage as by studying the philosophical texts of the time (Vernant, 1982, 1983).

It is readily apparent, then, that sociologists are far more idealist[8] when they speak of 'subjective', 'psychic', 'mental' or 'symbolic' realities than when they deal with so-called material realities, whilse the language and ways of acting by which these realities make themselves 'visible' are the most material and objectifiable of realities (even if oral language and ways of acting have a more ephemeral existence, which lasts only for the time of their implementation).

The singular folds of the social

> Even two twins, dressed and fed in the same fashion, are not treated identically by each of their parents. Is it surprising that they diverge so quickly? Is it surprising that two children of the same age, brought up in different families (even if from a common background) respond differently to similar stimuli?
> (Pierre Naville, *La Psychologie, science du comportement*)

There is a too common tendency, among non-sociologists as well as many sociologists, to see the social as reducible to differences between groups or classes of individuals. As soon as social differences are introduced, the focus is on differences between social classes, social positions, socio-professional and socio-cultural categories, etc. Rather more rarely, attention turns to socially constructed differences between the sexes, or differences between generations (which are often differences between frameworks of socialization). But almost never without prompting is there any idea that 'cognitive', 'psychical' and 'behavioural' differences between two individuals from the 'same' social milieu (or, better, the same family) are also social differences, in the sense that they have been socially generated in social relations, from social (socializing) experiences, or that cases which are atypical, exceptional in terms of probability, can also be interpreted sociologically (Lahire, 1995a). In the same way, it is rather rare to view the social (social differences) from the standpoint of the variety of different social situations which one and the same actor constantly deals with in everyday life (Goffman, 1991; Boltanski and Thévenot, 2006).

It is important to emphasize, therefore, that the social cannot be reduced to social relations between groups, and particularly to socio-professional, socio-economic or socio-cultural differences, if we are not to give the impression that more fine-grained differences are no longer socially generated, so that individual cognitive structures, and those of emotionality and sensitivity, etc., would lie outside the range of sociology. Social means relationship. And not all social differences are reducible to differences between social groups (whatever the criteria used to characterize these).

Intersubjectivity or interdependence is logically prior to subjectivity, and consequently social relationships (the specific and historically variable forms that these relationships take) come first, because they are constitutive of each individual social being (Lahire, 1995a, pp. 283–9). Taking the individual actor as object of study thus does not mean – against all atomistic individualism – making this into the 'ultimate unit' or 'logical atom' of all analysis (Boudon, 1984, p. 26; 1981, p. 36). No more does it mean endowing all these actors with 'autonomy' and 'rationality', by taking the same rudimentary psychological feature aprioristically as the origin of all their practices. Actors are what their multiple social experiences make of them; it is their vocation to have varied behaviours and attitudes according to the contexts in which they are led to develop. Far from being the most basic unit of sociology, the actor is undoubtedly the most complex of social realities to grasp. And we can understand how sociology could not begin with the analysis of these complex composites of heterogeneous social experiences that are individual actors. In the end, and contrary to what elementaristic and atomistic conceptions may lead us to believe, it is less complex to study social worlds, fields, groups, institutions or micro-situations, etc., than the individual folds of the social. Actors have passed and continue to pass through multiple social contexts (worlds, institutions, groups, situations, etc.); they are the fruit (and the bearers) of all the experiences (not always compatible, not always cumulatable, and sometimes highly contradictory) that they have undergone in various contexts.

The metaphor of the fold or folding of the social has a double use. First of all, folding denotes a particular modality of the existence of the social world: the social (and its plural logics) in its embodied and individualized form. If social space is represented in all its dimensions (economic, political, cultural, religious, sexual, familial, moral, sporting, etc., these coarsely designated dimensions being themselves in part indissociable and in part decomposable into sub-dimensions) in the form of a sheet of paper or a piece of cloth (geometrically, that is, a flat surface), then each individual is comparable to a crumpled sheet of paper or a creased piece of cloth. In other words, the individual actor is the product of multiple operations of folding (or internalization) and is characterized therefore by the multiplicity and complexity of the social processes, dimensions, logics, etc., they have internalized. These dimensions, processes or logics (these contexts) are always folded in a unique fashion in each individual actor, and the sociologist interested in individual actors finds the social space creased and crumpled in each one of them. If the individual actor is the most complex of beings, this is because a variety of dimensions, logics and processes are folded up in each of them. For a long while sociology was in the habit of basically studying flat structures (social processes, social groups or social structures) – i.e. the social in its unfolded and de-individualized form. But it has gradually turned its interest to these multiple operations of folding that are constitutive of the individual actor, to the always particular creasings that make each actor both a relatively singular being and one relatively analogous to many others.

The second interest in the metaphor of folding lies in the fact that it leads us to realize that the 'inside' or 'interior' (the mental, the cognitive, etc.) is simply an 'outside' or an 'exterior' (forms of social life, institutions, social groups and processes, etc.) that is folded.[9] In this image, there is no possible exit from the social fabric (whether unfolded or folded); the 'interior' is nothing more than the 'exterior' creased or folded, and thus does not enjoy any primacy or anteriority, or any irreducible specificity. To understand the 'inside' there is only one solution: to study the 'outside' in its finest grain, its greatest detail, and as systematically as possible. The economy of the mind does not follow a different logic from that which rules the economy of forms of social life. Its only specificity lies in the fact that the social reality studied in its folded, crumpled, creased state (that of the individual actor) is differently organized from how it can be grasped in its unfolded, flattened state (transindividual reality of groups, structures, institutions, types of interaction or systems of action).

Multi-determinism and the sense of freedom

As we have seen, social determinism is never as unambiguous as physical or chemical determinism. This does not mean that an actor's behaviours are not completely determined socially – i.e. that they could be explained only in terms of a kind of free will lacking attachment or roots in the social world. Those anti-determinist declarations that enjoy a certain currency in the social sciences today naively deduce, from the constant activity of construction of the social world (activity of perception, interpretation, representation, etc.) by its actors, the idea that the latter have a fundamental freedom. The critique of the present author's views as 'hyper-socialized' (as if there could be a question of degrees of socialization) blandly confuses determinism and passivity, as if social determinism could act on dead bodies, as if this does not presuppose a certain determination and 'personal' engagement on the part of actors. To be resolutely *determined* to commit this or that action is a common way of feeling and living the social determinisms of which we are the products.

But if social actors – from the most ordinary to the most scientific – very largely resist the idea of a social determinism, this is for reasons that bear on the nature of individual life in the social world. It is impossible to predict the appearance of a social behaviour in the way that the fall of a body is predicted from the universal law of gravity. There is a considerable difference between the relative regularity of social behaviours (relative, that is, to socio-historical contexts that are always limited) and the absolute regularity of certain physical or chemical facts, and an unwarranted use of the term 'law' in the social sciences cannot change anything about this situation. There simply are no social facts so regular and general that they would authorize researchers to explain their existence in the language of 'social laws'.

This situation is the combined result of two elements – on the one hand the impossibility of reducing a social context to a limited series of pertinent parameters that make it possible to predict a social behaviour, as in the case of chemical experiments,[10] and on the other hand the internal plurality of actors whose stock of habits (schemes) is more or less heterogeneous, made up of more or less contradictory elements. It is impossible to predict with any certainty, for actors and researchers alike, what in a specific context will 'weigh' on the actor and which of the various schemes the actor has embodied will be triggered in and by this or that context. Because the actor is plural, and affected by different 'forces' according to the social situation in which he or she happens to be, he or she is bound to have the feeling of a freedom of behaviour. We could say that we are all too multi-socialized and too multi-determined to be able to give an account of our determinisms. If there was only one powerful determining force affecting us, then perhaps we would have a vague intuition of determinism. There is nothing wrong if some people insist on using the term 'freedom' or, more precisely, 'feeling of freedom' for the product of this multi-determinism – i.e. the complexity of social determinisms that are never easy to predict. But this freedom then has nothing in common with the sovereign and conscious freedom that certain social philosophers describe. The feeling of freedom is simply the product of the complexity of determination.[11]

The only freedom the sociologists can seriously consider is a freedom of action (political, economic, cultural, etc.) relative to determinate socio-historical situations. Imprisonment, for example, is a clear deprivation of freedom – i.e. of a series of possible actions. Those individuals not incarcerated enjoy, relative to those who are, a greater freedom of action. It would be quite absurd, however, to view those actors outside the prison context as 'free' in the sense of not being caught up in social determinisms. In the same way, those individuals, groups, categories, communities, etc., who experience the effects of economic exploitation, political and police oppression, sexual domination, ideological or cultural censorship, or moral repression are certainly limited in their action by other individuals, groups, categories or communities. If 'freedom' does have a sociological meaning, it is indeed this freedom dearly won in the everyday or 'historic' struggles of liberation. But both oppressors and oppressed, dominant and dominated, exploiters and exploited, censors and censored, are equally subject to social determinisms. The actions, tastes, representations, etc., of one set are no less determined than those of the other.

New methodological requirements

> That is why, to judge a man, we must follow his traces long and carefully.
>
> (Montaigne, *The Complete Essays*)

With the exception of certain sociolinguistic studies,[12] only a few sociological investigations have undertaken to 'follow' the same actor (and not just the same group of actors) in the very different situations of life (different domains of existence, different social worlds, different types of interaction). In studying actors in particular settings, the most common practice is to deduce general dispositions, habitus, worldviews or general relationships to the world from the analysis of behaviours observed in these settings. As I have shown, however, it is impossible to deduce a general 'habitus' from behaviour observable in particular and limited circumstances.

The sociology of action that I propose implies, therefore, new methodological requirements. In order to grasp the internal plurality of actors, we have to equip ourselves with methodological procedures that make it possible to observe directly or reconstruct indirectly (from various sources) the variation of individual behaviours according to social context. Only methodological procedures of this kind will make it possible to judge the extent to which certain schemes of action are transferable from one situation to another, and others not, or to assess the degree of heterogeneity or homogeneity of the stock of schemes embodied by actors in the course of their previous socialization. If the direct observation of behaviours still remains the most pertinent method, it is rarely completely possible, given that 'following' an actor in the different situations of life is a task both heavy and ethically questionable. But even interviews and work on assorted archival material – when one is as sensitive to differences as to constancies – can reveal many little contradictions, heterogeneities of behaviour that are unperceived by the actors themselves, who very often seek, on the contrary, to maintain an illusion of the coherence and unity of their self.

It is not just a question of comparing the practices, manners, behaviours, etc., of the same actors in such varied social worlds (which can in certain cases, though not systematically, take the form of fields of struggle) as the world of work, the family, school, neighbourhood, church, political party, leisure activities, etc., but also of differentiating situations within these various broad domains of social reality – not always so clearly separated in practice – by taking into account 'internal' differences (i.e. within the family, work, etc.). It is common for sociologists to study the behaviours of actors in the context of a single domain of activity (sociology of the family, of education, of work, of religion, etc.). The actor is then always situated on just one single social stage. He or she is, according to the particular case, a worker, a pupil, a parent, a father or mother, a husband or wife ... The custom of classical sociology recording the sociological coordinates of a subject in terms of 'level of qualification' or 'socio-professional category' always leads researchers summarily to reinject into their analysis elements that are external to the context being studied. Even when subjects are viewed only from the angle of their religious or family behaviour, they are always characterized by a rather crudely defined socio-professional position.

If it is rather rare for sociologists to compare subjects in two different settings, this is, however, already the custom for those trying to grasp phenomena of cultural contradiction or difference. The sociology of education, for example, is well versed in this type of comparison: family educational practices versus those of school; popular knowledge versus formal knowledge; modes of exercise of parental authority versus educational mode of exercise of authority . . . Even if the emphasis is often more particularly on one setting (family or school), with the other often assumed as known or the researcher drawing on the work of others, this kind of study marks a first step towards developing the sociological approach that I would like to see. It is very hard, on the other hand, to cite studies that have systematically 'observed' the same actors across more than two settings, or beyond two types of social situation.

Partial responsibility for this state of affairs certainly lies with the specialization of research, which follows the internal organization of scientific and academic disciplines – especially as the number of researchers in the social sciences has increased – as well as the way in which the legitimate 'formulators' of social problems (the state above all) divide up social reality. Research financed by national grants is thus tacitly inscribed by ministerial divisions; the object of study is the city, the school, the family or work, because there are ministries of the city, national education, culture, social affairs and labour, etc. What ministry in what government could take an interest in the social actor across different domains of existence? And yet we should not attribute the basic responsibility for the state of research in the social sciences to these external conditions; they simply contribute to maintaining the existing state of affairs. Within these broad domains of social existence, or types of social activity, sociologists could have tested – and can test today – hypotheses of variation in practices and the heterogeneity of the stock of schemes embodied by actors. But, to do so, hypotheses of this kind would have to be proposed, formulated, made precise and explicit. If the sociological imagination does not develop without empirical study, it is never the 'terrain' that itself generates new ways of considering it. 'The perspective creates the object', as Ferdinand de Saussure put it, and not the other way round.

When researchers study only one setting, and there is no reason why they should not, they should at least try not to generalize excessively from their limited findings. However modest these may be, they at least have a contextual relevance. But by blocking the view of the limits of the knowledge produced, and at the same time encouraging an empirical laziness that consists here in dispensing with the long work of comparing behaviours according to context, the demon of generalization (well explained by the far greater symbolic profits it procures) constitutes a genuine obstacle to scientific understanding of the social world.

— Scene 2 —

PERTINENT FIELDS[1]

On excessive generalization

> It remains true that one can adopt any kind of description in practice, as long as no more is asked of it than it can supply, and no attempt is made to use it outside the necessarily limited domain in which it can be applied in a satisfactory manner.
> (Jacques Bouveresse, *Le Mythe de l'intériorité*)

If we wanted to sum up the attitude adopted towards the various theories of action and the actor throughout this book, we could say that this is the opposite of the kind of polemical critique that is customarily practised between the champions of these different theories. This is not a matter of timidly seeking an undiscoverable 'just mean', but rather one of a pragmatic and historicizing relationship to sociological concepts and theories.[2]

It is because study of the social world teaches us that there is not a single model of the actor or action, but rather very variable types of actor and action – historically, socially, geographically – that we cannot claim universal applicability for sociological concepts. A large part of my own 'theoretical' contribution on this question is thus paradoxically not theoretical, in the sense of championing a particular perspective – an original one, of course! – on action and the actor. It constitutes, rather, a necessary epistemological framework for guiding empirical research, but one that does not prejudge what can be discovered only empirically, by way of original empirical research programmes. By proceeding in this way, new concepts and new theoretical options can be gradually constructed, which in turn will only have scientific relevance within certain limits of validity.

The same holds for theories of action, cognition and practice as for any other tool: none is adequate or applicable irrespective of the type of action under consideration. They do not all speak of social reality in the same fashion, and do not all speak of the same social realities. There is no unambiguous manner of placing in hierarchical order the scientific results of theories that privilege collective action and those that privilege individual action, those that insist on the relationship to action and those that prefer to grasp the various sequences or phases of action from outside, those that study long sequences of action and those that study actions of short duration. To claim otherwise does offence to social reality and to the diverse well-founded scientific perspectives that grasp it.

One of the main defects of theoretical discourses, in both philosophy and the social sciences, is to generalize unwarrantedly from a particular case of the real. Like those specialists in 'games' who present the 'rules of basketball' as 'universal rules of the game', valid for every kind of game that exists (from chess to rugby, via real tennis), theorists of action – even the most lucid of their number – quite seriously defend partial theories as if they were general ones. They most often imagine that a general theory is possible, whereas the only theories that exist are partial ones. As Jacques Bouveresse reminds us, Wittgenstein was close to holding that all philosophical theories are 'false': 'from excess of ambition, partiality, lack of attention or complexity, etc.' (Bouveresse, 1987, p. 36).

Whether the actor is viewed as rational or an automaton, conscious or unconscious, etc., this reasoning is conducted in an aprioristic, general and universal manner that is not appropriate for the social sciences (Passeron, 1991).[3] One could call for greater modesty on the part of those who make such ascents into generality, since the underlying point at issue in these generalist theoretical positions is prestige. If taking the most general perspective[4] – i.e. the highest and most transcendent one – were not in the end the 'dream model', researchers could possibly find personal glory in demonstrating the relative and limited applicability of their analyses. It goes without saying that the model of the highest perspective is that of our state hierarchies, as it previously was that of absolute monarchies, theocracies and tyrannies. Whether it concerns the president of a democratic republic, a monarch, a theocrat or a tyrant, in every case absolute prestige lies at the summit of the pyramid. *Mutatis mutandis*, theorists sometimes execute the same strategies in the order of theory as those of soldiers or politicians, deploying analogous operations. The loss of theoretical lucidity is sometimes amazing, but in no way surprising once we understand where it comes from: a loss of lucidity is a gain in scope.

Everything happens as if, seeking to take the hilltop and stretching their heads towards the sun, they end up no longer seeing the details on the ground. Too remote means too blinded. It is good then to exclaim with Wittgenstein: 'Back to the rough ground!' (1972, p. 46).

The varying scale of context in the social sciences

Faced with the diversity of definitions of objects in the social sciences, whether implicit or explicit, there is a strong temptation to decide in a summary fashion which is the right definition, the most pertinent scale of observation, the most correct angle of view, and this is often the way in which researchers actually proceed, aiming at a monopoly of the legitimate definition of their objects of study. But if there is no transcendent and integrating point of view, and this cannot in fact exist, it should be possible for researchers to act as if they each took into consideration, from their own particular perspective, other constructions of the object.

It is more productive scientifically, however, to note the variation in knowledge effects according to the way that the object is divided up. As soon as people stop placing themselves in an adversarial relationship with other ways of constructing social facts (a position that leads, for example, to saying that someone else's object is 'reductive'), the knowledge effects specific to each mode of construction are revealed, and greater awareness is taken of the constructed character of every scientific object. The active position of the analyst is then made clear, and at the same time the importance of the operations and procedures of construction in relation to the results of these procedures.[5] We thus move from ontological reality (a reality that is unquestioned and taken as the right and proper reality, no matter the object of study) to constructed reality.

This constructivist – in fact, Weberian – point of view makes it possible to see that the 'inside' and 'outside' of a social fact (its internal and external readings) are basically a matter of the construction of the object, and are not defined once and for all. It is possible, for example, to constitute the immediate context of verbal interaction as the pertinent context, so as to avoid, as Erving Goffman does, autonomizing the exchange of speech. He considers grammatical or linguistic analysis, even the strict analysis of conversation, to be committing 'the sin of non-contextuality' by their study of 'self-sufficient sample sentences' (Goffman, 1981, pp. 31–2), and makes a sharp demarcation between what is internal (the utterance related to its grammatical properties, and even verbal exchange considered as a self-sufficient exchange) and what is external (and is to be reconstructed).

But it is possible to criticize Goffman, from the standpoint of an alternative construction of the object and the pertinent context, for autonomizing linguistic exchange and to maintain that the truth of interaction is not entirely contained in the interaction itself: 'The "interactionist" approach, which fails to go beyond the actions and reactions apprehended in their directly visible immediacy, is unable to discover that the different agents' linguistic strategies are strictly dependent on their positions in the structure of the distribution of linguistic capital, which can in turn be shown to depend, via the structure of chances of access to the educational system, on the structure of class relations' (Bourdieu, 1991, p. 64).

The pertinent context, in this view, is not the immediate context of interaction but rather the linguistic market. The operation of constructing the object then converts another researcher's 'external' into the 'internal'. If, however, one author seems to include the other in a broader framework, it is still not possible to deduce from this that the former is correct while the latter – as 'reductionist' – is wrong. It is impossible to banish the objects of others from 'reality' simply by claiming that they do not exist: 'What exists in the social world are relations – not interactions between agents or intersubjective ties between individuals, but objective relations' (Bourdieu and Wacquant, 1992, p. 97). It is simply not the same phenomena that are explained in the two cases, and not the same pertinent contexts that are being applied. On the one hand, the focus is particularly on analysing the phenomena of assumptions (or grasping the interpretative procedures applied by the members of a community);[6] on the other hand, it is on relationships of symbolic domination between interlocutors who are unequally endowed (particularly in cultural capital and legitimate language).

Experimental variation and loss of illusions

Rather than deploring sociological polytheism (interpreted as a symptom of the youth and scientific weakness of the social sciences) – in other words, the notable variability of sociological ways of constructing objects – we should on the contrary see the experimental variation of scientific constructions[7] as the site of the most interesting knowledge effects in the social sciences.

Whether the decision is made to study frameworks of interaction, individual experiences or fields, the structures of domination relationships between classes or individual action, it is quite impossible to say in a general fashion that one is right and another wrong, one true and another false, one has the right definition of objects and another with the wrong one – as impossible as saying that basketball players are real players whereas footballers are wrong to play in the way they do. To refine the metaphor, we could simply add that, no matter what the game, it is on the ground that professional players distinguish themselves from amateurs, the more skilled from the less, and so on. To recognize the legitimate plurality of ways of constructing the objects of research is thus not a veiled or underhand way of maintaining that all kinds of scientific production are equally valid (Lahire, 1996b). The fact is that different constructions of the object do not speak of the same things, and cannot claim – no matter what their champions say – to explain the same realities. To each level of context there corresponds a specific order of complexity as well as specific pertinent information, different from that which other researchers are working with at other levels. No theory or construction of the object can ever make it possible to accede to real practices, to reality as such. They simply give us in each case a plausible 'version'.[8]

The experimental variation in levels of context or modes of scientific construction of objects does assume, however, saying farewell to a number of scientific illusions that are still very current today, and in most cases interconnected. It implies breaking with a certain kind of realistic epistemology, with the idea of a linear accumulation of scientific work in history, and with the view of possibly arriving at a theory that would integrate all existing perspectives (past and present).

Realist epistemology does not accept a distinction between scientific theory and reality. By way of its concepts, the researcher believes it possible to gain access, one way or another, to reality itself. As Max Weber wrote, this 'confusion between theory and history' takes a variety of forms:

> In some cases it is believed that the 'genuine' content or 'essence' of historical reality can be fixed in these theoretical and conceptual figures, in other cases they are used as a kind of Procrustean bed which history is pressed into by force, in others again 'ideas' are hypostatized to make them the 'true' reality hidden behind the flux of events or the 'real' forces that act themselves out in history. (Weber, 1992, p. 178)

Weber thus positioned himself in relation to Marxism more from an epistemological perspective – criticizing it for a propensity to take concepts or figures of thought as real acting forces – than from a theoretical one (he recognized, in any case, 'the eminent and even unique heuristic importance' of Marxist theory).

This realist epistemology very often leads the researcher to believe, in an evolutionist fashion, that the history of scientific theories in the social sciences is the history of successive advances, assuming a linear accumulation of scientific knowledge, a progress in the complexity of scientific theories and methods. This view of things thus implies seeking an integrating standpoint that would make it possible to view the object from all perspectives. In their relationship to other theories (and other theorists), researchers aiming at the theoretical integration of other viewpoints (past and present), or believing that they have reached this objective, are then led to judge between scientific correctness and error, the right scale of context and the less pertinent scale, the most complex theory and the more reductive theories, etc., measuring them by their own standard. If we can draw once more on Max Weber's valuable words, we can say that 'there are sciences that have the gift of remaining eternally young' (1992), and that cannot pretend either to a simple historical accumulation or to a total theoretical integration. This is understandable once it is accepted that the diversity of value relationships leads researchers to investigate social reality differently (to illuminate different aspects and dimensions), and that the various possible types of analysis, the various possible scales of context, do not produce knowledge effects that can be immediately cumulated (there is a problem of translation of results from one level of analysis to another, one scale of context to another, one type of method or theoretical language to another, etc.).

The way in which Pierre Bourdieu conceives the place of his own theory of the social in the sociological field (and in that of the social sciences more broadly) is close to the epistemological position I am criticizing here. In fact, his theory of fields, and particularly of fields of cultural production, though it proposes an original and complex research programme, is presented or defended in a manner that sometimes resorts to a realist epistemology,[9] to the idea of an accumulation of scientific knowledge,[10] and to that of a theoretical integration of existing viewpoints.[11] On the basis of this kind of conception, alternative theoretical constructions are cast onto the side of scientific error, of lesser complexity or regression. Pierre Bourdieu thus believes that the notion of the 'art world' current in the United States 'marks a regression in relation to the theory of the field' (1996b, p. 204). In an interview with an English sociologist, he declared in similar terms, without any ambiguity: 'For example, the notion of field of power is an immense advance. If I had to list all the articles and studies in which people make enormous mistakes, even empirical ones, because they don't have this notion . . .' (Bourdieu and Grenfell, 1995, p. 8). In taking up such positions, this author does not seem willing to recognize the plurality of possible scientific models (and interests) other than in an evolutionist and hierarchical manner:[12] some models are more complex, more scientific, less reductive, than others. Even if the theory of fields is open to modification, perfection, etc., it still constitutes the most historically complete scientific theory.

But if we accept that sensory, phenomenal reality is unlimited and susceptible of a multiplicity of methodological approaches, scientific investigations and viewpoints – for reasons that our relationships to values, as well as the diversity of forms of social life, help to explain – then models cannot be placed in any simple hierarchical order, as they do not all speak of the same social world. When we read scientific work hailing from a diversity of theoretical traditions, we do not learn the same 'things' about the social world, and cannot claim that one or other of these works makes it possible to grasp in a more complex fashion the same realities that the others apprehend. They present us with different versions of a social world that is still susceptible, with the perpetual variations in cultural values and interests, of a multitude of other descriptions and analyses. The diversity of theoretical and methodological languages current in the social sciences, the variety of scales of contextualization of social phenomena, cannot be read according to a unique axis measuring the degree of scientific credentials of research works.

The historicizing of universal theories and fields of pertinence

Since by virtue of the inevitable variation in the guiding ideas of value, he could not have truly definitive historical concepts, such as could be viewed as ultimate and general, he will accept that, precisely because rigorous and unambiguous concepts have been constructed for the singular point of view that orients work in each case, he can each time be clearly aware of the limits of their validity.
(Max Weber, *Essais sur la théorie de la science*)

A philosopher's job is not to produce a view X and then, if possible, to become universally known as 'Mr. View X' or 'Ms. View X'.
(Hilary Putnam, *Representation and Reality*)

By recalling the importance of contexts of 'measurement' or observation (and the procedures for constructing these contexts), historical limits of validity are inevitably attached to any sociological concept (and any conceptual system in the social sciences). It is difficult in the social sciences, therefore, to win on two fronts at the same time: the extension of a concept (its ability to embrace a very large number of social situations) and its empirical richness (meaning that it still tells us things about relatively singular segments, sections and contexts within the social world) (Weber, 1992, p. 159). By wanting to say too much, the risk is no longer to say anything. If historians are accustomed to placing spatial and temporal limits on their objects, even in the titles or subtitles of their publications, sociologists have more commonly bent themselves to generalizing their theoretical contributions on the basis of a relatively restrained context (a particular geographical zone, historical period, sector of activity, etc.).

Becoming aware of the historical character of sociological concepts, however, makes it possible for us to orient our relationship to competing theories of the social differently, by historicizing the theoretical debates that have generally taken polemical forms. Thus, rather than joining theoretically the 'theoretical' debate on relationships between individuals and society, the primacy of one or the other in analysis, etc., Norbert Elias historicized these notions by bringing the terms of the debate back to their socio-historical conditions of possibility. These categories, no matter how broad they might be, are always valid only within such socio-historical limits. Elias (1991) thus sketched the origin of the notion and experience of a subjectivity distinct from an (objective) external social reality by placing this problem in the framework of a (long-term) history of the transformations of the mental economy (structures of the personality) bound up with the processes of civilization. In this way he defined the historical field of relevance of a conceptual opposition that is still sometimes deployed with complete theoretical unawareness.

We could mention a range of examples of fruitful and illuminating application of this historicizing of sociological concepts or theories. There was Durkheim criticizing the apriorism of political economy, which saw 'interest' or the 'maximization of profit' at the root of all action (1975, p. 16), while being careful not to champion in his turn any *a priori* principle of all human action; Marcel Mauss, who would not definitively decide between formalism and pragmatism on the question of studies of prayers (more or less autonomous in relation to religious rituals and ceremonies), but adapted his method to the nature of the object studied (1968–74, vol. 1, p. 451); Peter Berger and Thomas Luckmann defining part of the field of relevance of the 'Goffmanian model' (1979, p. 281); Jack Goody (1977) defining that of the structural-graphic method, and showing in particular the limits of usefulness of graphic methods and procedures for grasping the specific logic of oral cultures; and Pierre Bourdieu (1976) defining the respective fields of relevance of interactionism (social worlds with a low degree of objectification, which place great importance on face-to-face contact) and structuralism (worlds in which hierarchies are guaranteed, objective, codified and made official in and through institutions – educational, state, legal, economic, etc.).

But this often remains an implicit and partial attitude: e.g. the case of Mikhail Bakhtin, who showed the connections that existed between formalist, structural theories in linguistics and educational practices, but continued to believe that these theories were 'false' and that those who used them never systematically drew all the necessary conclusions, whether of an epistemological order or in terms of the social forms of scientific debate.

It is in Ludwig Wittgenstein, however, that formulations are to be found closest to what I myself understand by field of relevance. In his *Conversations on Freud*, for example, what Wittgenstein criticizes Freud for is not his theory of dreams, but his attempt to interpret *all* dreams on the basis of this theory, and the idea that being only partly right is tantamount to being wrong: 'It is probable', wrote Wittgenstein,

> that there are many different sorts of dreams, and that there is no single line of explanation for all of them. Just as there are many different sorts of jokes. Or just as there are many different sorts of language. Freud ... wanted to find some one explanation which would show what dreaming is. He wanted to find the essence of dreaming. And he would have rejected any suggestion that he might be partly right but not altogether so. If he was partly wrong, that would have meant for him that he was wrong altogether – that he had not really found the essence of dreaming. (1966, pp. 47–8)

In similar vein, when he was led to criticize the concept of meaning in Saint Augustine, Wittgenstein did not confine himself to saying that this was a 'false' theory of meaning, but tried to understand what Augustine was talking about:

> Augustine, we might say, does describe a system of communication; only not everything that we call language is this system. And one has to say this in many cases where the question arises: 'Is this an appropriate description or not?' The answer is: 'Yes, it is appropriate, but only for this narrowly circumscribed region, not for the whole of what you were claiming to describe.' It is as if someone were to say: 'A game consists

in moving objects about on a surface according to certain rules ...' – and we replied: 'You seem to be thinking of board games, but there are others. You can make your definition correct by expressly restricting it to those games.' (1972, p. 3)

Even when they are conceived by their authors as universal, theories always speak – and most commonly without their authors being aware – of a category or class of relatively singular socio-historical facts; they systematize different aspects of our social life. Why should we be surprised that theoretical models which are fruitful for explaining certain social phenomena suddenly prove very weak when moved further from the centre of their field of relevance? They often then try – desperately – to relate to these fields realities that escape them. Once we are aware of this situation, we can advance sociological knowledge by a movement of contextualization or historicization of what is posited as theoretical, abstract, decontextualized, and ultimately universal and transcending any particular socio-historical situation. We could even say that such advance in the social sciences is all the greater when we know what the abstract theories that generally present themselves as universal means for conceiving every socio-historical situation are actually talking about (what social characteristics, what forms of social life, what types of social phenomenon). To escape from this generalizing ascent to extremes, however, it has to be no longer necessary to maintain the universal character of the heuristic power of one's method, mode of construction of the object, scale of contextualization or mode of sociological writing in order to guarantee these their legitimate place in scientific debate.

The first (epistemological) lesson to be drawn from these reflections on the fields of relevance of theories may be formulated as follows: in their theoretical oppositions, researchers in the social sciences are always partly wrong not to see how their opponents are partly right. This leads them to take issue with one another over results produced on the basis of completely different scales of context, ways of constructing objects, etc., which because of this are not directly comparable; also to develop (necessarily) partial theories of the social by taking these for what they are not – i.e. universal and universally pertinent theories – and ruling out any competing theory without asking in what way this might be partly well founded. Non-adversarial critical work, therefore, consists in saying: 'This concept that you believe general and universal is only applicable to this or that category of facts, practices, or scale of observation ...' This way of conceiving scientific debate aims neither at finding a 'just mean' nor at proposing an academic consensus. It is rather a way of ruling out all those attitudes in the social sciences that are so keen on totally and abruptly ruling out others.

The second (practical) lesson bears on the very identity of researchers in the social sciences. This seems to be still based largely on the adoption or invention of a theoretical vocabulary (a theory of the social) that can be given a clear label, the definitive and stable choice of a particular method (so that there are specialists in statistical methods, in interviews, in life stories, in analysis of discourse, in observation, etc.) and a scale of context (more micro or macro). These three aspects go broadly together, even if they do not systematically coincide. At the conceptual level, we can observe that a recognized author in the social sciences is a researcher identified on the basis of a recognizable grid of theoretical interpretation. This state of affairs more often incites potential authors to seek originality in terms of such a theoretical grid, with the concern to maintain a certain theoretical coherence throughout their work and publications, rather than to effect shifts or transformations in their languages of description and analysis.[13] If this were not the case, it would be impossible to understand the curious and exotic interest frequently aroused in the social sciences between the Wittgenstein of the *Tractatus logico-philosophicus* and the Wittgenstein of the *Philosophical Investigations*.

As for methods, the authors of *The Craft of Sociology* already criticized strongly the 'monomaniac use' that was made of these. They cited A. Kaplan's humorous remark: 'Give a child a hammer, and you'll see that everything seems suited to being hit with it' (Bourdieu, Chamboredon and Passeron, 1991, p. 71). We might have the feeling, from reading contemporary sociological works, that the researchers had learned in the past twenty years how to combine and articulate, with greater or lesser reflectivity, data produced with the help of different investigative methods.

Finally, as to the scale of contextualization, this still seems to resist variation, despite the intermixing of methods. Even when they combine different methods, researchers very often confer a particular privilege on certain of these, and thus on a particular scale of observation. The researcher's identity thus continues to crystallize around the constant and non-explicit choice of a particular scale of context. Everything happens as if, accustomed to view the world from a particular distance, researchers were unwilling to let their vision cloud, even for a moment, in order to get closer or further away. It is even rather surprising that simple experimental curiosity has not pushed researchers further in the direction of observing what happens to their objects, problems or objects of study, how these are transformed or deformed, under the effect of such variation in the focus of their lens.

The constant experimental search for the pertinent context on the part of Italian micro-historians is in this sense an undeniable advance in sociological knowledge, which the discipline of sociology has not itself managed to produce. And in my own transition from the macro-sociological analysis of educational inequalities to the analysis of 'educational failure' that I now have under way, with the shift of gaze this involves from the educational world to the world of work and then the family, leaving the terrain of statistical analysis of phenomena of cultural inheritance to reach the field of investigation of the concrete modalities of the 'transmission' of 'culture' and the constitution of cultural schemes, I have tried on each occasion deliberately and experimentally to change the angle of scientific approach to social realities, testing the limit of sociological concepts, schemes of interpretation or the methods of observing reality. My purpose has not been first to criticize statistics, for example, then to proceed to a defence of ideographic ethnographic descriptions. It has rather been an attempt to determine, on the basis of a particular problem, fields of relevance for the different approaches. Instead of proceeding, as we often do, to champion the universally fruitful character of our constructions of the object, I have preferred to defend the experimental character of my procedure, which remains aware of the limits of its validity, the field of relevance of the model employed.

The sketch of a theory of the plural actor that this book comprises, its reflections and interpretations on the wellsprings of action, forms of reflexivity and different logics of action, on how the polymorphous processes of embodiment should be grasped and the most singular folds of the social studied, as well as the way of debating with existing theories, the manner (neither realist nor universalist) in which we conceive the relationship of concepts to the social world, the multiple investigations on which sociological imagination and its lines of investigation of the social are based – all this has aimed to constitute an opening. An opening both towards more theoretical modesty and less theoretical guilty conscience, towards more anchoring of assertions in the social world and less empirical laziness, towards more historicization and pragmatism in the use of concepts and less universalization and generalization, towards more sociological passion and less respect for academicism and institutional divisions, towards more experimentation and less fetishizing of methodology, towards more scientific inventiveness and less scholarly dogmatism. A wide programme with a low probability of realization? The future will decide.

NOTES

Preface

1 I also indicate in this book the social and historical limits of validity of the concept of 'field', whereas a number of people who use Bourdieusian concepts believe *a priori* that every context of action is necessarily a 'field'. This reflection is continued in 'Champ, hors-champ, contrechamp', in Lahire (1999, pp. 23–57), and especially in Lahire (2006).
2 Bourdieu and his school, in fact, steadily slipped towards a *contextualism of the field*, omitting to study what the theory of habitus should have impelled them to examine more closely. See Lahire (2010).
3 Luc Boltanski, a former disciple of Bourdieu, had broken several years before with his sociology and turned towards a contextualistic view of action. He proposed focusing interest exclusively on those 'constraints' tied to 'the arrangement of the situation in which individuals are placed' (Boltanski, 1990, p. 69) and caricatured *dispositionalist* approaches by suggesting that they 'intend to bring to light determinations that, inscribed in actors once and for all, guide their actions whatever the situation in which they find themselves' (ibid., p. 65) or, again, 'grasp properties that, inscribed irreversibly in actors and their physical habits, determine their conduct in every circumstance' (ibid., p. 69). He did, however, endow actors – and how could he have done otherwise? – with naturalized 'competences' whose sociogenesis (historical and individual) remained mysterious. ('We consider that it is part of the competence of all normal members of a particular society to be able to grasp these and take account of them'; ibid.). I have criticized this rather cavalier and summary way of viewing the problems of the theory of action in Lahire (2002).
4 It is not by chance, as I emphasize in this book, that it was for Kabyl society, a traditional society far less differentiated than modern societies, that Bourdieu started to forge the concept of habitus.
5 I insist here on the dispositional nature of this pluralism, which has sometimes been forgotten by users of and commentators on my work. It is not in fact without a certain surprise that I have seen in the past ten years the theses of this book summed up by authors mentioning a 'pluralism of identity'

that I am supposed to have brought to light. Reflection on the more or less conscious and strategic use of multiple individual identities, a reflection that sometimes traces a portrait of actors perpetually seeking or asserting their identity, is so far from the ideas inspiring the researcher working on the plurality of dispositions that it should not be necessary to explain these differences in detail. And yet, since rigour in reading texts seems to be a characteristic less frequently met with in the social sciences than the 'intoxication of inexactness' of which Bachelard speaks, and since the mere similarity of the questions raised (with the use of the term 'plurality') triggers hasty convergences in common academic classifications, it would seem far from useless to mention this point.

6 Taking up in this way expressions used in particular by Émile Durkheim and Marcel Mauss. See Lahire (2005).
7 By more frequently now using the expression 'sociology on the individual scale', I aim to avoid all those (disappointed) expectations that the expression 'psychological sociology' raises in relation to certain works of social psychology. See Lahire (2003a).
8 'Probable', in our societies.
9 Lahire (2004).
10 A change to which he was not very sensitive. Cf. in particular Revel (1996) and Lahire (1996a).
11 Cf. Lahire (1995a). Those who have situated my work on the side of microsociology and qualitative analysis of cases should at least not have been surprised by the fact that I worked, at the same time, as a member of the scientific advisory board of the Observatoire national de la vie étudiante (Paris), on very large-scale national quantitative studies (those of 1993 and 1997, each representing around 28,000 respondents). Cf. Lahire (1997a).
12 Lahire (2002).
13 Based on a new treatment of data from the study of the Ministry of Culture on 'cultural practices of the French in 1997' (n = 3,000), the analysis of more than a hundred interviews and a more contextualized study of certain cultural practices and a section of the cultural supply. Cf. Lahire (2004) and also Lahire (2008).
14 Cf. Lahire (2006).
15 Cf. Lahire (2003b).
16 It is by not excluding *a priori* any subject from its field of study that sociology is able to advance towards greater scientific autonomy. It has to show that there is no empirical limit to what it is capable of studying – i.e. that no objects are more sociological than others, that the essential thing lies in the sociological mode of dealing with subjects. By making it possible to embark on the analysis of the singular folds of the social, sociology on the individual scale inscribes itself in the long sociological tradition that, from Émile Durkheim via Maurice Halbwachs to Norbert Elias, aims to connect the mental economy of individuals ever more finely with the frameworks of social life.
17 Elias (1991).

Prologue

1 'When I was a "scientific realist" I felt deeply troubled by the difficulties with scientific realism; having given up scientific realism, I am still tremendously aware of what is appealing about the scientific conception of philosophy. I hope that the present book at least partly reveals this "being torn"' (Putnam, 1988, p. xii).
2 Pierre Naville thus wrote that 'one of the aims of a true science of behaviour is the transformation of the personality' (1942, p. 237).

Act I, Scene 1, The Plural Actor

1 All the same, there is sometimes a transition from constructivist caution (what is unitary is the scientific construction) to the philosophically realist idea that this singleness lies in the social reality. The concept of habitus then has the function of 'account[ing] for the unity of style, which unites the practices and goods of a single agent or a class of agents' (Bourdieu, 1998, p. 8).
2 With an interval of almost twenty years in between, Bourdieu twice indicted a certain psychology. His first critique was addressed above all at the 'atomist approach of social psychology' (1984, p. 573n) that 'breaks the unity of practice'; subsequently he criticized 'the atomistic view put forward by some experimental psychology' (Bourdieu, 2000, p. 64).
3 Lloyd more generally points out the problems involved in 'the inference *to* belief *from* either statements or behaviour', as well as those arising from 'inference *from* belief to what are supposed to be underlying thought processes' (1990, p. 4).
4 'Our ordinary practice is to follow the inclinations of our appetite, to the left, to the right, uphill and down, as the wind of circumstance carries us. We think of what we want only at the moment we want it, and we change like that animal which takes the colour of the place you set it on' (Montaigne, 1958, p. 240).
5 Only rational change, i.e. based on reason, is generally perceived more positively than (psycho-rigid) 'stupid stubbornness' despite evidence of mistakes committed: 'It's only imbeciles who don't change their ideas.' This formula is ritually recalled in particular by the most opportunist of our political figures, precisely to escape being trapped in the image of the 'weathercock' lacking other principles of orientation than the direction of the wind.
6 This is already what Bourdieu maintains in declaring that he aims to

> rediscover the kernel of truth in the approach characteristic of common-sense knowledge, namely, the intuition of the systematic nature of lifestyles and of the whole set which they constitute. To do this, one must return to the practice-unifying and practice-generating principle, i.e., class habitus, the internalized form of class condition and of the conditioning it entails. One must therefore construct the objective class, the set of agents who are placed in homogeneous conditions of existence imposing homogeneous conditionings and producing homogeneous systems of dispositions capable of generating similar practices. (Bourdieu, 1984, p. 101)

7 While not challenging the legitimacy of a very fine differentiation of social reality, it seems to me that this infinite fragmentation makes it difficult to structure the objects of study. Thus Jean-Claude Kaufmann writes:

> At each point in the cycle, at each stage in the cycle of circulation, the part of the Self deposited in the dance with the object is different, and markers determine a chain of particular gestures. The individual leaving a pile of dirty clothes in his room in the evening is not the individual of the morning who puts the same pile in the washing-machine. He does not touch things in the same way, with the same ideas in his head. He is genuinely someone else, in a different system of thought and action, changed by the different perception of the same objects. (1997, p. 43)

I can understand the author's intention here, but would not follow the same route.

8 We should none the less emphasize the fact that in our social formations it is generally only men who bear the same surname throughout their life, most women still changing theirs on marriage.

9 Everyone knows that not being 'registered', remaining outside these official registrations, being 'undocumented', means being relegated to a kind of symbolic and social non-existence.

10 The essential problem raised by the 'life story' told to social scientists is that of the variation of the totalizing syntheses according to the moment in the trajectory (professional, family, cultural, etc.) at which these are solicited. For example, in the case of a conjugal trajectory of the kind 'happy period of marriage'/ 'tormented period of divorce'/ 'enthusiastic formation of a new couple', the same inquiry could produce three very different biographical stories, according to the moment at which the story was given: (1) the story of a happy conjugal history; (2) the story of a long descent into nightmare; (3) the story of a trajectory punctuated by tests overcome (perhaps necessary in order to know what true happiness is . . .), which gave fresh impetus to a new and far more passionate life.

11 Ulf Hannerz writes, quite correctly, that 'the most extreme type of folk society, or, for inmates, the total institution without an underlife', would represent 'a society which is only a single stage' (1980, p. 232). But, even for representing the least differentiated societies, the model of the 'single stage' remains too much of a caricature, more appropriate to animal societies whose members are in constant interaction with one another, without an institutional context that makes it possible to distinguish timeframes of practice and avoid encroaching on any member at any moment, in any interaction.

12 Durkheim explains very well the historical exceptionality of this realization, by recalling how 'the French system of boarding derives from that excessive passion for uniform regimentation which imbued the university in the fifteenth century with an intensity which is matched nowhere else' (Durkheim, 1977, p. 122).

13 In a certain fashion, indeed, Bourdieu can be played against himself in order to advance towards resolving the problem of the singleness and plurality of the actor, following here, moreover, an advice on general orientation in reflective work that this author often gave and that his most faithful epigones are unable to apply to him: 'One does science – and above all sociology – against one's training as much as with it' (1982, p. 9).

14 'In short, unable to speak the two cultural languages well enough to keep them clearly separate, he is condemned to the interferences and contradictions that make up the cultural pidgin' (Bourdieu and Sayad, 1964, pp. 167–8); 'like the sub-proletariat, the wrongly occupied peasant refers constantly, when he lives, thinks or judges his condition, to two different and even opposing logics' (ibid., pp. 164–5).

> The models of behaviour and the economic ethos imported by colonization coexist within each subject with the models and ethos inherited from ancestral tradition; the result is that behaviours, attitudes or opinions appear as fragments of an unknown language, incomprehensible both to someone who only knows the cultural language of tradition, and to someone who refers only to the cultural language of colonization. Sometimes the words of the traditional language are combined according to modern syntax, sometimes the reverse, and sometimes it is the syntax itself that appears as the product of a combination. (Ibid., p. 163)

15 When statistical inquiries ask junior high-school students to classify a list of activities that include playing, practising sport, watching television, listening to music, and reading, variations according to the social milieu of the family are naturally conspicuous, but so too is the fact that reading is never placed at the top of the hierarchy of preferences. At this level reading is thus clearly out of favour, even among young people from the most culturally privileged milieus, and our investigations show very well how the production of a taste for the reading of texts, like many other aspects of children's education, presupposes a struggle and an asceticism on the part of the parents. A struggle to make children read when they prefer to play, a struggle to make them read other things besides comics, a struggle to integrate reading into ordinary moments of family life. When these students are asked about their preferences in reading matter, we note that in all social milieus comics come top (around two-thirds). In the same way, when asked if they have regular or occasional conversations about literature, or none at all, it is notable that social homogeneity dominates social heterogeneity (Singly, 1990b).

16 These findings are confirmed in the studies conducted by Roger Establet (1987, pp. 200–32).

17 Pierre Bourdieu sees the state as the means that differentiated societies give themselves in order to 'impose and inculcate in a universal manner . . . identical or similar cognitive and evaluative structures', playing here a similar role to institutional rituals in weakly differentiated societies: 'As organizational structure and regulator of practices, the state exerts an ongoing action formative of durable dispositions through the whole range of constraints and through the corporeal and mental discipline it uniformly imposes upon all agents' (1998, pp. 53–4).

18 This implies that we are never completely in the same group at different moments in this group's history – e.g. two children belonging to the same set of siblings are not born into or grow up in exactly the same family.

19 Halbwachs – who was appointed professor of social psychology at the Collège de France just a few months before being deported by the Nazis – has finally found successors on this fruitful path. I believe, even if this is shocking for some French sociologists, that it is in a school of contemporary American sociology that came out of interactionism that this type of interest

has managed to persist through to today. Anselm L. Strauss, for example, made this plural membership of social worlds and sub-worlds (not always mutually compatible and sometimes even in conflictual relationship) one of the fundamental conditions of contemporary social life (1993, pp. 41–2). He stresses, on the other hand, the fact that few social formations are made up of actors acting and engaging in a single social universe.

20 As against what James M. Ostrow writes: 'I am a white, Jewish, suburban-bred son of a lawyer, a man, a husband, a father, a teacher, a colleague – I am all of these things at once' (1990, p. 91), we are precisely not all these things 'at once', but rather – for some of them at least – often at different times and places in the day.

21 Leslie McCall notes how, for Bourdieu, 'the social structure . . . is defined by occupations and the capitals associated with them', and that habitus contains a dimension that is 'in large part political' (1992, p. 841). As a consequence of this, the social practices of women, who are more present in the private spheres, enters little into this definition – professional and public – of the sociologist's social space.

22 The author compares 'the interpretation of the text of an interview with a mere layperson' with that of 'the work of a celebrated author', and says that the second case none the less 'pose[s] particular problems, notably the belonging of its author to a field' (Bourdieu 1996b, p. 392, note 25).

23 One might say that even this is not so bad.

24 From Bergson's 'storehouse of auditory images' or 'reservoir', via Schütz's 'reserve of experiences' to Bourdieu's metaphor of the body as 'depot', 'storage' metaphors have long been current in sociology. But if we do employ a metaphor, it is better to take it to its logical conclusion (also as a way of finding its limitations).

25 George Herbert Mead (1863–1932), a contemporary of Proust (1871–1922), proposed a theory of the 'diversity of selves' that is very similar. According to him, 'the organization of the whole self with reference to the community to which we belong . . . varies, of course, with different individuals' and 'a multiple personality is in a certain sense normal' (1967, pp. 142–3). More generally, Proust's literary work and his presentation of the synchronic and diachronic plurality of actions certainly owe much to the psychology of his time, and especially to the work of Théodule Ribot on *Les Maladies de la personnalité* (1885). Ribot maintains here that 'everyday observation shows us how much the normal self has lost cohesion and unity', and that 'there is in each one of us tendencies of all kinds, all the possible opposites, and between them all intermediate shadings, with all combinations between these tendencies. If moralists, poets, novelists and playwrights have amply shown us these two selves struggling within the same self, everyday experience is still more rich: it shows us several, each one excluding the others as soon as it comes to the fore' (cited in Raimond and Fraisse, 1989, p. 40). The idea of the existence of several 'provinces of the self' was also proposed by the psychologist Ignace Meyerson (1888–1983). Cf. Malrieu (1996).

26 Thus Pierre Bourdieu was recently led to maintain the existence of 'cleft, tormented habitus bearing in the form of tensions and contradictions the mark of the contradictory conditions of formation of which they are the product' (2000, p. 64).

27 This raises the question as to the historical conditions of appearance of

scientific interest in the duplication of the personality and in what came to be called 'schizophrenia'. This is one of the lines of socio-historical investigation in the research programme that I have established in the context of the Institut universitaire de France.

28 Pierre Bourdieu speaks of 'destabilized habitus, torn by contradiction and internal division, generating suffering' (2000, p. 160).
29 Rather than speak of 'mental conflict' or 'internal conflict', it seems more exact to speak of conflicts of habits (of thought, taste, language, bodily movement, etc.) or schemes of action.
30 These contradictions or double constraints can even be characteristic of 'normal' social positions. We can think today of the lower-level supervisory staff (e.g. foremen or contractors) wedged between the social logics of hierarchically superior positions and those of hierarchically inferior ones. But we could also evoke the case of the artist at the eighteenth-century court as described by Norbert Elias in the case of Wolfgang Amadeus Mozart (1993, pp. 10–27). Mozart occupied like all artisans a subaltern position in respect to 'the court society'. As a musician, he was a servant with slightly more prestige than others (coachmen, cooks, goldsmiths . . .). As a bourgeois of the court, he lived in two social worlds: a bourgeois world and a world of the court nobility within which he had to respect specific norms of behaviour. But Mozart, overprotected by his father, never completely managed to integrate these norms and consider himself really as a subaltern (he wrote to his father that he had a horror of 'begging'; ibid., p. 20). His biography supplies a case of internalization of the highest and most noble musical canons without internalization of the manners that generally accompanied this. Mozart, a prodigious individual, possessed a musical knowledge that implied a profound embodiment of noble tastes (for him, as for the nobility, opera was the pinnacle of musical categories), but he kept the style of behaviour of a commoner. He found it particularly hard to conceal his frankness, whereas court behaviour demanded more euphemistic behaviour (not to shock, to be diplomatic, etc.). He adopted only the most outward norms of the court (i.e. dress), not its conduct.
31 Less is known about social ascent by the economic path, in so far as these cases of upward social mobility leave little in the way of written testimony, and so attract correspondingly little attention.
32 Naville even mentions the existence of 'attempts at double, triple (and sometimes multiple) predominance of systems of habits' (1942, p. 222), unfortunately without giving examples of these.
33 Annie Ernaux, born 1940, is a French writer whose literary work is autobiographical, focusing notably on the process of moving into adulthood and away from her social origins.
34 Even after establishing themselves in their new social position, these *transfuges* are not always free of their past. Their feeling of being 'uprooted' and their sense of 'unease' can sometimes even lead to them becoming 'psychotic' (Hoggart, 1998, p. 225); having 'left his class of origin, at least in spirit', the 'odd man out' remains none the less 'ill at ease with the middle classes' (ibid., p. 233).
35 For anyone ready to look at them and decipher them, contradictions, omissions, silences and lapses are present in any in-depth interview of any length. It is the practice of homogenizing interpretation, rather than the discourses

themselves, that wipes out any awkward trace of their presence, or one judged insignificant in the selected theoretical framework. Besides, while remaining in the register of discourse, the practice of interweaving interviews, such as those I conducted with teachers, parents and children in *Tableaux de familles* (Lahire, 1995a), makes it possible patiently to reconstruct heterogeneous social contexts.

ACT I, SCENE 2, THE WELLSPRINGS OF ACTION

1 J. Laplanche and J.-B. Pontalis, however, point out that, with the idea of the 'deferred revision' of the past (reinscription of memory traces) bound up with a new event or new situations, Freud ruled out 'the summary interpretation which reduces the psycho-analytic view of the subject's history to a linear determinism envisaging nothing but the action of the past upon the present' (2006, p. 111–12).

2 In *Cadres et mécanismes de la socialisation dans la France d'aujourd'hui* (1977, pp. 81–2), Jean-Claude Passeron very clearly expressed, in a paragraph entitled 'First socialization: towards a sociology of primary experiences', the implicit assumptions shared by many French sociologists of the time, and a number of them still today: 'The object that theoretical consideration raises most clearly for empirical research is undoubtedly the socialization exercised in the first three years of childhood, since both psychoanalysis and the ethnological and sociological theories of constitution of the personality agree, in different terms, in conferring a prototypical importance to such early experiences.' The same is expressed more recently by a North American author, Peter E. S. Freund: 'The quality, degree, and intensity of social construction and bio-social interaction depend on the time and timing. We are more open when we are very young than as adults. Socialization begins when the human organism is unfinished ... Primary socialization has a deep impact on the organism' (1988, p. 849).

3 If Bourdieu recently made clear that this was 'a particular but particularly frequent case' (2000, p. 145), this rhetorical concession changes nothing in the fact that texts continue to be cited in which this author makes this the general model of all practices. We have here a case that infringes both the principle of charity and the principle of non-contradiction.

4 Leslie McCall describes the case of an Islamic woman, Shabano, who had been married for forty years, with several children, before being thrown out of her house following a divorce. This rupture abruptly questioned the ordinary routines of everyday life and the values that these bore, and led Shabano to 'a sharp consciousness' of the situation of women in a patriarchal culture. After emerging from such situations of domination, these women may say some years later: 'That's not me'. Leslie McCall concludes by saying: 'The ontological complicity between habitus and field breaks down: *fit* no longer explains the relationship between positions and dispositions' (1992, p. 850).

5 It is not by chance that these big moments are when personal diaries are most frequently kept: divorce, retirement, adolescence, etc. (Fabre, 1993, p. 82).

6 See Christine L. Williams's study on women in the US Marines and men practising nursing (1989).

7 Novels by Albert Memmi (1984) and Degracia (1968) are excellent illustrations of these gaps: 'When I am at your place, with Christian friends, I suffocate, I feel ill at ease, as I'm always asked questions which I'm forced to reply to in with lies. When I find myself back in a Jewish milieu, I also feel awkward, as I realize that I no longer belong completely to this community. Then I tell myself: you don't have a place anywhere. And I get sad' (Degracia, 1968, p. 96).

8 Which leads Rogers Brubaker to remark on the basis of the findings presented in *Distinction* that the relationships between the indicators Bourdieu selects to 'measure' conditions of existence and those that he uses to grasp dispositions are 'discouragingly weak' (1985, p. 763).

9 This is what I myself did with respect to the world of students, by taking the relative weight, according to domains and dimensions of educational practice, of the school and university situation and the 'outside' social situation (Lahire, 1997a).

10 Bourdieu (in Labov, 1983, p. 71) refers to the 'relative weight' of educational level or social origin according to the cultural domain in question (painting and cinema, for example). We could say that it is not the same schemes or cultural habits that are activated in every case. The domain of cinema, or better still that of sports activities, may activate cultural tastes constructed in the social universe of origin, whereas the literary domain may trigger schemes that are educationally acquired.

11 It is important to make clear how rare it is – I shall give an example of this further on with the case of university students – for actors to make a 'choice' to activate or not habits or experiential schemes. In the great majority of cases, it is the situation that 'decides' on these inhibitions or triggers.

12 Bergson also uses formulas that seem in total contradiction with the elements I am stressing here. He writes, for example, that 'our character, always present in all our decisions, is indeed the actual synthesis of all our past states', or again that a person 'collects' and 'organizes the totality of its experience in what we call its character' (1912, pp. 188, 225).

13 Rather than 'cause' and 'effect', certain philosophers prefer to speak of *'reciprocal disposition partners'*: 'when salt dissolves in water, the salt and the water are reciprocal partners' (Crane, 1996, p. 9).

14 As Paul Ladrière writes: 'Thus it is not that the stone, which naturally falls, might have acquired the habit of rising, even if one tried to accustom it to this thousands of times by throwing it up in the air. . . . For the virtues, on the other hand, their possession presupposes a previous exercise, as is also the case for other arts. In actual fact, we learn them by doing the things that have to be learned to do them' (1990, p. 24).

15 It goes without saying that scientific debate about any given study leaves open the question whether the series of facts observed really can be interpreted as manifestations of a single underlying disposition.

16 Dispositions, Pierre Bourdieu writes, 'are revealed and fulfilled only in appropriate circumstances and in the relationship with a situation. They may therefore always remain in a virtual state, like a soldier's courage in the absence of war' (2000, p. 149).

17 'The difficulty is that understanding is not just a capacity but also an act, and that we do not manage to give ourselves a satisfactory image of the relationship that exists between the act of understanding and the ability that makes

it possible; to understand a sentence is not to understand the language at the moment that one understands this sentence' (Bouveresse, 1987, p. 319).

18 This is how it is possible to speak of ascetic and hedonistic dispositions in order to characterize the multiple usages or non-usages of the practices of writing within the household space. The notion of disposition, in a case such as this, makes it possible, in a context of study that is clearly circumscribed, to avoid dividing the analysis practice by practice (list of tasks, list of things to do, jotter, diary, calendar . . .). It is impossible all the same to generalize such dispositions to all the (non-studied) dimensions of existence of the actors on which this study bears (Lahire, 1993b, 1995b).

19 Richard Hoggart explains, for example, how members of the working classes can infringe a certain number of 'rules' or neglect certain fundamental values of their group when they are in contact with other social groups located on the other side of the divide (us/them). On the one side, 'never do the dirty on your mates', and, on the other, 'screw the "others", bosses or foremen'. 'You will not fiddle from your mate, but you will flog anything you safely can from the "firm" or the Services. You will not twist a neighbour, but a middle-class customer is fair game' (Hoggart, 1998, p. 212).

20 Adolescence, a critical period (and a period of criticism) *par excellence*, constitutes a particularly interesting moment for the sociologist studying the phenomena of embodiment of habits. It is in effect a time in the life cycle during which habits are formed both despite and thanks to (or at least by way of) the conscious resistance that is actively opposed to them. Refusal to tidy the bedroom, to listen to parents' advice on all manner of subjects, 'adolescents' resistant to different family constraints internalize these all the same in these moments of crisis in habits and demands, that are reactivated as if by magic in post-adolescent periods. Adolescents are against their parents in both senses of the term: 'close to' and 'opposed to'.

21 One woman studied by Anne Muxel, for example (forty-four years old, a teacher), explained how, despite her critical feminist discourse and her active resistance until the age of twenty ('I did absolutely nothing at home, I didn't even boil an egg until I was twenty'), rediscovered aptitudes of her mother ('a very good cook') without any particular effort ('from having seen her do it, it came by itself') with her son (1996, p. 87). In the same way, J.-C. Kaufmann describes the situation of a male respondent living in a couple who, following a course in Paris that led him to live by himself for several days each week, found that 'the (bad) old bachelor habits, which he thought were behind him, re-emerged and his old untidiness came back with astonishing ease and familiarity' (1998, pp. 101–2).

22 J.-C. Kaufmann describes the missing act of a woman who, although devoted to housekeeping and domestic organization, forgets each morning to iron her husband's shirt – like an act of resistance.

23 Calm/Agitated; Attentive/Distracted; Gentle/Aggressive; Agreeable/Disagreeable; Polite/Impolite; Active/Passive; Regular work effort/Irregular work effort; Hard-working/Lazy; Babyish/Mature; Assured/Fearful; Reserved/Talkative; Participating/Not participating; Relaxed/Anxious; Keen to work/Not keen to work; Influenced by schoolfriends/Not influenced . . .; Emotional/Not particularly . . .; Autonomous in work/Not autonomous . . .; Disciplined/Undisciplined; Stable/Unstable; Serious/Unserious; Applied/Not very applied; Careful/Not very careful; Organized/Disorganized; Fast/

Slow; Self-confident/Lacking self-confidence; Good memory/Bad memory; Logical mind/Lack of logic; Often asks for explanations/Doesn't ask much ...; Gifted/Not gifted; Quick on the uptake/Hard-going on the uptake; 'Brilliant'/'Pedestrian'; Rigorous/Not very rigorous; Well mannered/Not well mannered; Curious/Incurious; Reflective/Unreflective; Organized/Unorganized; 'Imaginative'/'Stubborn'.

24 We can note in passing that this twofold division of our everyday reasonings is common to our own social formations, in the differences they make between, on the one hand, gifts and their exchange in the family or between friends and, on the other hand, commodity exchanges. More generally, François de Singly sees this kind of tension between the spirit of rivalry and competition, the pursuit of one's own interest and the demand of 'disinterestedness', 'humanity', 'love' or 'friendship', as a fundamental – and rarely highlighted – characteristic of individualism in our societies. This double constraint sometimes finds its resolution in a dissociation of the types of relationship to others between 'private life' and 'public life' (Singly, 1990a).

25 Thus Ulf Hannerz writes: 'There may be occasions which one would prefer to keep well insulated from another because of the contradictory demands they make on the self, but which impinge on each other so that at least certain of its accoutrements must be made to match them all. At worst, the experience may be like that of a chameleon on a multicolor patchwork' (1980, p. 237). Analysing the novels of Albert Cohen, Clara Lévy shows very well the separation that the character Solal has to live so as not to experience a feeling of shame towards some people close to him, immediately doubled by a shame at being ashamed: 'As soon as he has understood that the two facets of his personality must never come publicly into contact, Solal clearly separates his life into two parts – one of which is lived in the Western way and the other in the Eastern, without the two ever colliding' (1998, pp. 371–2).

26 'Ideas and experiences associated with the speaker's Hispanic past . . . trigger a communication in Spanish' (Gumperz, 1989, p. 89).

27 The way in which Paul Connerton refers to the work of David Efron is revealing with regard to the unifying conception of culture, completely ignoring this key point of his thesis (1989, pp. 79–82).

28 The very nature of 'individual' work within the different establishments varies: the objectives of individual work are made more or less explicit by the different establishments of higher education; the different acts of work are more or less prescribed; the different injunctions for the submission of individual work more or less frequent. The distant objective of the final dissertation in the faculties of letters and humanities, which leaves the students 'free' to determine the most adequate means of arriving at this, is thus quite contrary to the denser micro-injunctions that constitute 'homework', exercises or revisions that are prescribed almost daily, especially within the preparatory classes. Whereas university students are led to organize their individual work themselves, with a view to reaching objectives that are more or less clearly laid down by their teachers, pupils in higher-education establishments with a strong pedagogic formation are literally led by the institution, and their 'individual' work is thus very largely a directed work.

29 Personal lodgings and the parental home are today the main workplaces of students, far ahead of the library or the university premises.

30 Oscillations of this kind are also to be observed in domestic practices. Cf. a

case of household oscillation between 'doing the essentials' and 'everything must be just so' in Kaufmann (1997, p. 154).

Act I, Scene 3, Analogy and Transfer

1. Anne Muxel (1996) offers a phenomenological approach to these different ways of triggering memory that is very suggestive.
2. Despite its evident limitations, the metaphor of jurisprudence makes it possible to draw on a strong historic opposition that distinguishes (and sometimes opposes) Anglo-Saxon jurisprudential law from that of continental Europe, which arose from Roman law and is based on a code deemed applicable to all possible circumstances. Legal work in the first case consists in comparing each new situation with similar situations judged previously (the logic of analogy and 'precedent'). In the second case it presupposes the construction of general rules (laws), impersonal and universal, on the basis of which various decisions can be deduced for various future cases. On the one hand we have a movement from one particular case to another, on the other a movement leading from the general rule to the case that depends on it (Weber, 1978). By using the metaphor of jurisprudence here, I thus wish to emphasize the extreme formalism of those theories of action that invoke, with no sense of distinction, the 'norm' or the 'rule'. By being too widely used, these end up on the one hand giving the impression that actors, in their most everyday actions, are engaged in a fastidious work of guidance or orientation of their behaviour as a function of norms or rules, while on the other hand no longer making visible, when this would be particularly useful, the specific social effects on practice of the effective presence of express (written) rules or norms to which reference can be made, and which can be contested. Cf. on the 'educational rule', Lahire (1994a).
3. 'We thus note that Marie-Line's conflicts with her husband reactivate conflicts with her father. The question for her is always to maintain the right to be her own person, against a retaliatory threat from the man' (Schwartz, 1990, p. 237).
4. 'In essential aspects of her relationship to her husband, the woman thus occupies a position of mother, homologous to that which she fulfils in relation to her children' (ibid., p. 177).
5. James M. Ostrow gives on this subject the very fine example of an extract from Virginia Woolf's *To the Lighthouse* in which we see a theme from Cam's childhood resurface several years later, without Cam having any need to 'recall' his mother, the environment he finds himself in being 'saturated with his mother's presence' (1990, pp. 47–8).
6. Anne Longuet Marx recalls how 'Proust always defined metaphor and involuntary memory in the same way, as the "miracle of analogy", the encounter and superposition of two objects or two sensations' (1986, p. 181).
7. It is not by chance, moreover, that Piaget could write, in certain formulas that are not very happy but are symptomatic of the proximity of the two orders of phenomena (memory and habit): 'The child no longer merely tries to repeat or prolong an effect which he has discovered or observed by chance ... he adapts the familiar schema to the particulars of [the present] situation' (1952, pp. 212–13).

8 We should note that these quotations from Bergson do not imply a general acceptance of his theses. On questions such as the dualism between memory and habit, 'motor mechanisms' and 'memory-images', the idea of a 'true memory' or 'pure remembrances' or the idealism of certain propositions, Bergson's reflections do not all seem pertinent. It must be recognized, however, that this author, unloved by sociologists and little read for historical and institutional reasons that can readily be imagined, correctly accounted in some of his formulas for the operation of habit-memory, or what he also calls 'memory of the body' ('the ensemble of sensory-motor systems that habit has organized').

9 I should note in passing that, if 'habitus as incorporated acquisition' is the 'presence of the past – or to the past – and not memory of the past' (i.e. in Bergsonian terms, habit-memory and not remembrance-memory), then the theory of habitus is powerless to conceive 'remembrances' (or does it see the latter as outside the field of sociological investigation?), which is not without its problems (see Bourdieu, 2000, p. 210).

10 See, in Kaufmann (1997, pp. 133–47), chapter 10 devoted to habit.

11 The model 'habit or routine'/'crisis situation'/'reflection or consciousness' is already present in Durkheim's work. It was variously examined by James Dewey, Anselm L. Strauss and Pierre Bourdieu.

12 Paul Connerton, for example, criticizes the conception of habits as competences or skills 'waiting to be called into action on the appropriate occasion'. He gives the example of 'bad habits', to emphasize the fact that habits are tendencies or strong impulses to act in a certain way, even when the actor does not consciously desire this. This tends none the less towards a model of self-propulsion, in which embodied habit no longer needs any support, encouragement or external trigger (1989, p. 93).

13 We are then dealing with what certain psychologists call 'modularization': 'Modularization refers to all processes by which a motor action that constitutes a sequence acquires a relative constancy of duration, quantity of energy required, and form, and ends up being accomplished without any need to be interrupted in order for information to be processed' (Bruner, 1991, p. 146).

14 'When, for example, the traffic light turns red as I approach in my automobile, I do not in general deliberate and then choose to release the accelerator and apply the brakes. Indeed, most of the actions we perform are done without deliberation or choice. In most cases habits, desires and impulses prevail – we act as we do as a matter of course, straight off, without reflection or pondering of any kind' (Melden, 1968, p. 28).

15 Olivier Schwartz describes the case of a woman who embarks on a critical discussion of her condition and her husband only when she is alone with the researcher (1990, p. 237).

16 We need only think of the 'self-evident' choice (but one that no linguist, psycholinguist or psychologist had the idea of making before him), made by William Labov (1972a, 1972b), of asking a black researcher (who had himself come from the ghetto) to record 'natural' speech in black American vernacular in the black ghettos of New York. When I myself had to conduct interviews with women teachers (Lahire, 1993a) or with the specialized staff of primary schools (Lahire, 1993b), a large part of these interviews owed their richness – and I believe their quality – to a kind of relationship that was sometimes not spoken, sometimes explicitly mentioned ('I have a son or

daughter of your age'; 'You remind me of my son') of the mother–child kind. This transfer of the mother–son relationship into the context of the sociological interview was sometimes accompanied by other complicities based on common family or cultural experiences.

17 'According to this usage, habit is the durable and generalized disposition that suffuses a person's action throughout an entire domain of life or, in the extreme instance, throughout all of life – in which case the term comes to mean the whole manner, turn, cast or mold of the personality' (Camic, 1986, p. 1046).

18 'The same privileged-class habitus can generate radically opposed political or aesthetic opinions' (Bourdieu and Passeron, 1977, p. 35).

19 The question still remains unanswered whether it is the researcher who 'sees' a combination scheme in both situations, or whether in actual fact, from the standpoint of the cognitive functioning of the child, there is indeed a transfer of the same scheme from situations of material manipulation to more logical and abstract situations.

20 As some findings in cognitive psychology suggest, 'the development of rationality cannot be reduced to the improving substitution of new structures, whether symbolic or sub-symbolic . . . but development also frequently means inhibiting a competing structure' (Houdé, 1995, p. 3).

21 The heroes of various novels by Jean-Philippe Toussaint, for example (1990, 1991, 2008).

22 What are the various manifestations of educational 'difficulty' in children from working-class milieus, if not the expression of a feeling of foreignness that they experience in particular social forms and their resistance – not necessarily conscious – towards these? Those unable to engage in the educational forms of apprenticeship, who 'dis-invest' educational practices, pragmatically reappropriate into their own dialogue the most formal educational exercises, and – out of the necessity of adaptation – apply 'imitations' and 'automatisms', undergo the curious experience common to everyone compelled to enter into a logic that they have no means of understanding systematically, being forced to live in forms in relation to which they remain foreign. The 'automatisms' or 'imitations' that can give the illusion of 'success' enable these pupils to supply 'good' results even when they lack mastery of the principles of educational production of these results. But at the least trap set by a new exercise, the 'automatism' appears in broad daylight and ceases to cast its illusion, thus showing the weak degree of mastery of the educational situation or, more precisely, the extremely low transferability of the knowledge, techniques, modes of reasoning, skills, etc., that are acquired there. The behaviours at school that I referred to as 'educational dis-investment', 'oral imitation' and 'automatisms' are in any case revealing indicators of the effort of adaptation to an educational world perceived as strange and foreign.

23 'It surely should not require such elaborate efforts to demonstrate transfer effects if in fact it is the major mechanism for knowledge deployment in cognitive theory and Western socialization practices. But the news in this ethnographic excursion is how little transfer there is, rather than how much' (Lave, 1988, p. 34).

24 In the same fashion, faced with evidence of the existence of specific intellectual capacities in practices as different as writing a letter or keeping an

account book, the British anthropologist Jack Goody has suggested 'the generalization of skills exhibited by an individual in one realm of activity to other spheres in open to doubt' (1987, p. 206).

25 There are no syllabic lists, or tables of graphic signs, that would provide material for a specific apprenticeship in reading and writing.

26 As I have been able to show by offering an analysis of it in Lahire (1993a, pp. 36–40).

27 But, whatever their general character, schemes always remain marked by and attached to the singular circumstances of their constitution (content of knowledge, type of activity, domain of existence, etc.). These 'summaries of experience' always preserve in them a trace of the nature of the experience on the basis of which they were established. It is this fact that explains how it is possible to discover in one and the same individual disparate tastes or cultural dispositions according to the cultural domain in question: the same actor who applies an aesthetic disposition in relation to literary reading (for reasons of educational formation) may apply a less educated ethico-practical disposition when watching television or going to the cinema.

28 'When we asked an informant to tell us the names of the various Vai clans ordinarily represented at funerals in his town we ... obtained an impressively long list ... [This] stands in sharp contrast to the many experimentally contrived situations in which populations such as the Vai fail to demonstrate conceptually ordered recall' (Goody, 1987, p. 207).

29 'Our handwriting is recognizable whether we trace letters on paper with a pencil held by three fingers or on the blackboard with chalk held at arm's length – for our handwriting is more than simply a power that our body has of circumscribing a certain absolute space, limited once and for all by certain conditions and the use of certain muscles rather than others. It is a general capacity to formulate a constant type (of gesture?), handling all the transpositions that may be necessary' (Merleau-Ponty, 1973, p. 76).

Act I, Scene 4, Literary Experience

1 This type of reading is displayed in Bernhard Schlink's novel *The Reader* (1998). The illiterate Hannah has texts read aloud to her by her young lover Michael, and reacts to the characters' adventures as if they were real people: 'She was an attentive listener. Her laugh, her sniffs of contempt, and her angry or enthusiastic remarks left no doubt that she was following the action intently, and she found [the two heroines] to be silly little girls. Her impatience when she sometimes asked me to go on reading seemed to come from the hope that all this imbecility would eventually play itself out. "Unbelievable!"' (ibid., p. 41). And, in connection with reading Eichendorff's *Good for Nothing*, 'she held it against him he's a good-for-nothing who doesn't achieve anything, can't do anything, and doesn't want to besides' (ibid., p. 58).

2 We could cite here Gustave Flaubert, James Joyce, Alain Robbe-Grillet or Claude Simon, considering them – wrongly – as in a way theorists or ideologists of the cultivated relationship to literature. For example, Flaubert well expressed this pure aesthetic conception in a letter to Louise Colet of 16 January 1852:

> What strikes me as beautiful, what I would like to do, is a book about nothing, a book with no external attachment, which would maintain itself by the internal strength of its style, like the earth floats without being held.... This is why there are neither good nor bad subjects, and one could even establish it as an axiom, situating oneself at the standpoint of pure Art, that there is nothing of the kind, style being in and of itself an absolute manner of seeing things. (1980, p. 31)

3 'As if', since in the end what is sought is as much the 'real' or the 'true to life' (which leads to reading romanticized biographies, documentaries, history books, stories hinging on a real drama of some kind) as the effect of reality or authenticity (which leads to reading novels knowing that the story did not really take place, but written in such a way that 'you believe it'). Readers can thus 'act as if' they were reading real, true, authentic stories, while still not being completely duped by their fictitious character.

4 Erich Schön (1993) mentions the role of reading in the ego-formation of children and adolescents. Among the young people he interviewed, girls 'privilege reading that can help them "assume" analogous situations in their everyday life' (ibid., p. 32).

5 See above, 'The many occasions for maladjustment and crisis', p. 45–7.

6 My research shows, moreover, that the same circumstances of rupture, disconnection and crisis are propitious to the keeping of personal diaries for actors who have already acquired a certain familiarity with writing. The diary is then a catalogue of situations experienced, which is written down, re-read and reworked, or of fictitious situations in preparation for real actions. It is a place for reflection on oneself, one's past and one's future.

7 An exception to this is the work of Jacques Leenhardt and Pierre Jósza (1982), as well as the arguments of François de Singly (1993b). Besides the innovative work of historians of reading (Chartier, 1993, 1994), however, there is also the sociological research into cultural reception. Cf. in particular Passeron and Pedler (1991). For my part, I place these reflections on literary experience in the more general context of a sociology of the social uses of writing (produced or received).

8 See, for example, Donnat and Cogneau (1990).

9 See, on ways of defining reading in education, Chartier and Hébrard (1989), and in particular 'Troisième partie: Discours d'école', pp. 169–394.

10 At a lecture – 'The World of the Reader and the World of the Text: Readings and Readers in the Renaissance' – given at the Villa Gillet in Lyon in January 1993, Roger Chartier mentioned the importance of age and family situation in understanding the interest for certain literary genres in Spain at that time. Crossing social milieus that were classically divided, novels of chivalry on the one hand and devotional literature on the other circulated among readers who were either young and single, or else elderly and married or widowed.

11 A model of writing based on 'trying out' can be found in Montaigne's *Essays*. The *exempla* that the author cites are ones that have an echo in his own experience, as Fausta Garavini emphasized:

> But how to discover oneself if not by identifying with the agent or subject of a moral act – i.e. with the character of a story? Montaigne's 'examples' are not responses to the need to compose a mosaic of the varieties and contradictions of human nature in general, which is the customary intent

of compilers. He does not choose them at random: 'I prefer to note the examples that affect me.' These anecdotes signify that the subject is directly concerned by the attitudes he observes in people like himself, and that he records by way of evidence dispositions that he recognizes in himself or, on the contrary, tendencies that are foreign to him. If he reflects in this way on the diversity and incoherence of our nature, this is in a certain sense secondary. The main point is the question that surfaces from each example: What would I, Michel de Montaigne, do in similar circumstances? A question that ultimately sums up the whole undertaking of the *Essays*: 'trying out' also means putting oneself in someone else's skin ('In my imagination I completely insinuate myself into their place'), trying to experience, by slipping into another person, all the experiences that one cannot experience in everyday life, expanding one's real life by the boundless directions of possible lives. The person who has renounced being always the same individual finds in the protagonists of the *exempla* the means of being many people. (Garavini, 1995–6, p. 723)

12 The dreams of certain subjects seem to be anticipations or rehearsals of experiences that they will have to confront in the future, such as the death of a loved one. When one of the subjects was asked if he dreamt of his brother, who suffered from a cancer of the spinal column that was rapidly progressing, he replied: 'I don't know: only dreams of the sleeping kind [*sic*]. I see my thoughts going in this direction. Sometimes I wonder, after his latest bout of surgery, how it would be if he wasn't there any more, if he died. This haunted me for a while. It disturbed me: what would I do? How would all this affect my life, my family? It was quite a morbid thought. After thinking about it I feel calm when I think of the possibility that something might happen. But if it did, I think I'd be better able to confront it than I was before. It wouldn't be the same shock as it would have been earlier.' (Wunder, 1993, p. 121)

13 The characters in dreams are thus very often members of the dreamer's family: 'Hall makes the hypothesis that we dream of members of our family because it is they whom we are emotionally involved with and towards whom we have mixed feelings of affection, antagonism and unresolved tensions (Hall, 1966, p. 33)' (Wunder, 1993, pp. 118–19).

14 A similar case of parapraxis is found in context in my *Portrait de configuration no. 20*, titled 'Un surinvestissement scolaire paradoxale' (Lahire, 1995a, pp. 217–25).

15 Erving Goffman puts it as follows: 'A back region or backstage may be defined as a place, relative to a given performance, where the impression fostered by the performance is knowingly contradicted as a matter of course' (1956, p. 69).

16 'It was not that I denied daydreams could be idle, playful or merely expressive, but I was focusing on their relation to action' (Strauss, 1993, p. 6).

Act II, Scene 1, School, Action and Language

1 Writing was considered for a very long time as 'derived' from 'oral language' and 'external' to it, so that its invention left intact an 'oral language' that

pre-existed it. For Rousseau, Condillac, Warburton, Locke, Leibniz and Hegel, as well as Saussure, 'writing' was conceived from an instrumentalist perspective as a 'representation' of 'language'. 'Representation', 'vehicle', 'communication technique', 'duplicate', 'means of expression' are all images and metaphors that completely demolish any possibility of considering writing as tracing a kind of homogeneous and continuous space of meaning. But the privilege conferred on the 'voice' in relation to 'writing' in much scientific discourse is not to be taken literally. For example, contrary to his proclaimed intentions, Saussure, like so many others before him, never stopped referring unconsciously to writing, written language, practices of writing and the relationship to language formed in these practices.

2 'The men who invented and perfected writing were great linguists, and it is they who created linguistics' (Meillet, 1912–13, p. cxiv).

3 As I remarked above, we actually have a tendency to reverse the historical course of events by thinking that writing is simply a duplicate of speech, whereas it is because we are accustomed to perceiving speech through the categories that alphabetic writing and grammar have enabled us to construct (e.g. letters, syllables, words, sentences . . .) that we are able to believe that speech and writing resemble one another like two drops of water.

4 To illustrate, for example, the cases of misunderstandings that revolve around the opposition between passive, grammatical, paradigmatic comprehension, on the one hand, and active, dialogical, pragmatic comprehension, on the other, I presented the situation that Wittgenstein describes on the basis of a 'a boy . . . who had to say whether the verbs in certain sentences were in the active or passive voice, and who racked his brains over the question whether the verb "to sleep" meant something active or passive' (1972, p. 22). The pupils who committed misunderstandings of this kind reappropriated the grammatical categories and questions (which presuppose a perspective on language as such, as a world of its own) on the basis of a *pragmatic relationship to language* (language as indissociable from a possible situation, real or imaginary) (Lahire, 1993a, pp. 181–2).

5 One could also say Platonic, referring to E. A. Havelock's magnificent *Preface to Plato* (1963).

6 We know that the first scribes made very formal exercises for themselves, copying and recopying the names of the months, lists of names in an arbitrarily chosen order, model sentences ('dogs bark', 'cats miaow'), etc. (Goody, 1987, p. 169).

7 'Associative relations, on the contrary, hold in absentia. They hold between terms constituting a mnemonic group' (Saussure, 1960, p. 122).

8 'Syntagmatic relations hold *in praesentia*. They hold between two or more terms co-present in a sequence'; 'In its place in a syntagma, any unit acquires its value simply in opposition to what precedes, or to what follows, or to both' (ibid., pp. 121–2).

9 A similar criticism is made by David Sudnow:

Almost without exception, the contemporary analysis of oral discourse objectifies the discourse, completely depriving it of its characteristics of a motivated movement that make up its essential experiential qualities. Someone speaks and their discourse is transformed into text by language itself. Instead of the fluxes and refluxes that circulate from one place to another (a continuous and developing performance that consists in intelligent movements going this way and that and organized on the temporal plane), we are immediately dealing with a 'text', a silent and immobile collection of objects visible on the page. We are confronted – in transformational analysis, in sociolinguistic analysis, in the analysis of everyday discourse – with a range of visible objects. These are examined at leisure, inspected from all points of view, and as is generally the case when modern thought attacks visible objects, their different parts are named – here a pronoun, there a noun, a morpheme, and so on. These classifications and 'parts of discourse' (a mistaken designation *par excellence*) are subsequently subjected to an exhaustive taxonomic treatment by using the same system of movements that we are supposed to analyse. Thus these visible objects become the reality of the discourse.... But to speak is to move. (1978, p. 86)

Yet Sudnow still does not see how school proceeds exactly in the same fashion as the linguistics he criticizes.

10 This holds also for the Bourdieu's Bakhtinian critical remarks on the grammarian way of dealing with language (1990, p. 32).
11 We need only read the statistical tables given in Bourdieu's *Distinction* to convince ourselves of the fact that it is the (longer or shorter) experience of schooling that is determinant in this matter, and not general social position in social space (upper, middle or working class) or amount of economic capital (1984, pp. 36–8).
12 I used this distinction in *Les Manières d'étudier* (Lahire, 1997a, pp. 137–8, 159).
13 The Hoggart family, consisting of mother and three children, received support from the Committee of Guardians and public assistance, and lived in very precarious material conditions.
14 Scientific analysis here is no different from a kind of critique addressed to the school by certain educationalists: that this is 'inconsequential', 'futile', 'artificial', 'inauthentic', and opposed to 'life' – which life? – as the place of the 'real', 'useful', 'functional', 'natural', 'authentic', etc .
15 The same economism is to be found in Bourdieu's books on Algeria, which explain rational dispositions in terms of the material conditions of existence. Thus, 'rational calculation, initially conducted in an imaginary and abstract mode, is gradually embodied in behaviour, insofar as the improvement of material conditions permits this' (Bourdieu, Darbel, Rivet and Seibel, 1995, p. 342). These authors refer to the 'objective heritage of a different civilization, techniques of remuneration or commercialization, methods of accounting, calculation, organization, the system imported by colonization', which 'appears as an infinitely complex game which workers find themselves plunged into' (ibid., 313), but this aspect of things seemed secondary in the given scientific context. Today I would see it as central, if we are to grasp the precise modalities by which dispositions or schemes are established. And it was not accidental that the Algerian small peasants, artisans and market traders were incapable of rational conduct, given that the majority at that time were illiterate and in unstable and precarious economic conditions.

Act II, Scene 2, The Everyday Practices of Writing in Action

1 My discussion here is based on the results of a number of studies (in total, around 100 interviews and 500 questionnaires) devoted to practices of domestic writing in different social milieus. These were partly conducted with the efficient and wise help of Luc Bourgade (1993) and Mathias Millet (1993).
2 Itineraries based on reading maps. But the commonplace of using road maps has ended up making us forget the revolution in relationship to space that this miniaturized representation of space presupposes. The map presents in synoptic fashion, in the form of a single image visible at a glance, a spatial and geographical reality that can generally be crossed only in a discontinuous fashion, in the succession of different moments of a real movement in space. This fantastic abstraction gives 'a visible simulacrum of what in reality has always escaped the human gaze' (Jacob, 1988, p. 275).
3 Cf. above, 'The many occasions for maladjustment and crisis', pp. 45–7.
4 Among these conditions, we should certainly mention the familiarity with writing that comes from having acquired through education a certain mastery of written language (as confirmed by statistical inquiries as to the educational level of subjects). Besides, the individual keeping a diary cannot be completely forgetful of themselves, sacrificing themselves (and their time and attention) to other members of the family: the 'family-ization' of which Richard Hoggart (1988) speaks restrains any move in this direction and explains why diaries kept by women frequently end on marriage or the birth of the first child.
5 It should be noted that one of the presuppositions of our interview grid was that discussion should bear on and remain at a very particular level of reality – i.e. the level of language. We were speaking in fact of practices of writing in relation to very different practices in everyday life, and not really dealing directly and in depth with each of the dimensions of family activity with which domestic writings are connected (purchases, travel, relationships with family and friends, etc.). This tacit pact, however, was quite often broken during interviews with working-class families, who are precisely not very great users of writing. If we asked about shopping lists, these respondents spontaneously ended up talking about purchases and tastes in food; if we mentioned lists of things to take for a new school year, they slipped from writing to the reality of the new year and commented on that event. The sociologist had each time to refocus these statements back to practices of writing; each subject, each theme might have been commented on not specifically from the standpoint of practices of writing but that of the general feelings that they had towards it. Fundamentally, however, the tacit pact that underlay the whole interview rested on a relationship to language – in other words on the dissociability of language from the world of situations, events and things experienced. To break the pact thus meant resisting this dissociation.
6 Cf., on cognitive artefacts, *Sociologie du travail*, 36 (1994).
7 But the embodiment of information depends on the relationship that one has with the domain of activity in question. For instance, if women who are responsible for the cohesion of the family group generally know the birthdays of their nearest and dearest by heart and without particular effort, this

is not necessarily the case on the male side; one subject (teacher of German in a *grande école*) wrote down the birthdays of his family in his diary.

8 It seems that senior managers are statistically those most inclined to conceive and manage their everyday family life as an 'organization' and cultivate a form of asceticism (Establet, 1987). However, if rational domestic dispositions are unevenly distributed in society, the lines of division do not always follow the boundaries of classes or social groups (Lahire, 1995b).

9 As do Bernard Conein and Eric Jacopin: 'Routine seems to explain quite well the behaviour of customers in the supermarket: they use certain spatial bearings to find the products they want, without thinking or deliberating, since every gesture is controlled by a perception guided by these bearings' (1994, p. 491).

10 Certain occasions of speech can be 'prepared' without the mediation of writing being needed. Nevertheless, on the one hand, writing makes it possible to increase the degree of precision of preparation, while, on the other hand, as Jack Goody suggests at many points in his work (see in particular, 1987, pp. 115–22), the existence of a written culture has cognitive consequences on the relationship to language, including 'oral' practices. I have myself shown the fundamentally written character of the 'oral' educational practice of language – in structures of language that are acceptable at school, but also and especially in the educational relationship to language (Lahire, 1993a, pp. 193–242).

11 A woman respondent (maintenance agent), for example, describes her partner (a cook) as follows:

> When he phones it's enough, he knows very well how to tell you, he knows exactly what he means and no one puts him off. For me it's easier. Certain places, it's him who goes because he knows very well that it's like that, it's like that and it's finished, and the person can say what they want. It doesn't make any difference at all. Besides, he knows very well, there are certain places he goes and I don't. For example he goes to the tax office and things like that. 'It's like this, it's like that, you've made a mistake!' 'No, I'm sorry, we've not made a mistake.' 'But I assure you, and I don't want to wait in line like this.' He goes to the head of the queue. Yes, he's bold. [Laughter] And it's true that, when you're in the right, you're in the right, when you're sure of yourself. You're sure, you've done everything needed, they send you more and more forms to fill in. Well, he never fills in a form, he just goes there. When he goes there, he's sure of himself – that he's in the right. And the last time, that's how it went, he went there and straight to the head of the queue. And it ended up, well, he was quite right, they apologized to him and everything. If it was me, I'm sure I'd have gone back two or three times. Whereas him, it's like that.

Once again, men from a working-class milieu echo the classic critique addressed to rhetoric from its very invention: only open, spontaneous, direct and improvised relationships are acceptable (morally and politically). Cf. Desbordes (1991, pp. 26–7, 40).

12 Thus we can express some reservation as to the first hypothesis of the action theory proposed by Anselm L. Strauss: '*No action is possible without the body*: that is, the body is a *necessary condition for action*' (1993, p. 23).

13 'The emigrants were not content to sent money to their families. They

continued to manage and direct their properties. The ties that they maintained with their family and their village could be secured by friends returning home. But the freemason able to read and write was kept in touch with incidents that happened on his land. He could thus keep economic control of his domain, decide the rotation of crops, set the date for sale and the price of animals' (Dauphin, Lebrun-Pezerat and Poublan, 1991, p. 74).

14 We can add to this the practices of writing that participate in reflexivity and self-control: personal diaries, poems, autobiographies, proto-literary commentaries accompanying photographs . . . (Lahire, 1993b, pp. 148–51). The case of personal diaries shows that, apart from any practical necessity, actors make reflexive returns on past events, whether happy or otherwise, reflexively prepare actions (things to say or do) and, in particular, interactions, or invent fictitious scenes and characters (a lover, a friend, a big brother, an elder sister, a father, etc.). Writing can thus intervene before the experience of events, helping one to be stronger, more calm, less agitated . . . It can also intervene subsequently, making it possible to 'work through' scenes outside of the torment of action. Some diarists even speak of returning to the past consigned to their journal with a view to resolving problematic situations in the present, thus effecting, as in the reading of literary texts, jurisprudential comparisons between past and present. They thus draw points of support for future action from their own objectified experience.

15 On the basis of a sociology of action regimes, Laurent Thévenot (1995) adopts the same attitude towards the notion of the plan.

16 This author compares a plan made to decide major operations before the action proper with descending the rapids in a canoe (Suchman, 1990).

17 'They [forecasts] are more like resources that the actors construct and consult before and after the performance of the action' (ibid., p. 159).

18 'Instructions intervene directly on action and define the content of performance, i.e. a precise operation to be realized, whereas advice qualifies the objectives of the task but remains vague on the way in which the action should be accomplished: it gives an orientation and leaves part to improvisation, attenuating control' (Conein and Jacopin, 1993, pp. 71–2).

19 A good example of deliberate interruption of activity for reasons of safety is the use of checklists in industry, and especially in civil aviation. In this field, the checklist is generally consulted by two pilots; one reads aloud the items on the list, while the other confirms and responds aloud as each item is read out. The aim of these actions is to force a deliberate and conscious interruption, controlled behaviour, to deliberately interrupt the normal flow of activity. The controls and precautions bound up with safety are supposed to create a disturbance that stimulates an effort of conscious attention. Automatic actions are exposed to two kinds of problem: errors caused by forgetting an action (action slip) and disturbances caused by external events and interruptions. Even the checklist may fail in its function. After being used thousands of times and after years of experience, its use may become so routine that it becomes automatic, which may have very serious consequences. (Norman, 1993, pp. 27–8)

20 'But in no case – and this is the crucial point – do such plans control action, whatever the particular sense is given to the word "control". Whatever their number or the scope of the possible use, plans stop where the work of descending the rapids begins' (Suchman, 1990, p. 158).

21 Long confined to the strictly economic order, these practices are now permeating the domestic world by force of circumstance.
22 The notion of 'rational calculation', whether used or rejected, which is part of the vocabulary of economics or a certain sociology, may be usefully put in perspective by asking what are the intellectual techniques, and in particular the written and visual practices, without which no rational calculation could exist. Max Weber already described, in *The Protestant Ethic and the Spirit of Capitalism* (2001), the keeping of rational accounts (regular, rigorous, etc.) as a precondition for the rationalization of economic practices.
23 Jürgen Habermas remarks, for example, that theories of strategic activity 'bear hypotheses about rationality that only apply (approximately) to limited sectors of social reality' (1995, p. 18).
24 On the notion of 'field of relevance' as a tool of epistemological reflexivity, but above all as a concrete (historicizing) attitude that the researcher deploys in relation to 'theories', see below, 'Workshops and Debates', pp. 220–2.

Act II, Scene 3, The Plural Logics of Action

1 See below, 'The Place of Language', pp. 163–74.
2 'A particularly clear example of practical sense as a proleptic adjustment to the demands of the field is what is called, in the language of sport, "a feel for the game"' (Bourdieu, 1990a, p. 66).
3 More generally, the theory of practical reason is based on the phenomenology of Husserl and Merleau-Ponty. In 'The dead seize the living' (1980, p. 7, note 10), Bourdieu refers to the 'late Heidegger' and to Merleau-Ponty, who 'sought to express in the language of ontology' and in terms of a '"wild" or "barbaric" beyond' . . . the intentional relationship to the object', what he himself denotes as a 'practical' relationship to the world.
4 If an academic or group of academics decide, for example, to put on a conference in a year's time, they will have to plan preparatory meetings, draw up a budget, book premises, fix dates and deadlines for proposed contributions, etc. All these are acts that are consciously posited as such with a view to very explicitly attaining a goal consciously aimed at. It would be ridiculous here to say that the conference can be held simply thanks to a sense of the game (even if the sense of the academic game is present from the moment that round tables or symposia, for example, are formed), in the immediate, obscure, pre-reflexive relationship of the habitus to a situation, or that it will be present without anyone having targeted it as an explicit goal to attain, a goal to be realized . . .
5 We may note, moreover, that the players taken as examples are often 'excellent' or 'good' ones. Cf., for example, Bourdieu (1990b, pp. 63–4).
6 Practices could be seen here as varying according to the preparation or training time that they require. For example, if there are sites and times for the preparation of a good tennis player, footballer, engineer, car mechanic, etc., for the formation of a 'good father' there are no other 'sites' than those of our own family experience and the example of the role of father with which everyday life supplies us. It is hard to imagine – and this therefore makes it worth questioning the reasons for this improbable situation – the latter in a situation of simulation and training, constantly rehearsing the

gestures to make or not make with his child, the reactions to have or not to have.

7 'In a more general way, habitus has its "blips", critical moments when it misfires or is out of phase: the relationship of immediate adaptation is suspended, in an instant of hesitation into which there may slip a form of reflection which has nothing in common with that of the scholastic thinker and which ... remains turned toward practice and not towards the agent who performs it' (Bourdieu, 2000, p. 162).

8 'To live only in the present, to respond to a stimulus by the immediate reaction which prolongs it, is the mark of lower animals: the man who proceeds in this way is a man of *impulse*' (Bergson, 1912, p. 198).

9 This perspective is best expressed in the qualified way that M. Crozier and E. Friedberg pose the question of rationality in action:

> The actor rarely has clear objectives and, even more rarely, coherent projects. His objectives are diverse, more or less ambiguous, more or less explicit, and more or less contradictory. Some will be changed in the course of action, some rejected, others discovered during the process or even after the fact, if only because the unforeseen and unforeseeable consequences of his action require him to 'reconsider his position' and 'readjust his aim.' What is a 'means' at one moment will be an 'end' at another, and vice versa. It follows that it would be illusory to regard such behavior as deliberate and reasoned, i.e., mediated by a lucid subject calculating his moves as a function of objectives established at the outset. (1980, pp. 24–5)

10 An example of this way of conceiving the debate between theories of action, from the standpoint of the theory of practical reason, can be found in Wacquant and Calhoun (1989).

11 A critique of utilitarianism offered on the basis of anti-utilitarianism, and presupposing an alternative *a priori* conception of human action, is thus not any more pertinent. To oppose to the calculating satisfaction of interests the 'desire for intersubjective recognition', and maintain that 'the real motor of social practice is the search for prestige, or more modestly for a tolerable social identity', is to believe that there exist 'fundamental motives of human action' or 'real motors' of practices (Caillé, 1988, p. 196). But 'motives' and 'motors' are always the product of socio-historical forms of life. Durkheim, moreover, would not have failed to say about anti-utilitarianism what he said about utilitarianism – i.e. that it theorizes what it desires.

12 Cases range from those in which nothing that seems at all relevant happens except the occurrence of the bodily movement – one responds to the situation in which one finds oneself almost automatically, guided as it were by habit and the whole accumulation of past experience – to the cases in which force of mind, great effort, or internal struggles are involved as habit is resisted or passions and temptations conquered ... The characteristic philosophic vice of generalizing from special cases is involved in the familiar summary explanation of the concept of action in terms of various psychological factors or processes. (Melden, 1968, pp. 30–1)

13 'Even when the action-present is brief, performers can sometimes train themselves to think about their actions. In the split-second exchanges of a game of tennis, a skilled player learns to give himself a moment to plan the next shot. His game is the better for this momentary hesitation, so long as he gauges

the time available for reflection correctly and integrates his reflection into the smooth flow of action' (Schön, 1983, p. 279). See also Détienne and Vernant (1978).
14 We even find a series of oxymorons in Bourdieu: 'unconscious strategy', 'intentionality without intention', 'finality without purpose', 'regulated improvisation', etc. Pierre-Michel Menger is right to point out the theoretical contortions and semantic torsions that these expressions involve. A precise analysis, he writes, 'would show the whole effort deployed to correct each word by its opposite' and reveal operations comparable with 'a game of snap played by a single player' (1997, pp. 591–2).
15 Is it giving in to bad habits of thought to raise this kind of question and proceed by empirical verification and the hunt for counter-examples, rather than by peremptory *a priori* assertion? At all events, the habit of empirical work in sociology is always better than the inclination to settle theoretical questions by philosophical quotations, no matter how seductive these are. To reply to theoretical problems with philosophy constitutes – for sociologists, not of course for philosophers – a clear sign of weakness and empirical laziness. As Paul Valéry ironically said: 'Pascal "found", but undoubtedly because he stopped looking.'

Act III, Scene 1, The Place of Language

1 To this we must add the metaphor of great depths: 'the pugilistic *illusio* – the half-inarticulate, quasi-organismic belief in the value of the game and its stakes, inscribed deep within the body' (Wacquant, 1995b, pp. 492–3); 'The pugilistic *illusio* is found lodged deep within the body' (Wacquant, 1995a, p. 88); 'Habitus can be understood as virtual "sedimented situations" . . . lodged inside the body' (Bourdieu and Wacquant, 1992, p. 22); 'the emotion . . . that touches the depths of our organic being' (Bourdieu, 2000, p. 140).
2 'What we are tempted to consider as raw experience often presupposes, in reality, the existence of a whole world of concepts and the manipulation of a certain technique', writes Jacques Bouveresse (1987, p. 69).
3 'It is language that must be internalized above all' (Berger and Luckmann, 1979, p. 155).
4 After noting this critical reading, I discovered a similar text from Jean-Paul Bronckart (1997) on Jean Piaget. Bronckart in fact conducts a re-reading of a body of interaction situations between adult and child that Piaget commented on, bringing to light, in a particularly illuminating fashion, the fact that the psychologist omits or neglects language in his interpretation of these situations in the perspective of a theory of development of the child (the formation of symbols).
5 'To acquire the specific *bodily sensitivity* that makes one a competent pugilist is a slow and protracted process; it cannot be effected by an act of will or a conscious transfer of information. It necessitates, rather, an imperceptible embodiment of the mental and corporeal schemata immanent in pugilistic practice that admits no discursive mediation or systematization' (Wacquant, 1995a, p. 72).
6 My intuition is that having the words to say what one is doing facilitates subsequent execution. By drawing children's attention repeatedly to points

of particular observation, by asking them to name these themselves, I would like to help them construct an ordered protocol that accompanies and then guides the order of gestures to be subsequently executed, aiding them with a kind of internal language. What I desire is that the child faced with a new task should be increasingly well armed to regard a complex form, recognize it immediately from the simple forms she is able to reproduce, knowing where to begin in order to combine them in the right order and end up with the complex form. (Chartier and Janssens, 1996, p. 17)

7 Cf. the operation of hospital services and the use of notebooks 'recording the state of each sick person and the care they have received' (Lacoste, 1994).
8 All formalisms (grammatical, linguistic or semiological) abstract (in the sense of extract), from different types of language practice, elements to reconstitute them, recompose them into systems (language types made possible thanks to written and graphic practices).
9 If the systematic relating of sociologically constructed characteristics (social milieu, educational level, age class, sex, place of residence . . .) and linguistically constructed characteristics (phonological, lexical, syntactical, stylistic . . .) is a way of questioning the autonomy of language, it tacitly accepts none the less the legitimacy of the division between language and society, the linguistic and the sociological. In a construction of this kind, linguistic facts, situations of utterance, serve only, as Goffman writes, 'to banalize, in some way, the geometrical intersection between actors who speak and actors who offer certain particular social indices' (1988, p. 146).

ACT III, SCENE 2, WHAT EXACTLY IS EMBODIED?

1 From Peter Berger and Thomas Luckmann (1979) to Pierre Bourdieu (1990a).
2 An interesting contribution to the study of the first phase can be found in Freund (1988).
3 For the modalities of educational socialization in primary school, see Lahire (1993a).
4 As evidence of the vagueness that surrounds these notions, and is largely explained by the very secondary attention that has so far been granted to these terms in sociological models, it is possible to internalize, according to the particular case, 'significations', the 'principles' of a 'cultural variable', 'social structures', 'roles' and 'attitudes', 'schemas of interpretation and motivation', etc.
5 Michael Cole notes the results of certain studies showing how children who have been left alone for a long time in front of television programmes in a foreign language do not manage to acquire this language:

> It seems an inescapable conclusion from this kind of evidence that in order for children to acquire more than the barest rudiments of language they must not only hear (or see) the language but also participate in the activities which that language is helping to create . . . Note that I am not saying that adults must deliberately teach language; rather, that they must arrange/allow children to participate in culturally organized activities mediated by language. (1996, p. 203)

6 'The common people represent the doing twice over, when they make lightning flash – that is being doubled by another doing: it posits the same event once as cause and then once again as effect' (Nietzsche, 1996, p. 29).
7 Of course, some solicitations are non-existent, just as certain kinds of collaboration are not invited in certain families, on account of the place socially ascribed to the child and the representations that adults may make about what is possible and conceivable (in the sense of 'competence' and 'right') at the age of eight to nine, or ten and eleven. Children may thus be forbidden to write on visible supports – calendars, photos, photo albums, video cassettes – out of fear that these will be damaged, to answer the phone or to make a phone call themselves, to go out without first asking (oral) permission from an adult, etc. Children may even be considered too young to write letters (the case of Marouan, eight years old, father a boilermaker and mother a housewife), to want to write stories or poems by themselves, to be able to read children's novels or magazines (the case of Chaouki, eight years old, father a plasterer/painter and mother a housewife), to be able to look up for themselves in a dictionary or little encyclopedia (the case of Damien, nine years old, father and mother run a butcher's shop). Limits of this kind imposed on learning – bound up with a rather closed conception of roles and a particular relationship to childhood – seem almost non-existent in the higher social classes.
8 Julien (eight years old, father a skilled worker and mother a nurse) is thus a good example of the infrequent reader with a good knowledge of French that François de Singly discusses: 'a boy from a working-class milieu, excellent in maths' (1993a).
9 We should note that such cases provide interesting examples of heterogeneous dispositions activated as a function of the situation. On the one hand, the parents do not like reading and writing but, on the other hand, they incite and 'push' their children relentlessly to practise these, so that they turn out different from themselves.
10 Concerning family conditions of access to reading, large-scale studies have shown that the share of great readers is higher among those who benefited from their mother telling them stories each day than among those who never (or rarely) heard these, and that this share is also higher among those with a bookshelf in their bedroom than among those with no books in their bedroom (Singly, 1993a).
11 At the opposite extreme we have the parents of Damien (see above), who don't like writing at all and whose pronunciation of certain words, and grammatical mistakes, are the sign of a poor internalization of the specific linguistic norms of written culture.
12 The 'rule' may be suddenly modulated as a function of the context: if it is impossible to apply it in town, then the environment has to be rigorously respected when in the countryside. Cf. Madec (1996, pp. 119–20).

Act IV, Scene 1, Psychological Sociology

1 Pierre Bourdieu wrote that habitus was 'one of the 'intermediate concepts and concepts which mediate between the subjective and the objective' (Bourdieu, 1990d, p. 3).

2 We can often find in Max Weber, though he was far from excluding the individual actor from his comprehensive sociology, the idea that an isolated individual act is not a social act. Religious behaviour, for example, is not a social activity 'if it is simply a matter of contemplation or of solitary prayer' (1978, p. 22). But a solitary behaviour is every bit as social as a behaviour with someone else, because an 'isolated individual' is intersubjective by nature, and her 'internal' mental activity is dependent on her past and present experiences. See 'Une anthropologie de l'interdépendance', in Lahire (1995a, pp. 283–9). One might reply to Max Weber, indeed, with the words of Maurice Halbwachs: 'In reality we are never alone. Other men need not be physically present, since we always carry with us and in us a number of distinct persons' (1980, p. 23).

3 It was Georg Simmel, however, who made the strongest division, and also the most realist (in the sense of epistemological realism), between what was social and what was not. We may note in passing that this division, fixing an *a priori* limit to sociological analysis, holds a high place in the historical honours of the abdication of sociological interpretation. Simmel conferred on 'individuals' and their behavioural and mental schemas a life of their own, independent from social 'forces' and 'forms' (1981, p. 137). For Simmel, instincts, interests, impulses, ends, inclinations, tendencies, etc., are in themselves not social (since they denote 'the matter of socialization, the materials that fill up existence, these motivations that stimulate it but do not yet form either in or for themselves a social being'; ibid., p. 122), but simply 'have the effect that men engage in coexistence with others' (ibid., p. 121). Simmel did not adopt the sociological orientation that would have enabled him to conceive that, on the contrary, it is because they are engaged in historical forms of coexistence that people have particular interests, motivations, impulses, inclinations, etc. Here again, if sociology makes this division between the individual (the mental, the psychic, inclinations, intentions, impulses, etc.) and the social, it plays a bad trick of sociological magic on us by reintroducing underhand those products denoted as sociologically illicit. If individual thoughts and behaviours are not the business of sociology, then sociologists are unable to integrate these into their discourse. But the temptation, as can be readily seen, is stronger than the principle of division initially proclaimed.

4 I have criticized pluridisciplinarity and interdisciplinarity in Lahire (1998a).

5 Gabriel Tarde, as is well known, opposed Durkheim's sociology, which he referred to as an inter-mental psychology; for him, to believe that there exists anything but individual acts or deeds 'is pure ontology' (Durkheim, 1975, p. 165).

6 See, among other less well-known works, Cole (1996); Shweder (1991); Bruner (1991).

7 *Why has it proven so difficult for psychologists to keep culture in mind?* A short answer might be: Because when psychology treated culture as an independent variable and mind as a dependent variable, it broke apart the unity of culture and mind and ordered them temporally – culture is stimulus, mind response. The entire history of cross-cultural psychology can be viewed as a long struggle to put back together that which was torn apart as a consequence of the division of the humane sciences into the social sciences and humanities. (Cole, 1996, pp. 327–8)

8 They also very often remain in thrall to a mentalist conception which claims

that the 'said' is only the 'thought' made public. Now, given that public language is our only tool for tracing this 'thought', it is hard to understand the interest that scholars have in placing a 'thought' that is invisible in itself at the root of a public language that constitutes its one and only trace and proof of existence. The idea that language is only the public expression of a mental structure, a mental reality, totally reverses – quite unreasonably – the order of realities that are tangible, observable and open to study. It is surprising, therefore, to see the disproportionate place granted to this supposed reality, inherently invisible, in relation to that assigned to objective and objectifiable realities (verbal, para-verbal, written, gestural, iconic . . .), reduced to the rank of a mere 'trace' or 'index' of a mental activity deemed fundamental. From this point of view, the work of Ludwig Wittgenstein amounts to a real linguistic therapy. Cf. in particular the presentation of Wittgenstein's philosophy by Jacques Bouveresse (1987).

9 'The inside as an operation of the outside: in all his work, Foucault seems haunted by this theme of an inside which is merely the fold of the outside' (Deleuze, 1999, p. 81).

10 'The description of a historical context is never exhausted by a finite list of variables' (Passeron, 1991, p. 364). This does not mean that sociologists cannot effect a reduction of this kind, or even that they should not do so on certain occasions, simply that they should not be mistaken as to its application.

11 It makes no more sense to view actors as free electrons subject to magnetic fields, or as independent bowling balls moving in an alley that would leave them a certain 'play' (in the mechanical sense of the term) or a 'margin of movement'. It is hard, in fact, to see what advantage there can be (apart from the benefit of a rhetorical union of opposites) in calling actors 'free in a system of constraints', or speaking of 'social determinism in indeterminacy', 'constraint accompanied by free play', 'choices in the limits of a social structure', etc.

12 I have in mind here the works of John Gumperz and William Labov, which inspired psychologists working on language, in particular Michael Cole: 'The strategy we employed in two other studies, both carried out in New York City, was to contrast the behaviour of the same children in their classrooms, when they were being tested, and in an activity outside the school' (1996, p. 221).

Act IV, Scene 2, Pertinent Fields

1 This section is a shortened and modified version of Lahire (1996a).
2 This is the conception of debate in the social sciences that I began to develop in Lahire (1991b).
3 We can again mention Wittgenstein here, as he thought similarly about philosophy.
4 Rogers Brubaker expresses some doubt as to the generalist claim made by Pierre Bourdieu in his preface to the English edition of *Distinction* – i.e. that the theoretical model developed in this work is valid for all stratified societies. Brubaker asks whether this generality is of a meta-theoretical order (e.g. bearing on relationships between conditions of existence, habitus and

practices) or of a more historical order (e.g. changes in modes of domination or in the increased value of cultural capital in relation to economic capital). 'The uniqueness of the Parisian *haute bourgeoisie* and the French educational system would seem to restrict the scope of at least some of Bourdieu's generalizations about the relationships between class and culture' (1985, p. 774, n. 60).

5 Thus C. Jouhaud writes: 'Contexts do not exist prior to the operation that constructs them, or rather they are only assumptions. What exists is not contexts, but rather operations, procedures, experiments of contextualization which bear on a part of the historical reality in a partial, specific and relative fashion' (1994, p. 273).

6 The analysis of frameworks proposed by Erving Goffman (1974) studies 'the structures of individual experience of social life'. For his part, Aaron V. Cicourel, in *Cognitive Sociology* (1974), takes as object, among other things, the interpretative procedures of the members of a community.

7 As practised by the Italian micro-historians, in particular Giovanni Levi (1988).

8 This term is proposed by Jacques Revel, who maintains that the 'macro' and 'micro' versions of reality, 'and many others at intermediate levels that may be noted by means of experiment', are equally 'true' (1994, p. 319). A similar position is found in Lepetit (1993, p. 137): 'The macro-phenomena are no less real, micro-phenomena no more real (or conversely): there is no hierarchy between them.'

9 Bourdieu speaks of 'the impression of heuristic strength often gained by the application of theoretical schemas expressing the very moment of reality' as having 'its counterpart in the permanent feeling of dissatisfaction aroused by the immensity of work necessary to obtain the full return on the theory in each of the cases considered' (1996b, p. 184).

10 The author appeals to 'the direction which should be taken by a social science concerned with converting into a really integrated and cumulative programme of empirical research that legitimate ambition for systematicity which is imprisoned by the totalizing pretensions of "grand theory"' (ibid.).

11 For Marxists I am a Durkheimian, for Durkheimians I am a Weberian, for Weberians a Marxist . . . No one asks: 'But what if he were all these at the same time?' And if the task of science were to accumulate instead of these ritual antagonisms? I believe this is completely possible. It is very pretentious, but these people Marx, Weber, Durkheim developed their thoughts in relation to one another, and we may come to see that each saw the others synthesize and thus accumulate in a non-eclectic manner. (Bourdieu and Grenfell, 1995, pp. 15–16)

12 Cf. the severe criticisms he makes of textual genetics on the basis of his own scientific objectives and interests, acting as if all researchers shared (or should share) the same research objectives and interests: 'I could . . ., at the risk of seeming unjust, evoke the disproportion between the immensity of the work of erudition involved and the slightness of the results obtained' (Bourdieu, 1996b, p. 197).

13 Besides, whenever there is too much worry about how to manage their conceptual heritage and draw profit from it, the temptation to dogmatic and hypostatizing defence of sociological concepts is never far away, even though these concepts, by their nature, are always subject to revision.

REFERENCES

Agre, P. E., and Chapman, D. (1987) 'Pengi: an implementation of a theory of activity', in *Proceedings of the Sixth National Conference on Artificial Intelligence* (Los Altos, CA: Morgan Kaufmann, 1987), pp. 261–72.
Allam, M. (1996) *Journaux intimes: une sociologie de l'écriture personelle* (Paris: L'Harmattan).
Aristotle (1998) *The Nicomachean Ethics*, trans. D. Ross (Oxford: Oxford University Press).
Aune, B. (1977) *Reason and Action* (Dodrecht and Boston: D. Reidel).
Bachelard, G. (2001) *The Formation of the Scientific Mind: A Contribution to a Psychoanalysis of Objective Knowledge* (Manchester: Clinamen).
Bakhtin, M. (1973) *Marxism and the Philosophy of Language* (New York and London: Seminar Press).
Bakhtin, M. (1984) *Esthétique de la creation verbale* (Paris: Gallimard).
Bakhtin, M. (1987) *Freudianism: A Critical Sketch* (Indianapolis: Indiana University Press).
Bally, C. (1926) *Le Langage et la vie* (Paris: Payot).
Becker, H. S. (1994) '"Foi por acaso": conceptualizing coincidence', *Sociological Quarterly*, 35: 183–94.
Benoliel, R., and Establet, R. (1991) 'Jeunesse et habitus: pertinence de l'hypothèse des enquêtes', *Cahiers du CERCOM*, no. 6: 9–29.
Benveniste, É. (1971) *Problems in General Linguistics* (Coral Gables, FL: University of Miami Press).
Berger, P., and Luckmann, T. (1979) *The Social Construction of Reality* (Harmondsworth: Penguin).
Bergson, H. (1912) *Matter and Memory* (London: George Allen).
Bernstein, B. (ed.) (1974) 'Social class, language and socialization', in *Class, Codes and Control: Theoretical Studies towards a Sociology of Language* (2nd edn, London: Routledge & Kegan Paul).
Bernstein, B. (1992) 'La Construction du discours pédagogique et les modalités de sa pratique', *Critiques Sociales*, no. 3–4: 20–58.
Berry, J. W. (1976) *Human Ecology and Cognitive Style: Comparative Studies in Cultural and Psychological Adaptation* (Beverly Hills, CA: Sage).
Boltanski, L. (1990) *L'Amour et la justice comme compétences : trois essais de sociologie de l'action* (Paris: Métailié).

REFERENCES

Boltanski, L., and Thévenot, L. (2006) *On Justification: Economies of Worth* (Princeton, NJ: Princeton University Press).
Boudon, R. (1981) *The Logic of Social Action: An Introduction to Sociological Analysis* (London: Routledge & Kegan Paul).
Boudon, R. (1984) 'Introduction', in G. Simmel, *Les Problèmes de la philosophie de l'histoire* (Paris: Presses universitaires de France), pp. 7–52.
Bourdieu, P. (1976) 'Les Modes de domination', *Actes de la recherche en sciences sociales*, no. 2–3: 122–32.
Bourdieu, P. (1980) 'Le Mort saisit le vif', *Actes de la recherche en sciences sociales*, no. 32–3: 3–14.
Bourdieu, P. (1981) 'Men and Machines', in A. Knorr-Cetina and A. V. Cicourel (eds), *Advances in Social Theory and Methodology: Toward an Integration of Micro- and Macro-Sociologies* (London and Boston: Routledge & Kegan Paul), pp. 304–17.
Bourdieu, P. (1982) *Leçon sur la leçon* (Paris: Minuit).
Bourdieu, P. (1984) *Distinction: A Social Critique of the Judgement of Taste* (London: Routledge & Kegan Paul).
Bourdieu, P. (1986a) 'L'illusion biographique', *Actes de la recherche en sciences sociales*, no. 62–3: 69–72.
Bourdieu, P. (1986b) 'Habitus, code et codification', *Actes de la recherche en sciences sociales*, no. 64: 40–4.
Bourdieu, P. (1989) 'Intérêt et désintéressement', *Cahiers de recherche du GRS*, no. 7.
Bourdieu, P. (1990a) *The Logic of Practice* (Cambridge: Polity).
Bourdieu, P. (1990b) *In Other Words: Essays Towards a Reflexive Sociology* (Cambridge: Polity).
Bourdieu, P. (1990c) 'La domination masculine', *Actes de la recherche en sciences sociales*, no. 84: 3–31.
Bourdieu, P. (ed.) (1990d) *Photography: A Middle-Brow Art* (Cambridge: Polity).
Bourdieu, P. (1991) *Language and Symbolic Power* (Cambridge: Polity).
Bourdieu, P. (1994) 'Stratégies de reproduction et modes de domination', *Actes de la recherche en sciences sociales*, no. 105: 3–12.
Bourdieu, P. (1996a) *The State Nobility: Elite Schools in the Field of Power* (Cambridge: Polity).
Bourdieu, P. (1996b) *The Rules of Art: Genesis and Structure of the Literary Field* (Cambridge: Polity).
Bourdieu, P. (1998) *Practical Reason: On the Theory of Action* (Cambridge: Polity).
Bourdieu, P. (2000) *Pascalian Meditations* (Cambridge: Polity).
Bourdieu, P., and Grenfell, M. (1995) *Entretiens: Pierre Bourdieu et Michael Grenfell*, Centre for Language in Education, University of Southampton, Occasional Paper no. 37.
Bourdieu, P., and Passeron, J.-C. (1977) *Reproduction in Education, Society and Culture* (London: Sage).
Bourdieu, P., and Sayad, A. (1964) *Le Déracinement: la crise de l'agriculture traditionelle en Algérie* (Paris: Minuit).
Bourdieu, P., and Wacquant, L. J. D. (1992) *An Invitation to Reflexive Sociology* (Cambridge: Polity).
Bourdieu, P., Chamboredon, J.-C. and Passeron, J.-C. (1991) *The Craft of Sociology: Epistemological Preliminaries* (New York: Walter de Gruyter).

REFERENCES

Bourdieu, P., Darbel, A., Rivet, J.-P. and Seibel, C. (1995) *Work and Workers in Algeria* (Stanford, CA.: Stanford University Press).
Bourgade, L. (1993) *Des pratiques d'écriture ordinaires* (Lyons: University Lumière Lyon 2).
Bouveresse, J. (1987) *Le Mythe de l'intériorité: expérience, signification et langage privé chez Wittgenstein* (Paris: Minuit).
Bouveresse, J. (1995) 'Règles, dispositions et habitus', *Critique*, no. 579–80: 573–94.
Bronckart, J.-P. (1997) 'Semiotic interaction and cognitive construction', *Archives de Psychologie*, 65: 95–106.
Brubaker, R. (1985) 'Rethinking classical theory: the sociological vision of Pierre Bourdieu', *Theory and Society*, 14(6): 745–75.
Bruner, J. S. (1991) *Le Développement de l'enfant: savoir faire, savoir dire* (Paris: Presses universitaires de France).
Caillé, A. (1988) 'Esquisse d'une critique de l'économie générale de la pratique', *Cahiers du LASA*, no. 8–9: 103–213.
Camic, C. (1986) 'The matter of habit', *American Journal of Sociology*, 91: 1039–87.
Carraher, T. N., Carraher, D. W., and Schliemann, A. D. (1985) 'Mathematics in the streets and in schools', *British Journal of Development Psychology*, no. 3: 21–9.
Certeau, M. de (1984) *The Practice of Everyday Life* (Berkeley: University of California Press).
Chartier, A.-M., and Hébrard, J. (1989) *Discours sur la lecture (1880–1980)* (Paris: BPI).
Chartier, A.-M., and Janssens, F. (1996) 'Les Interactions maître–élèves dans l'apprentisage de l'écriture en grande section de maternelle', paper given at the Piaget centennial conference 'The Growing Mind', Geneva, 14–16 September.
Chartier, R. (ed.) (1991) *La Correspondence: les usages de la lettre au XIXe siècle* (Paris: Fayard); part trans. as *Correspondence: Models of Letter Writing from the Middle Ages to the Nineteenth Century* (Cambridge: Polity, 1997).
Chartier, R. (ed.) (1993) *Pratiques de la lecture* (Paris: PBP).
Chartier, R. (1994) *The Order of Books* (Cambridge: Polity).
Chervel, A. (1981) *Histoire de la grammaire scolaire* (Paris: PBP)
Chevallier, D., and Chiva, I. (1991) 'L'introuvable objet de la transmission', in D. Chevallier (ed.), *Savoir fair et pouvoir transmettre* (Paris: MSH).
Cicourel, A.-V. (1974) *Cognitive Sociology: Language and Meaning in Social Interaction* (New York: Free Press).
Cole, M. (1996) *Cultural Psychology: A Once and Future Discipline* (Cambridge, MA: Belknap Press).
Cometti, J.-P. (1996) *Philosopher avec Wittgenstein* (Paris: Presses universitaires de France).
Conan Doyle, A. (1992) 'A case of identity', in *The Adventures of Sherlock Holmes* (Ware: Wordsworth).
Conein, B., and Jacopin, É. (1993) 'Les Objets dans 'l'espace: la planifaction dans l'action', in *Les Objets dans l'action, Raisons pratiques*, no. 4: 59–84.
Conein, B., and Jacopin, É. (1994) 'Action située et cognition: le savoir en place', *Sociologie du travail*, 36(4): 475–500.
Connerton, P. (1989) *How Societies Remember* (Cambridge: Cambridge University Press).

REFERENCES

Crane, T. (1996) 'Introduction', in D. M. Armstrong, C. B. Martin and U. T. Place (eds), *Dispositions: A Debate* (London and New York: Routledge), pp. 1–11.
Crozier, M., and Friedberg, E. (1980) *Actors and Systems: The Politics of Collective Action* (Chicago: University of Chicago Press).
Dauphin, D., Lebrun-Pezerat, P., and Poublan, D. (1991) 'L'Enquête postal de 1847', in R. Chartier (ed.), *La Correspondence: les usages de la lettre au XIXe siècle* (Paris: Fayard).
Degracia [Gracia Cohen] (1968) *Mariage mixte* (Paris: Presses du temps present).
Delbos, G., and Jorion, P. (1984) *La Transmission des savoirs* (Paris: MSH).
Deleuze, G. (1999) *Foucault* (London: Athlone Press).
Delon, M. (1997) *Usages et fonctions des pratiques d'écriture professionels des professeurs d'école* (Lyons: University Lumière Lyon 2).
Desbordes, F. (1991) *La Rhétorique antique: l'art de persuader* (Paris: Hachette Supérieur).
Détienne, M., and Vernant, J.-P. (1978) *Cunning Intelligence in Greek Culture and Society* (Hassocks: Harvester Press).
Dolle, J.-M. (1988) *Pour comprendre Jean Piaget* (Toulouse: privately pubd).
Donnat, O., and Cogneau, D. (1990) *Les Pratiques culturelles des Français, 1973–1989* (Paris: La Découverte/La Documentation français).
Dostoyevsky, F. (1965) *Memoirs from the House of the Dead*, trans. J. Coulson (Oxford: Oxford University Press).
Dostoyevsky, F. (2008) *A Writer's Diary, 1873–1876* (Evanston, IL: Northwestern University Press).
Durkheim, É. (1956) *Education and Sociology* (New York: Free Press).
Durkheim, É. (1975) *Textes*, vol. 1: *Éléments d'une théorie sociale* (Paris: Minuit).
Durkheim, É. (1976) *The Elementary Forms of the Religious Life* (London: Allen & Unwin).
Durkheim, É. (1977) *The Evolution of Educational Thought* (London: Routledge & Kegan Paul).
Durkheim, É. (1982) *The Rules of Sociological Method* (New York: Free Press).
Durkheim, É. (1987) *La Science social et l'action* (Paris: Presses universitaires de France).
Efron, D. (1941) *Gesture and Environment* (Morningside Heights, NY: King's Crown Press).
Elias, N. (1991) *The Society of Individuals* (Oxford: Blackwell).
Elias, N. (1993) *Mozart: Portrait of a Genius* (Cambridge: Polity).
Elias, N. (1994) *The Civilizing Process* (Oxford: Blackwell).
Ernaux, A. (1974) *Les Armoires vides* (Paris: Gallimard); available in English as *Cleaned Out* (Elmwood Park, IL: Dalkey Archive Press, 1990).
Ernaux, A. (1983) *La Place* (Paris: Gallimard); available in English as *Positions* (London: Quartet, 1991).
Establet, R. (1987) *L'École est-elle rentable?* (Paris: Presses universitaires de France).
Fabre, D. (ed.) (1993) *Écritures ordinaires* (Paris: POL).
Faure, S. (1994) *Processus de transmission et d'appropriation des savoir-faire de la danse classique et contemporaine* (Lyons: University Lumière Lyon 2).
Flaubert, G. (1980) *Correspondances*, vol. 2 (Paris: Gallimard).
Foucault, M. (1972) *The Archaeology of Knowledge* (London: Tavistock).

REFERENCES

Freund, P. E. S. (1988) 'Bringing society into the body: understanding socialized human nature', *Theory and Society*, 17: 839–64.

Furet, F., and Ozouf, J. (1977) *Livre et écrire: l'alphabétisation des Français de Calvin à Jules Ferry*, vol. 2 (Paris: Minuit).

Garavini, F. (1995–6) 'Montaigne (M. de)', in *Encyclopædia Universalis*, vol. 15, pp. 720–5.

Garvey, C. (1974) 'Some properties of social play', *Merrill-Palmer Quarterly*, 20, no.3: 163–80.

Goffman, E. (1956) *The Presentation of Self in Everyday Life* (Edinburgh: University of Edinburgh Social Sciences Research Centre).

Goffman, E. (1961) *Asylums: Essays on the Social Situation of Mental Patients and Other Inmates* (Ann Arbor: University of Michigan Press).

Goffman, E. (1974) *Frame Analysis: An Essay on the Organization of Experience* (Cambridge, MA: Harvard University Press).

Goffman, E. (1981) *Forms of Talk* (Oxford: Blackwell).

Goffman, E. (1988) *Les Moments et leurs hommes* (Paris: Minuit).

Goffman, E. (1991) *Les Cadres de l'expérience* (Paris: Minuit).

Goody, J. (1977) *The Domestication of the Savage Mind* (Cambridge: Cambridge University Press).

Goody, J. (1987) *The Interface between the Written and the Oral* (Cambridge: Cambridge University Press).

Gruzinski, S. (1988) *La Colonisation de l'imaginaire: sociétés indigènes et occidentalisation dans le Mexique espagnol XVe–XVIIIe siècle* (Paris: Gallimard).

Gumperz, J. (1989) *Engager la conversation: introduction à la sociolinguistique interactionelle* (Paris: Minuit).

Habermas, J. (1995) *Sociologie et théorie du langage* (Paris: Armand Colin).

Halbwachs, M. (1980) *The Collective Memory* (New York and London: Harper & Row).

Halbwachs, M. (1992) *On Collective Memory* (Chicago: University of Chicago Press).

Hall, H. S. (1966) *The Meaning of Dreams* (New York: McGraw-Hill).

Hannerz, U. (1980) *Exploring the City* (New York: Columbia University Press).

Havelock, E. A. (1963) *Preface to Plato* (Cambridge, MA: Harvard University Press).

Havelock, E. A. (1976) *The Origins of Western Literacy* (Toronto: Ontario Institute for Studies in Education).

Hoggart, R. (1988) *A Local Habitation* (London: Chatto & Windus).

Hoggart, R. (1998) *The Uses of Literacy* (New Brunswick, NJ: Transaction Books).

Houdé, O. (1995) *Rationalité, développement et inhibition: un nouveau cadre d'analyse* (Paris: Presses universitaires de France).

Hughes, E. C. (1971) *The Sociological Eye* (Chicago: Aldine-Atherton).

Husserl, E. (1990) *Philosophie première*, vol. 1: *Histoire critique des idées* (Paris: Presses universitaires de France).

Jacob, C. (1988) 'Inscrire la terre habité sure une tablette: réflexions sur la fonction des cartes géographiques en Grèce ancienne', in M. Détienne (ed.), *Les Savoirs de l'écriture en Grèce ancienne* (Lille: PUL), pp. 273–304.

Jacobson, R. (1981) *Essais de linguistique générale* (Paris: Minuit).

Janet, P. (1988) *L'Évolution psychologique de la personnalité* (Paris: Masson).

REFERENCES

Jouhaud, C. (1994) 'Présentation', *Annales: Histoire, sciences sociales*, no. 2: 271–6.

Judd, C. H. (1908) 'The relation of special training and general intelligence', *Educational Review*, no. 36: 42–8.

Kaufmann, J.-C. (1994) 'Rôles et identité: l'example de l'entrée en couple', *Cahiers internationaux de sociologie*, 97: 301–28.

Kaufmann, J.-C. (1997) *Corps de femmes, regards d'hommes: sociologie des seins nus* (Paris: Nathan).

Kaufmann, J.-C. (1998) *Dirty Linen: Couples and their Laundry* (London: Middlesex University Press).

Labov, W. (1972a) *Sociolinguistic Patterns* (Philadelphia: University of Pennsylvania Press).

Labov, W. (1972b) *Language in the Inner City: Studies in the Black English Vernacular* (Philadelphia: University of Pennsylvania Press).

Labov, W. (1983) 'Le Changement linguistique: entretien avec William Labov', *Actes de la recherché en sciences sociales*, no. 46: 67–71.

Lacoste, M. (1994) 'Langage et travail: quelques perspectives', *Sociologie du travail*, 36: 45–56.

Ladrière, M. (1990) 'La Sagesse pratique: les implications de la notion aristotélicienne de *phronèsis* pour la théorie de l'action', in *Les Formes de l'action: sémantique et sociologie*, Raisons pratiques, no. 1: 15–37.

Lahire, B. (1990) 'Sociologie des pratiques d'écriture: contribution à l'analyse du lien entre le social et le langagier', *Ethnologie français*, 3: 262–73.

Lahire, B. (1991a) 'Les pratiques langagières orales en situation scolaire des enfants de milieux populaires', *Revue internationale de pédagogie*, 37: 401–13.

Lahire, B. (1991b) 'Linguistique/écriture/pédagogie: champs de pertinence et transferts illégaux', *L'Homme et la Société: Revue internationale de recherches et de synthèses en sciences sociales*, no. 101: 109–19.

Lahire, B. (1992) 'L'inégalité devant la culture écrite scolaire: le cas de l'"expression écrite" à l'école primaire', *Sociétés contemporaines*, no. 11: 171–91.

Lahire, B. (1993a) *Culture écrite et inégalités scolaires: sociologie de l'"échec scolaire" à l'école primaire* (Lyons: PUL).

Lahire, B. (1993b) *La Raison des plus faibles: rapport au travail, écritures domestiques et lectures en milieux populaires* (Lille: PUL).

Lahire, B. (1993c) 'Practiques d'écriture et sens pratique', in M. Chaudron and F. de Singly (eds), *Identité, lecture et écriture* (Paris: BPI-Centre).

Lahire, B. (1993d) 'La Division sexuelle du travail d'écriture domestique', *Ethnologie français*, 23: 504–16.

Lahire, B. (1993e) 'Un pragmatisme radical: modes d'appropriation du poste d'adultes de "bas niveaux de qualifications"', *Revue français des affaires sociales*, no. 1: 19–40.

Lahire, B. (1994a) 'Formes sociales scripturales-scolaires et formes sociales orales: modes de connaissance et formes d'exercice du pouvoir', in G. Vincent (ed.), *L'Éducation prisonnière de la forme scolaire? Scolarisation et socialisation dans les sociétés industrielles* (Lyons: PUL), pp. 20–38.

Lahire, B. (1994b) 'Remarques sociologiques sur le *linguistic turn*: suite au "Dialogue sur l'espace public" entre Keith Michael Baker et Roget Chartier', *Travaux de science politique*, no. 27: 189–92.

Lahire, B. (1995a) *Tableaux de familles: heurs et malheurs scolaires en milieux populaires* (Paris: Gallimard/Seuil).
Lahire, B. (1995b) 'Écritures domestiques: la domestification du domestique', *Social Science Information/Information sur les sciences sociales*, 34: 567–92.
Lahire, B. (1995c) 'Écrits hors école: la réinterrogation des catégories de perception des actes de lecture et d'écriture', in B. Seibel (ed.), *Lire, faire lire: des usages de l'écrit aux politiques de lecture* (Paris: Le Monde), pp. 137–55.
Lahire, B. (1995d) *Transmissions familiales de l'écrit et performances scolaires d'élèves de CE2* (Paris: Ministère de l'Éducation nationale et de la culture).
Lahire, B. (1995e) *Cultures familiales de l'écrit et rapports intergénérationnels* (Paris: Ministère de l'Éducation nationale et de la culture).
Lahire, B. (1996a) 'La Variation des contextes en sciences sociales: remarques épistémologiques', *Annales: Histoire, sciences sociales*, no. 2: 381–407.
Lahire, B. (1996b) 'Risquer l'interprétation: pertinences interprétatives et sur-interprétations en sciences sociales', *Enquête: Anthropologie, histoire, sociologie*, no. 3: 61–87.
Lahire, B. (1997a) *Les Manières d'étudier* (Paris: La Documentation français).
Lahire, B. (1997b) 'Masculin–feminine: l'écriture domestique', in D. Fabre (ed.), *Par écrit: ethnologie des écritures quotidiennes* (Paris: MSH), pp. 145–61.
Lahire, B. (1998a) 'Certitudes et incertitudes des sociologues', in M. Hardy (ed.), *L'École et les changements sociaux: un défi à la sociologie?* (Montreal: Éditions Logiques).
Lahire, B. (1998b) 'Décrire la réalité sociale? Place et nature de la description et sociologie', in *Sur la description* (Lille: Presses du Septentrion).
Lahire, B (ed.) (1999) *Le Travail sociologique de Pierre Bourdieu: dettes et critiques* (Paris: La Découverte).
Lahire, B. (2002) *Portraits sociologiques: dispositions et variations individuelles* (Paris: Nathan).
Lahire, B. (2003a) 'From the habitus to an individual heritage of dispositions: towards a sociology at the level of the individual', *Poetics: Journal of Empirical Research on Culture, the Media and the Arts*, 31 : 329–55.
Lahire, B. (2003b) 'Les Classes sociales: objet d'études ou instrument de disqualification?', *Mouvements*, no. 29: 179–80.
Lahire, B. (2004) 'Post-scriptum: individu et sociologie', in B. Lahire, *La Culture des individus: dissonances culturelles et distinction de soi* (Paris: La Découverte), pp. 695–736.
Lahire, B. (2005) 'Sociologie, psychologie et sociologie psychologique', *Hermès: Revue cognition communication politique*, no. 41: 146–52.
Lahire, B. (2006) *La Condition littéraire: la double vie des écrivains* (Paris: La Découverte).
Lahire, B. (2008) 'The individual and the mixing of genres: cultural dissonance and self-distinction', *Poetics: Journal of Empirical Research on Culture, the Media and the Arts*, 36: 166–88.
Lahire, B. (2010) *Franz Kafka: éléments pour une théorie de la création littéraire* (Paris: La Découverte).
Laplanche, J., and Pontalis, J.-B. (2006) *The Language of Psycho-Analysis* (London: Karnac).
Lave, J. (1988) *Cognition in Practice: Mind, Mathematics and Culture in Everyday Life* (Cambridge: Cambridge University Press).

REFERENCES

Leenhardt, J., and Józsa, P. (1982) *Lire la lecture: essai de sociologie de la lecture* (Paris: Le Sycomore).

Lefebvre, H. (2002) *Critique of Everyday Life*, Vol. 2: *Foundations of a Sociology of the Everyday* (London and New York: Verso).

Lepetit, B. (1993) 'Architecture, géographie, histoire: usages de l'échelle', *Genèses*, 13: 118–38.

Levi, G. (1988) *Inheriting Power: The Story of an Exorcist* (Chicago: University of Chicago Press).

Lévy, C. (1998) 'Les Écrivains juifs contemporains de langue français: déclinisations identitaires et modes d'expression littéraire', doctoral thesis, Paris: École des hautes etudes en sciences sociales.

Lloyd, G. E. R. (1990) *Demystifying Mentalities* (Cambridge: Cambridge University Press).

Loarer, E., Chartier, D., Huteau, M., and Lautrey, J. (1995) *Peut-on éduquer l'intelligence? L'évaluation d'une méthode d'éducation cognitive* (Berne: Peter Lane).

Longuet Marx, A. (1986) *Proust, Musil: partage d'écritures* (Paris: Presses universitaires de France).

McCall, L. (1992) 'Does gender fit? Bourdieu, feminism, and conception of social order', *Theory and Society*, 21: 837–67.

Madec, A. (1996) 'Chronique familiale en quartier impopulaire', doctoral thesis, University of Paris VIII.

Malrieu, P. (1996) 'La Théorie de la personne chez Ignace Meyerson', in F. Parot (ed.), *Pour une psychologie historique: écrits en homage à Ignace Meyerson* (Paris: Presses universitaires de France), pp. 77–93.

Marx, K. (1978) *Capital* (Harmondsworth: Penguin).

Mauss, M. (1968) *Oeuvres 2. Représentations collectives et diversité des civilisations* (Paris: Minuit), p. 451.

Mead, G. H. (1967) *Mind, Self, and Society* (Chicago: University of Chicago Press).

Meillet, A. (1912–13) *Bulletin de la société de linguistique*, 18.

Melden, A. I. (1968) 'Action', in S. Care Norman and C. Landesman (eds), *Readings in the Theory of Action* (Bloomington and London: Indiana University Press), pp. 27–47.

Memmi, A. (1984) *Agar* (Paris: Gallimard).

Menger, P.-M. (1997) 'Temporalité et différences inter-individuelles: l'analyse de l'action en sociologie et en économie', *Revue français de sociologie*, 38: 587–633.

Merleau-Ponty, M. (1962) *Phenomenology of Perception* (London and New York: Routledge).

Merleau-Ponty, M. (1965) *The Structure of Behaviour* (London: Methuen).

Merleau-Ponty, M. (1968) *The Visible and the Invisible* (Evanston, IL: Northwestern University Press).

Merleau-Ponty, M. (1970) *Themes from the Lectures at the Collège de France, 1952–1960* (Evanston, IL: Northwestern University Press).

Merleau-Ponty, M. (1973) *The Prose of the World* (Evanston, IL: Northwestern University Press).

Millet, M. (1993) 'Les Écritures du quotidien domestique', thesis, Lyons: Université Lumière Lyon 2.

Montaigne, M. de (1958) *The Complete Essays of Montaigne* (Stanford, CA: Stanford University Press).

REFERENCES

Muxel, A. (1996) *Individu et mémoire familiale* (Paris: Nathan).
Naville, P. (1942) *La Psychologie, science du comportement: le behaviorisme de Watson* (Paris: Gallimard).
Nicole, E. (1981) 'Personnage et rhétorique du nom', *Poétique*, 46: 200–16.
Nietzsche, F. (1996) *On the Genealogy of Morals* (Oxford: Oxford University Press).
Norman, D. A. (1993) 'Les Artefacts cognitifs', in *Les Objets dans l'action: de la maison au laboratoire, Raisons pratiques*, no. 4: 15–34.
Ostrow, J. M. (1990) *Social Sensitivity: A Study of Habit and Experience* (Albany: State University of New York Press).
Pagnol, M. (1989) *My Father's Glory and my Mother's Castle* (London: André Deutsch).
Panovsky, E. (1957) *Gothic Architecture and Scholasticism* (New York: Meridian Books).
Pascual-Leone, J. (1988) 'Organismic processes for neo-Piagetian theories: a dialectic causal account of cognitive development', in A. Demetriou (ed.), *The Neo-Piagetian Theories of Cognitive Development: Towards an Integration* (Amsterdam: North-Holland), pp. 25–64.
Pascual-Leone, J., and Baillargeon, R. (1994) 'Developmental measurements of mental attention', *International Journal of Behavioral Development*, 17: 161–200.
Passeron, J.-C. (1977) *Cadres et mécanismes de la socialisation dans la France d'aujourd'hui* (Paris: Ronéoté).
Passeron, J.-C. (1991) *Le Raisonnement sociologique: l'espace non-Poppérien du raisonnement naturel* (Paris: Nathan).
Passeron, J.-C., and Pedler, E. (1991) *Le Temps donné aux tableaux* (Marseilles: IMEREC).
Piaget, J. (1952) *The Origins of Intelligence in Children* (New York: International Universities Press).
Piaget, J. (1971) *Biology and Knowledge* (Chicago: University of Chicago Press).
Proust, M. (1981) *Time Regained* (New York: Random House).
Proust, M. (1988) *Against Saint-Beuve and Other Essays*, trans. J. Sturrock (Harmondsworth: Penguin).
Proust, M. (2002) *The Guermantes Way* (London: Allen Lane).
Proust, M. (2003) *The Way by Swann's* (London: Penguin).
Putnam, H. (1988) *Representation and Reality* (Cambridge, MA: MIT Press).
Raimond, M., and Fraisse, L. (1989) *Proust en toutes lettres* (Paris: Bordas).
Revel, J. (1994) 'Micro-analyse et construction du social', in P.-M. Menger and J.-C. Passeron (eds), *L'Art de la recherche: essais en l'honneur de Raymond Moulin* (Paris: La Documentation française), pp. 305–27.
Revel, J. (ed.) (1996) *Jeux d'échelles: la micro-analyse à l'expérience* (Paris: Gallimard/Seuil).
Ricœur, P. (1984–8) *Time and Narrative* (3 vols, Chicago: University of Chicago Press).
Rosset, C. (1995) *Les Choix des mots* (Paris: Minuit).
Sartre, J.-P. (1964) *Words* (London: Hamish Hamilton).
Saussure, F. de (1960) *Course in General Linguistics* (London: Peter Owen).
Schlink, B. (1998) *The Reader* (New York: Vintage Books).
Schön, D. A. (1983) *The Reflective Practitioner: How Professionals Think in Action* (New York: Basic Books).

REFERENCES

Schön, E. (1993) 'La "Fabrication" du lecteur', in M. Chaudron and F. de Singly (eds), *Identité, lecture, écriture* (Paris: BPI), pp. 17–58.

Schwartz, O. (1990) *Le Monde privé des ouvriers: hommes et femmes du Nord* (Paris: Presses universitaires de France).

Scribner, S., and Cole, M. (1981) *The Psychology of Literacy* (Cambridge, MA: Harvard University Press).

Sharrock, S., and Watson, R. (1990) 'L'Unité du faire et du dire: l'action et l'organisation sociales comme phénomènes observables et descriptibles', *Les Formes de l'action: sémantique et sociologie, Raisons pratiques*, no. 1: 227–54.

Shweder, R. A. (1991) *Thinking through Cultures* (Cambridge, MA: Harvard University Press).

Simmel, G. (1981) *Sociologie et épistémologie* (Paris: Presses universitaires de France).

Simon, H. A. (1980) 'Problem solving and education', in D. T. Tuma and F. Reif (eds), *Problem Solving and Education: Issues in Teaching and Research* (Hillsdale, NJ: Erlbaum), pp. 81–96.

Singly, F. de (1982) 'La gestion sociale des silences', *Consommation: revue de socio-économie*, no. 4: 37–63.

Singly, F. de (1990a) 'L'Homme dual: raison utilitaire, raison humanitaire', *Le Débat*, no. 61: 138–51.

Singly, F. de (1990b) 'Réussir à lire: la lecture chez les collégiens', *Cahiers de l'économie du livre*, no. 3: 71–83.

Singly, F. de (1993a) *Les Jeunes et la lecture*, Les Dossiers education & formations no. 24 (Paris: Ministère de l'éducation).

Singly, F. de (1993b) 'La Lecture de livres pendant la jeunesse: statut et fonction', in M. Poulain (ed.), *Lire en France aujourd'hui* (Paris: Cercle de la librairie), pp. 137–62.

Singly, F. de (1993c) 'Savoir hériter: la transmission du gout de la lecture chez les étudiants', in E. Fraisse (ed.), *Les Étudiants et la lecture* (Paris: Presses universitaires de France), pp. 49–71.

Singly, F. de (1996) 'L'Appropriation de l'héritage culturel', *Liens social et politiques-RIAC*, 35: 153–65.

Sperber, D. (1996) *Explaining Culture: A Naturalistic Approach* (Oxford: Blackwell).

Strauss, A. L. (1993) *Continual Permutations of Action* (New York: Walter de Gruyter).

Suchman, L. (1990) 'Plans d'action: problèmes de representation de la pratique en sciences sociales', *Les Formes de l'action, Raisons pratiques*, no. 1: 149–70.

Sudnow, D. (1978) 'Singing with the fingers', *Human Nature*, 1: 80–6.

Thévenot, L. (1995) 'L'Action en plan', *Sociologie du travail*, no. 3: 411–34.

Thorndike, E. L. (1913) *Educational Psychology*, vol. 2: *The Psychology of Learning* (New York: Columbia University Press).

Toussaint, J.-P. (1990) *The Bathroom* (New York: Dutton).

Toussaint, J.-P. (1991) *Monsieur: A Novel* (New York: Marion Boyars).

Toussaint, J.-P. (2008) *Camera* (Champaign, IL: Dalkey Archive Press).

Tralongo, S. (1996) 'Les Conditions d'une rencontre heureuse: analyse sociologique des conditions de possibilité de se sentir 'reconnu' et 'révélé' par des textes de Christian Bobin', thesis, Université Lumière Lyon 2.

Valéry, P. (1938) *Variety* (New York: Harcourt, Brace).

REFERENCES

Van Heerden, J., and Smolenaars, A. J. (1990) 'On traits as dispositions: an alleged truism', *Journal for the Theory of Social Behavior*, 19: 297–310.

Vendryes, J. (1959) *Language: A Linguistic Introduction to History* (London: Routledge & Kegan Paul).

Vernant, J.-P. (1982) *The Origins of Greek Thought* (Ithaca, NY: Cornell University Press).

Vernant, J.-P. (1983) *Myth and Thought among the Greeks* (London: Routledge & Kegan Paul).

Vygotsky, L. S. (1962) *Thought and Language* (Cambridge, MA: MIT Press).

Wacquant, L. J. D. (1989) 'Corps et âmes: notes ethnographiques d'un apprenti-boxeur', *Actes de la recherche en sciences sociales*, no. 80: 33–67.

Wacquant, L. J. D. (1991) 'Busy Louie aux Golden Gloves', *Gulliver: Revue littéraire*, no. 6: 13–33.

Wacquant, L. J. D. (1995a) 'Pugs at work: bodily capital and bodily labour among professional boxers', *Body & Society*, 1: 65–93.

Wacquant, L. J. D. (1995b) 'The pugilistic point of view: how boxers think and feel about their trade', *Theory and Society*, 24: 489–535.

Wacquant, L. J. D. and Calhoun, C. J. (1989) 'Intérêt, rationalité et culture: à propos d'un recent débat sur la théorie de l'action', *Actes de la recherche en sciences sociales*, no. 78: 41–60.

Weber, M. (1978) *Economy and Society* (Berkeley: University of California Press).

Weber, M. (1992) *Essais sur la théorie de la science* (Paris: Pocket).

Weber, M. (2001) *The Protestant Ethic and the Spirit of Capitalism* (London: Routledge).

Wertsch, J. V. (1979) 'From social interaction to higher psychological processes: a clarification and application of Vygotsky's theory', *Human Development*, 22: 1–22.

Williams, C. L. (1989) *Gender Differences at Work: Women and Men in Nontraditional Occupations* (Berkeley: University of California Press).

Witkin, H. A. (1967) 'A cognitive-style approach to cross-cultural research', *International Journal of Psychology*, 2: 233–50.

Wittgenstein, L. (1966) *Lectures and Conversations on Aesthetics, Psychology and Religious Belief* (Berkeley: University of California Press).

Wittgenstein, L. (1972) *Philosophical Investigations* (Oxford: Blackwell).

Wittgenstein, L. (1974) *Tractatus logico-philosophicus* (London: Routledge & Kegan Paul).

Wunder, D. F. (1993) 'Dreams as empirical data: siblings' dreams and fantasies about their disabled sisters and brothers', *Symbolic Interaction*, 16: 117–27.

Xenophon (1994) *Oeconomicus* (Oxford: Clarendon Press).

Zola, É. (1964) *The Experimental Novel and Other Essays* (New York: Haskell House).

INDEX

accounts, 116, 127, 141, 173
action, meaning, 71
actor, meaning, 2–3
administrative communications, 129–32
administrative identity, 16–17
adolescence, 122
Algeria, 19, 20–1, 60, 141, 241n15
analogies
   analogical transfer, 66–9, 88
   boxing language, 166–7
   dance, 168
   novels, 93
   triggers of action and memory, 66–9
anthropology, 6, 13–14, 83
anti-intellectualism, 163–5
anti-structuralism, 163
Aristotle, 7, 50, 52, 73
Athens, 203
Auerbach, Eric, 50
Augustine of Hippo, St, 219–20

Bachelard, Gaston, 1
Bakhtin, Mikhail, 89–90, 103, 108–10, 174, 219
Bali, 13
Bally, Charles, 131
Balzac, Honoré de, 34
Baudelaire, Charles, 34
behaviourism, 72, 202
Benoliel, Roger, 25
Benveniste, Émile, 174

Berger, Pierre, 27–8, 37, 165, 190, 218
Bergson, Henri, 49–50, 66, 69, 70–2, 246n8
Bernstein, Basil, 169–70, 176
Binet–Simon test, 84
Boltanski, Luc, 223n3
Bonenfant, Louis, 15
Boudon, Raymond, 204
Bourdieu, Pierre
   on Algeria, 19, 20–1, 60, 141, 241n15
   avoiding crisis, 45
   on case studies, 116
   on cultural production, 89, 90
   dispositions, 231n16
   freedom from urgencies, 111–14
   generalizations, 251n4
   habitus, xi, xiv, 3, 16, 79, 87, 141, 146–7, 247n1, 249n1
   on history, 47
   on intellectual trajectories, 154–6
   on language, 111–12, 172, 214, 241n10
   Panovsky and, 20
   on passing of time, 139
   Piaget and, 79, 82
   present past, 43, 44
   research methods and, 82
   scholarly reputation, viii, 3–4
   school, ix
   on silence, 164
   on singleness, 11–13, 15–16

INDEX

on social principles, 135
on the state, 227n17
tennis player, 147–8, 150
theory of fields, 28, 216–17, 219
theory of practice, 143, 145, 149, 151
transfer of schemes, 80
unconscious strategy, 247n14
on writing, 87, 139–40
Bourget, Paul, 33
Bouveresse, Jacques, 51, 174, 211, 212, 231–2n17
boxing, 159, 165–8, 169
Bronckart, Jean-Paul, 247n4
Brubaker, Rogers, 251n4
Bruner, Jérôme, 169, 170, 174
Burgess, E. W., 72

calendar notes, 115, 116, 117, 120, 121, 124–5, 126, 139, 140, 141
Camic, Charles, 72
Certeau, Michel de, 51
Chamboredon, Jean.-Claude, 82
Chartier, Anne-Marie, 153, 247–8n6
Chartier, Roger, 49, 238n10
checklists, 244n19
chemistry, 51–3
Chevallier, Denis, 180
children
  development, 79–80
  family transmission of written culture to, 183–9
  imitation, 185–6
  jigsaw puzzles, 176–8
  language learning, 101–7, 171, 174, 182, 248n5
  negative indications to, 189–91
  play, 89–90
  reading, 178
  undesirable dispositions, 181–2
  see also education; socialization
Chiva, Isaac, 180
Chomsky, Noam, 174
class
  déclassement, 46
  languages, 39–40
  middle-class reading, 90
  transfuges, 37–41, 56, 81
  working-class readers, 91–2, 189
  working-class school failures, 82

cock-fighting, 13
codes
  codification, 141–2
  language, 52–3, 93, 174
  switching and mixing, 60–2
  weakly codified societies, 146
cognitive style, 13, 15, 202
Cohen, Albert, 233n25
Cole, Michael, 83–5, 106–7, 248n5, 251n12
Colet, Louise, 237n2
colonialism, 21
Cometti, Jean-Pierre, 2
Conan Doyle, Arthur, 115
Condillac, Étienne de, 240n1
Conein, Bernard, 243n9, 244n18
Connerton, Paul, 235n12
consciousness
  collective and individual, 198
  context levels and, 154–6
  mysterious inside, 173–4
constructivism, 213
context, see social contexts
correspondence, 24, 49, 116, 130–1, 133, 185, 190
crises
  maladjustment, 45–7
  rational choice, 146
  reflexivity, 152
  writing and, 122
criticism, rehabilitation, 2, 3
crosswords, 116
Crozier, Michel, 246n9
cultural contradiction, 46
cultural inheritance, 178–82
cultural transmission, see transmission
curriculum vitae, 17

dance, 168
daydreams, 95–8
Degracia (Gracia Cohen), 231n7
déja vu, 67
Delbos, Geneviève, 169, 181
Descartes, René, 1, 174, 182
determinism, see social determinism
diary jottings, 115, 116, 117, 120–1, 124–8, 139, 141
discursive mediation, 165, 167, 168–9

265

INDEX

dispositions
  children's undesirable dispositions, 181–2
  conditional dispositions, 50–6
divorce, 46, 92, 122
Dostoevsky, Fyodor, 72, 115
dreams, 95–8, 219
Durkheim, Émile
  autonomy of sociology, 199, 200
  boarding-school regime, 18, 19–20
  collective and individual consciousness, 198
  Halbwachs and, 6
  legacy, 199
  nature of sociology, 5
  political economy, 157, 218
  sociology and psychology, 195, 198
  traditional societies, 18–19

education
  class *transfuges*, 39–40
  family transmission of written culture, 183–9
  language teaching
    departure from common sense, 101–7
    Saussure on, 108–10
    social conditions, 110–14
  middle classes, 24–5
  reading experience and, 94
  school culture and family worlds, 186–8
  sociology, 175–6, 209
  teachers' evaluations, 58–9
  teachers' timeframes, 153
  teachers' writing, 119–20
  university students' timetables, 62–3, 64
  working-class families, 31
  working-class school failures, 82
Efron, David, 61–2
Egypt, 103
Eichendorff, Joseph von, 237n1
Elias, Norbert, 180, 201, 218, 229n30
embodiment
  implicit injunctions, 189–91
  language, *see* language
  memory, 117–20
  multiplicity of fields of action, 32
  negative indications, 189–91

  processes, 175–82
  social structures, 176, 182
  written culture in families, 183–9
Ernaux, Annie, 36, 39–40, 183
esprit de corps, 22
Establet, Roger, 25
ethnomethodology, 42
experimental variation, 214–17

family worlds
  gender and, 190–1
  illiteracy, 186–7, 189
  interdependence, 67–8, 182
  school culture and, 186–8
  singleness, 23–5, 27–8
  transmission of written cultures, 183–9
  working-class, 31
  writing and complex practices, 128–9
  writing to the absent, 133–4
fields
  excessive generalization, 211–13
  experimental variation, 214–17
  historicizing, 217–22
  pertinence, 211–22
  theory, 28–30
  varying scale of context, 213–14
fire fighters, 85–6
Flaubert, Gustave, xiv, 15, 237n2
folds of the social, 203–5
Foucault, Michel, 4, 173
freedom of action, 206–7
Freud, Sigmund, 36, 75, 98, 219
Freund, Peter, 230n2
Friedberg, Erhard, 246n9

Galton, Francis, xvi
game theory, 160
Garavini, Fausta, 238n11
Geertz, Clifford, 13
gender
  family worlds, 190–1
  literacy and, 190–1
  role transmission, 185–6
generalization
  excessive generalization, 210, 211–13
  schemes of action, 85–6
Goffman, Erving

INDEX

backstage, 98
collectively organized activities, 63
daydreams, 97
interactionism, 132
  on language, 170, 213–14, 248n9
  on singleness, 15, 16
  total institutions, 19
Goody, Jack, 129, 139, 218–19
Gothic art, 20
Granet, Marcel, 1
Greece, 104, 203
Gumperz, John, 60–1, 251n12

Habermas, Jürgen, 245n23
habits
  concept, 144–5
  plurality of social contexts, 26–32
  role, 72–4
Halbwachs, Maurice
  corporate worlds, 22–3
  on heterogeneity, 26–7
  legacy, 6
  on memory, 36, 69, 70
  on musical language, 172
  reading and memory, 96
  on use of time, 63
handwriting, 87
Hannerz, Ulf, 226n11, 233n25
Havelock, Eric Alfred, 102
Hegel, Georg Wilhelm Friedrich, 240n1
Heidegger, Martin, xiv, 245n3
history
  single mentality, 14
  sociology and, 6, 217–22
Hoggart, Richard, 38, 39, 40, 113, 232n19, 242n4
hospitalization, 46, 50
Hughes, Everett C., 122
Husserl, Edmund, 13, 165

illness, 122, 135
imitation, 185–6, 200
implicit injunctions, 189–91
imprisonment, 46, 50, 207
inhibitions, 56–60
intentionality, context levels, 154–6
interactionism, 42, 73, 132, 214, 219
interdependence, 67–8, 172, 176, 182, 204

interdisciplinarity, 6–7, 199, 201
internalization, 175–82
interview, sociological interview, 75–6
itineraries, 115, 121–2, 126, 136–7, 141

Jacobson, Roman, 102–3
Jacopin, Eric, 243n9, 244n18
Janet, Pierre, 202
Janssens, Florence, 153, 247–8n6
jigsaw puzzles, 176–8
Jorion, Paul, 169, 181
Jouhaud, C., 252n5
Joyce, James, 237n2

Kabyls, 19, 141
Kaplan, A., 221
Kaufmann, Jean-Claude, 226n7, 232n21

labelling, 116, 185
Labov, William, 61, 235n16, 251n12
Ladrière, Paul, 231n14
language
  class *transfuges*, 39–40
  foreign languages, 248n5
  forms of social life and, 172–3
  gestural bilingualism, 62
  language games, 168, 177
  learning, 182
  linguistic pathology, 182
  mysterious inside, 173–4
  psychology, 170–1
  punctuation of action, 169–71
  Saussurian model, 52–3
  school teaching
    departure from common sense, 101–7
    Saussure on, 108–10
    social conditions, 110–14
  silence, 163–9
  switching, 61
  tongue and, 103
Laplanche, Jean, 49
Lave, C., 106–7
Lave, Jean, 82
Lefebvre, Henri, 173
legal precedents, 67
Leibniz, Gottfried, 1, 12, 146, 240n1
letters, *see* correspondence

INDEX

Lévy, Clara, 233n25
Liberia, 83–4
life stories, 17
lightning, 182
lists, 121, 125–6, 127, 129, 135, 136–9, 140, 141, 185
literacy, *see* reading; writing
literary experience, 89–98
Lloyd, Geoffrey, 14
Locke, John, 240n1
log books, 116
Longuet Marx, Anne, 234n6
Luckmann, Thomas, 27–8, 37, 165, 190, 218

McCall, Leslie, 230n4
maladjustment, 45–7, 92, 122
Marx, Karl, 172
Marxism, 215–16
Maspero, Henri, 1
Mauss, Marcel, 218
Mayas, 106–7
Mead, George Herbert, 228n25
Meillet, Antoine, 154–5, 156
Melden, A. I., 235n14, 246n12
Memmi, Albert, 231n7
memory
  'doing it like that', 123–4
  embodied and objectified, 117–20
  everyday writing and, 115–26
  for the unusual, 124–6
  gender and, 117–18
  involuntary actions and, 69–72
  Proust, 69, 70
  psychological approaches, 86
  reading and, 96
  transferential repetition, 75
mental conflict, splitting selves, 36–41
mental structures, 182
mentality, 14, 197, 202, 203
Merleau-Ponty, Maurice, x, 87, 102, 109, 147, 164–5
Mesopotamia, 103
Mestizos, 106–7
methodology
  methodological individualism, 42
  new requirements, 207–10
Mexico, 46, 106–7
migration, 46, 50, 133

military service, 46
minority groups, 61–2
modularization, 235n13
Montaigne, Michel de, 18, 26, 47, 77, 86, 207, 238n11
mountain rescuers, 85–6
Mozart, Leopold, 180
Mozart, Wolfgang Amadeus, 180, 229n30
multi-determinism, 206–7
music, 149, 172
Musset, Alfred de, 35
Muxel, Anne, 232n21

Naville, Pierre, 17–18, 38, 45, 202, 203
negative indications, 189–91
Nietzsche, Friedrich, 4, 182, 249n6
Norman, Donald, 153
novelists, 30
novels, 90–4

obituaries, 17
objective structures, 43, 146, 175, 177, 182, 195, 202
objectivity of the subjective, 201–3
opium, 51
Ostrow, James, 234n5

Pagnol, Marcel, 183
Panovsky, Erwin, 20
parapraxes, 98, 150
Park, R. E., 72
Parsons, Talcott, 72
Pascal, Blaise, 247n15
Passeron, Jean-Claude, 1, 82, 230n2
past
  presence, 42–4
  present openings and, 47–50
Peirce, Charles, 102–3
philosophy
  generalizations, 212
  sociology and, 5–6
phone calls, 129–31
Piaget, Jean
  Bourdieu and, 79, 82
  child development, 79–80
  language and, 174, 247n4
  legacy, 5, 87, 196
  memory and habit, 234n7

268

schemes of action, 78–9, 80–1, 82, 85, 86
school, 77
summaries of experience, 74
terminology, 195
planned behaviour theory, 160
planners, 126–7, 140
planning, 136–9, 153
Plato, 102, 119, 133
plural actor
  plural logics of action, 143–60
  plural social contexts, 26–32
  plurality, 10–41
  plurality of times, 156–60
  Proustian model, 32–5
  socio-historical conditions, 18–26
  splitting selves and mental conflict, 36–41
  wellsprings of action, 42–65
  see also singleness
pluridisciplinarity, 6–7, 199, 201
Pontalis, Jean-Bertrand, 49
power, fields of power, 30
practical sense, departure from
  language and social conditions, 110–14
  relative pertinence, 139–42
  sporting model, 147–54
  theory, 160
  writing
    everyday breaks, 120–3
    sporting model, 147–54
    temporary disturbances, 134–5
practice, theory of practice, 143–4
prayers, 218
precedents, 67
Protestantism, xiv, xv
Proust, Marcel, 6, 32–5, 69, 70, 89
psychoanalysis, 42, 49, 74, 97–8
psychological sociology
  exit from sociology, 197–201
  multi-determinism and sense of freedom, 206–7
  new methodology, 207–10
  objectivity of the subjective, 201–3
  overview, 195–210
  singular folds of the social, 203–5
psychology
  cognitive psychology, 199

cultural psychology, 200–1
generalization of cognitive problems, 86
language, 170–1
object, 202
sociology and, 5, 6, 72–3, 77
transfers, 82, 86
see also psychological sociology
pugilistic *illusio*, 247n1
punctuation of action, 169–71
Putnam, Hilary, 51, 217

Quine, Willard, 50, 51

rational choice theory, 42, 160
reading
  children's learning, 178
  daydreams and, 96–8
  experience, 89–95
  family transmission, 183–9
  incentives, 190
  memory and, 96
  middle-class models, 90–1
  one-to-one correspondence, 93
  sociology, 94–5
  therapeutic role, 92–3
  working-class readers, 91–2, 189
realism, 70, 215–16
recipes, 116, 185
reflexivity
  habits and, 72–3, 144–5
  reflexive habitus, 147
  school language teaching, 106, 110–14
reminder notes, 115
retirement, 46, 57, 92, 122
Revel, Jacques, 252n8
Ribot, Théodule, 228n25
rituals, 124, 218
Robbe-Grillet, Alain, 237n2
Rousseau, Jean-Jacques, 240n1
ruptures, 46, 92, 116, 122

Sainte-Beuve, Charles, 32–4
salt-cutters, 169, 181
Sartre, Jean-Paul, 183
Saussure, Ferdinand de, 52, 108–10, 172, 209, 240n1
Sayad, Abdelmalek, 21, 60

schemes of action
　embodiment, *see* embodiment
　general and partial schemes, 82–6
　Piaget definition, 78–9
Schlink, Bernard, 237n1
scholasticism, 20
Schön, Erich, 238n4, 247n13
School, *see* education
Schwartz, Olivier, 235n15
Scribner, Sylvia, 83–4, 106–7
self
　class *transfuges*, 37–41
　Proustian plurality, 32–5
　singleness, 11–14
　split and mental conflict, 36–41
Sharp, D., 106–7
shepherding, 180
shopping lists, 115, 116, 125–6, 129, 136, 137–8, 141, 185
signatures, 17, 185
silence, 163–9
Simmel, Georg, 250n3
Simon, Claude, 237n2
Simon, Theodore, 84
singleness
　ambiguity of singular practice, 143–7
　anthropology, 13–14
　corporate worlds, 22–3
　family worlds, 23–5
　history, 14
　social illusion, 15–18
　socio-historical conditions, 18–26
　sociology, 11–13
　total institutions, 19–20
　traditional societies, 20–1
Singly, François de, 189, 249n10
situated action theory, 160
Smolenaars, A. J., 50, 53
social contexts
　code switching and mixing, 60–2
　intentionality and, 154–6
　memory and, 69
　mentality and, 14
　negative power, 56–60
　non-contextuality, 213
　plurality, 26–32, 204–5
　varying scale, 213–14, 221–2
social determinism, 53, 206–7
socialization
　contradictory experiences, 37
　multi-socialization, 207
　personality and, 54
　plurality, 31
　primary, 27–8
　processes, 175–82
　school and language, 101–7
　secondary, 28
sociology
　concerns, 197
　daydreams, 97
　education, 175–6, 209
　facts, 199
　nature of discipline, 2
　philosophy and, 5–6
　psychology and, 5, 72–3, 77
　reading, 94–5
　value of epistemology, 6
　see also psychological sociology
Socrates, 119
Sophocles, 86
Sperber, Dan, 199–200
sport, 147–54
Stendhal, 34
stock metaphor, 32
Strauss, Anselm, 9, 49, 95–6, 150, 228n19, 243n12
students
　daydreams, 95–6
　use of time, 62–3, 64
subjective, objectivity of the subjective, 201–3
Suchman, Lucy, 136, 148, 244n20
Sudnow, David, 240n9
Sumerians, 103
syllogisms, 106–7
symbolic interactionism, 42

Taine, Hippolyte, 33
Tarde, Gabriel, 200
tennis players, 147–8, 150, 152, 153, 155
Thomas, W. I., 72
Tralongo, S., 97
transfers
　analogical transfer, 66–9, 88
　analytic transfer, 74–5
　contemporary psychology, 82, 86
　general to limited, 86–8
　relative transferability, 77–82

transmission
  channels, 20
  cultural transmission, 24, 175, 178–82
  gender role, 185–6
  implicit injunctions, 189–91
  meaning, 178
  negative indications, 189–91
  processes, 175–82
  skills, 142, 146
  written cultures in families, 183–9
  see also education
traumas, 179
twins, 203

United States, 72, 216
utilitarianism, 154, 156, 246n11

Vai peoples, 83–4
Valéry, Paul, 18, 247n15
Van Heerden, J., 50, 53
Vygotsky, L. S., 106, 174, 200

Wacquant, Loïc J. D., 11, 146, 159, 165, 165–8, 166–8, 214, 247n1
war, 50
Watson, John Broadus, 202
Weber, Max, 114, 191, 213, 215–16, 217–18, 245n22, 250n2
wellsprings of action
  analogy, 66–9
  code switching and mixing, 60–2
  conditional dispositions, 50–6
  habits, 72–4
  inhibitions, 56–60
  involuntary actions and memory, 69–72
  maladjustment and crisis, 45–7
  negative power of context, 56–60
  overview, 42–65
  past, 42–4
  plurality and present openings, 47–50
  uncertain swings, 62–5

Wertsch, James, 176–7
Wittgenstein, Ludwig, 66, 101, 107, 160, 182, 212, 219–20, 221
women
  correspondence, 49
  learning gender role, 185–6
  life cycle, 57–8
  literacy and, 190–1
  memory, 117–18
  working-class men and, 57
Woolf, Virginia, 50, 234n5
writing
  Bourdieu on, 87
  correspondence and literacy, 48–9
  crises and, 122
  'doing it like that', 123–4
  domestic writing, 116
  early writing, 103–4
  embodied and objectified memory, 117–20
  everyday practices, 115–42
  family transmission of written cultures, 183–9
  incentives, 190
  lists, 136–9
  longer-term planning, 126–7
  managing complex practices, 128–9
  memory for the unusual, 124–6
  objectification techniques, 140
  official and tense situations, 129–32
  planning, 136–9
  practical sense and
    everyday breaks, 120–3
    relative pertinence, 139–42
    temporary disturbances, 134–5
  presence of the absent, 132–4
  Vai peoples, 83–4
Wunder, Delores, 97

Xenophon, 125

Znaniecki, F., 72
Zola, Émile, 201